CREATING STRATEGIC READERS

Techniques for Developing Competency
in Phonemic Awareness, Phonics, Fluency, Vocabulary, and Comprehension

Second Edition

VALERIE ELLERY

INTERNATIONAL Reading Association
800 BARKSDALE ROAD, PO BOX 8139
NEWARK, DE 19714-8139, USA
www.reading.org

The International Reading Association attempts, through its publications, to provide a forum for a wide spectrum of opinions on reading. This policy permits divergent viewpoints without implying the endorsement of the Association.

Executive Editor, Books   Corinne M. Mooney
Developmental Editor   Charlene M. Nichols
Developmental Editor   Tori Mello Bachman
Developmental Editor   Stacey L. Reid
Editorial Production Manager   Shannon T. Fortner
Design and Composition Manager   Anette Schuetz
Project Editors   Charlene M. Nichols and Wesley Ford
Cover   Design and illustration by Six Red Marbles

Library of Congress Cataloging-in-Publication Data
Ellery, Valerie, 1964-
 Creating strategic readers: techniques for developing competency in
phonemic awareness, phonics, fluency, vocabulary, and comprehension /
Valerie Ellery -- 2nd ed.
    p. cm.
Includes bibliographical references and index.
ISBN 978-0-87207-469-9
1. Reading--United States. 2. Language arts--United States. I.
Title.
LB1050.E52E45 2009
372.41--dc22

                                                              2009028281

Dedicated in loving memory to Velma, my grandma, who believed in me and encouraged me to become a teacher. It was through her love for writing and inspiring words that the seed for writing was planted in my heart.

Velma, excited about receiving her copy of the 1st Edition.

Contents

Valerie Ellery has dedicated two decades to the field of literacy in various roles as a National Board Certified Teacher, curriculum specialist, mentor, reading coach, national consultant, and international author. Twenty years ago while teaching, she realized that her son, Nick, had a reading problem. This very personal experience launched her journey in the quest for understanding, What do proficient readers do?

On the first stretch of her journey, she spent over 10 years watching and analyzing students as they were learning to read. In 1998, she was certified as a National Board Teacher where she learned the importance of reflecting on her instructional techniques. This process was paving the road for further knowledge on how to better meet the needs of readers.

After acquiring her master's in reading K–12 at the University of South Florida, she became a district curriculum specialist. This new role gave her the opportunity to model reading strategies, mentor teachers, and construct a roadmap for creating strategic readers. In 2005, her first book, *Creating Strategic Readers: Techniques for Developing Competency in Phonemic Awareness, Phonics, Fluency, Vocabulary, and Comprehension*, was published by the International Reading Association. The book has been used internationally in universities as an undergraduate course, helping to propel the reading process into the forefront of education. Educators have shared that the techniques in the book are clear and concise and easy to implement in their classrooms.

Following the publication of her book, Valerie went back to her roots as a classroom teacher to continue fostering the concept of comprehensive literacy while applying strategies and maintaining the quest for action research. She then served as a part-time reading coach, which allowed her the opportunity to consult nationally and advise on literacy boards, as well as continue locally to reach readers and teachers.

In 2008, she published a staff development DVD/VHS series titled *Creating Strategic Readers: Teaching Techniques for the Primary and Intermediate Grades* based on her first book. She also coauthored the Facilitator's Guide to *What Research Has to Say About Reading Instruction* (third edition), published by the International Reading Association. Currently, Valerie is a nationally known reading consultant who offers innovative, interactive, and motivating techniques with relevant and practical application. She is truly passionate about creating strategic readers.

Valerie carries that same passion into her home in Bradenton, Florida. She is a devoted wife to Gregg, mother to four—Nick, Derek, Jacey, and Brooke—grandmother, and a women's ministry leader to thousands.

The journey that started with Valerie's oldest son continues today. Nick, who overcame his reading difficulties, graduated with a biomedical degree from the U.S. Navy and is currently working in a hospital in Naples, Italy. He, along with his wife, Virginia, is continuing the legacy of creating strategic readers with his daughter, Evelyn Marie.

Author Information for Correspondence and Workshops

Valerie Ellery has served the field of education as a National Board Certified Teacher, curriculum specialist, mentor, reading coach, staff developer, and an award-winning author and consultant. For more information or to reach Valerie, visit www .ValerieEllery.com.

Acknowledgments

There are always those special people in your life to whom you are forever grateful. I am so fortunate to have so many who believe in me and inspire me to be all that God has called me to be and live a life of integrity.

I am grateful for

- My loving husband, Gregg, who is my true north

- My children, Nick, Virginia (daughter-in-law), Derek, Jacey, and Brooke, who bring such a purpose to my life

- My granddaughter, little princess "Evie," who is one of the main reasons why I will stay passionate about creating strategic readers

- My parents, Roger and Laurie, who never give up on me

- My sister Connie, who is not only my friend but also my faithful travel partner

- My dear friends, Lisa Hanna, Tammy Thompson, and Michele Howard, who continue to encourage me with their genuine hearts

- My church family, Bayside Community, who never stops praying for me

- My colleagues and friends, Stephanie Dix, Bobbette Gilbertson, Lisa Lenton, Gena Junker, Shannon McCoy, Sherry Perny, and Jennifer Rosenboom, who never cease to amaze me with their support and love for the world of teaching

- My IRA team, Corinne Mooney, Teresa Curto, and Charlene Nichols, who bring an expertise to their profession and have inspired me more than they will ever know

Introduction

S ince the publication of *Creating Strategic Readers* in 2005, I have had the opportunity to travel and meet firsthand with teachers who have read and used the book and to hear their testimonies. *Creating Strategic Readers* has been overwhelmingly received by educators internationally, and it has been making an impact on the next generation of readers. It is inspiring to know that teachers all over are using the first edition to support their readers to think strategically and bring meaning to their learning.

Prior to the first edition of *Creating Strategic Readers*, research was proving—and is still proving—that teachers need to modify some of their traditional practices of teaching skills in isolation (Duffy & Roehler, 1986; Pressley et al., 1992; Pressley, Goodchild, Fleet, Zajchowski, & Evan, 1989). I wrote *Creating Strategic Readers* to support teachers who knew they did not want to teach skills in isolation. These educators know that our *goal* is to teach reading as a strategic, decision-making process that allows readers to use basic reading skills automatically and apply strategies independently to comprehend what they read. What I found that educators really needed was a way to strategically view the components of phonemic awareness, phonics, fluency, vocabulary, and comprehension as identified by the National Reading Panel (NRP) report (National Institute of Child Health and Human Development [NICHD], 2000).

However, because at that time reading initiatives were leaning so much toward explicit, direct instruction, my trepidation was that reading would be viewed as very skill driven without the emphasis being on why readers are doing what they are doing to read. With federal mandates reflecting on embedding the five components in effective instruction and the accountability for ensuring that all students read by the third grade within the Reading First legislation, it was my desire to equip educators with techniques that concentrate on effective instruction within these five components, promoting strategic reading.

Looking Back to Look Forward: Focusing on the Whole Child

As we continue to strive to help create these strategic learners, it is imperative that we assess the multitude of theories and initiatives that educators have researched and applied over generations in the name, and sometimes *game*, of education. It is time we revisit what has worked, and what has not, within educational mandates and bring forth a secure and steady system that will successfully propel learners in the 21st century. We need to analyze the art and science of how to support, rather than suppress, critical and creative thinking.

Prior to the No Child Left Behind (NCLB) act, the Goals 2000: Educate America Act of 1994 focused on preparing students for "a technologically sophisticated and competitive job market" (Short & Talley, 1997, p. 234). Standards embedded in this act focused more than NCLB on the whole child: critical thinker, creative learner, effective communicator, and cooperative worker to name a few. I believe if we take the cognitive, scientifically based knowledge and questions that surfaced from NCLB and weave it with the artistic standards incorporated in past educational acts, our focus will then become educating the whole child. It is a crucial time for all of us to support the education system in teaching the minds of tomorrow to empower them to lead the way. It will be necessary for 21st-century educators to have cognitive knowledge and artistic design of the whole child as they scaffold their instruction systematically. In order for students to become responsible for their learning, educators will need to cultivate them to be intrinsically motivated, engaged, strategic, and able to direct their own learning.

When working with teachers who were using the first edition, I found that many wanted to discuss and reflect on ways to motivate and engage their readers while focusing on the strategies. Therefore, I incorporated a section on motivation and engagement, which is explained in more detail in Chapter 1, and I emphasized the importance of teaching to reach all readers by reflecting on the whole child. The first edition presented timeless strategies that proficient readers apply, and all of those strategies are in this edition with updated research to support them and show why they are widely successful with independent readers. There are also 35 new techniques presented in this edition that support the strategies.

This second edition is a resource for teaching the strategies that will empower learners to bring meaning to their learning in all areas. Reading *needs* to be the forefront of all content area learning. According to the report by the Commission on Reading, *Becoming a Nation of Readers* (Anderson, Hiebert, Scott, & Wilkinson, 1985), "Reading is a process in which information from the text and the knowledge possessed by the reader act together to produce meaning" (p. 8). This interaction between the reader and the text generates critical thinking and problem solving while the reader is engaging in the reading process, allowing readers to be active thinkers rather than passive ones. Currently U.S. legislation is focusing on regaining the whole child. The American Recovery and Reinvestment Act (ARRA) 2009 lays the foundation for educators to focus on the science and art of educating the whole child.

The days of stressing the acquisition of reading skills *in isolation* are in the past even if some programs interpreted the NCLB act as bringing forth the isolation of skills to teach reading. Skills are valuable if it is understood how to apply them. Self-regulated readers apply their reading skills automatically, concentrating on the strategies rather than the skills. This form of self-regulation is the ultimate design of strategic readers (Hilden & Pressley, 2007; Paris, Wasik, & Turner, 1991; Parsons, 2008).

Educators may utilize this book as a source to better equip themselves in the craft of teaching reading while also focusing on the whole child. This book stresses embedding all five of the components (phonemic awareness, phonics, fluency, vocabulary, and comprehension), their strategies, their techniques, and teacher talk into a comprehensive literacy approach. This approach should include scaffolding: modeling for the students, interacting with the students, gradually guiding the students, and allowing ample time for independent application of skills and strategies by the students. This scaffolding, or gradual release of responsibility (Pearson & Gallagher, 1983), should occur repeatedly throughout teaching and learning opportunities. Scaffolding instruction according to the individual needs of readers will help students to become independent, strategic readers.

To move forward successfully, teachers need a plethora of research-based reading strategies at their disposal. That is the purpose of this second edition, to apply these timeless strategies and allow opportunities to engage and motivate the whole learner.

Overview of This Book

A curriculum, assessment, and instruction (CAI) framework, guided by addressing the whole child, is presented in Chapter 1 of this book. Chapter 1 also discusses the comprehensive literacy classroom and the developmental stages of reading, with the emphasis added in this edition on motivating and engaging the reader. Learning stations have also been aligned in Chapter 1 to many of the techniques in the book.

Chapters 2–6 focus on the NRP's (NICHD, 2000) five components of reading. Each chapter focuses on a specific component, beginning with an overview of that component and identifying strategies that students can use when implementing that component. The strategies do not need to be taught in a specific order; the order should be based on individual students' needs. Each strategy is defined and then followed by instructional techniques that support the application of the strategy. This edition includes 35 new techniques to support teaching the necessary strategies for self-regulated reading.

The CAI framework is demonstrated in each chapter. The *curriculum* section is identified as the reading component and strategies within the chapters (i.e., what you want your students to know about phonemic awareness and what strategies you want them to apply in the area of phonemic awareness).

Strategy *assessments* are embedded within each strategy for educators to evaluate students' strengths and weaknesses within a particular strategy. These assessments are guides to help keep the end results in mind as educators implement the various techniques that support the strategies. A review of appropriate teacher talk (e.g., statements, questions, and prompts) is provided at the beginning of each of the strategy sections and within each technique; using such teacher talk encourages readers to think strategically as they employ the given skills. See the appendix for an assessment matrix that aligns several assessments to each of the reading components. This is by no means an exhaustive list; it is only meant to support educators and be used as a starting point if necessary.

The *instructional* techniques support the strategies and are designed to reach the whole child. The techniques within the strategies are presented in order of the stages of reading (i.e., emergent, early, transitional, and fluent). The procedure for each technique should begin with the teacher modeling the entire technique using appropriate text and then be followed by ample time for students to work toward independent use of the strategy. Each technique identifies corresponding developmental reading levels and multiple intelligences. In this second edition, I also include additional ways to motivate and engage students. The added "Motivation/Engagement" sections are meant to help teachers differentiate their instruction when trying to reach the whole child. Thus, each section incorporates an additional intelligence or whole child standard. In addition, although the NRP report (NICHD, 2000) did not address some important areas of reading due to time constraints, I felt it was important to include techniques that best support English-language learners (ELLs); applicable techniques are identified in Chapters 2–6. However, it is important to note that the Center for the Improvement of Early Reading Achievement (CIERA) recommends that ELLs learn to read in their first language before being taught to read English (Hiebert, Pearson, Taylor, Richardson, & Paris, 1998).

A recommended resource list can be found at the end of the references. These resources are identified throughout the chapters. Many of the techniques in this book have accompanying reproducibles; these can be found on the CD 💿. See Table 1 for a listing of the CD materials. Note that the CD includes an assessment rubric for each chapter; these assessments include all of the strategy assessments from each chapter in one comprehensive format. In addition, a primary and intermediate DVD series is available illustrating many of the techniques presented in this second edition. If applicable, this is noted at the beginning of each technique.

My life's mission has always been to inspire, encourage, and transform lives. As a classroom teacher, I wanted my students to leave my doors *confident* who they were, *dedicated* to being life-long learners, and *driven* to apply their newfound knowledge. More than ever, the time has come for all of us to rise above the challenges that are all around and become *confident, dedicated,* and *driven* educators who believe that their students can achieve! The students in today's classrooms are tomorrow's future. It is time for all of us to believe that these students can be life-long, self-regulated, strategic readers. Do you believe that the children are our future? A well-known song by Whitney Houston says for us to "teach them well and let them lead the way." I do believe we need to provide opportunities for these young minds to fully develop so they are equipped to be *confident, dedicated,* and *driven* to successfully take this world into the next century. Use this book as an artist palette. Dip your brushes into the colorful ways (strategies and techniques) to create on your canvases (your students' minds) a masterpiece of learning that completes the whole picture (strategic readers)!

TABLE 1. Contents Listing for Accompanying CD

Book Chapter	Accompanying CD Material
Chapter 1: A Comprehensive Literacy Classroom	Emergent Reader Assessment Early Reader Assessment Transitional Reader Assessment Fluent Reader Assessment
Chapter 2: Phonemic Awareness	Musical Rhyme Pictures Rhyming Jar Sentences Draw a Rhyme Pair–Share Match Think Sounds Graphing Phonemes Graphing Phonemes Answer Key Chart Bingo/Bongo Word Changers Phonemic Awareness Assessment
Chapter 3: Phonics	Letterboxes Roll-Read-Record DISSECT Word Detectives Calculating Cues Onset and Rimes Vowel Pattern Jingles Working With Words Brain Tricks: Making Connections Brain Tricks: Visualize If I Can Spell Creating Words Look/Say/Cover/Write/Check 10 Ways to Help Know My Word Phonics Assessment
Chapter 4: Fluency	Teacher Talk Phrase Cards Phrase Strips Choices Reading Bookmark Listen to Me Express Yourself Punctuation Police Tickets Emotion Mat Fluency Assessment
Chapter 5: Vocabulary	Reflection Connection Puzzle Pieces Semantic Feature Analysis What Do You Mean? Context Complex Clues Alphaboxes List/Group/Label Four Corners Vocabulary Tree Word Jar Knowledge Rating Vocabulary Assessment

(continued)

TABLE 1. Contents Listing for Accompanying CD *(continued)*

Book Chapter	Accompanying CD Material
Chapter 6: Comprehension	Text Traits
	Connect and Reflect
	Anticipation/Reaction Guide
	Think Sheet
	Two-Column Note Prediction Form
	QARs
	Question Logs: 3Rs
	SQ3R
	Sensory Impressions: Form 1
	Sensory Impressions: Form 2
	Detail/Retell Rubric
	Story Mapping
	Narrative Pyramid
	Main Idea Wheel: Primary Grades
	Main Idea Wheel: Intermediate Grades
	Synthesizing Target
	Comprehension Assessment

A Comprehensive Literacy Classroom

The basis for a comprehensive literacy classroom is solid CAI. These three essentials are the infrastructure that gives educators a sound foundation upon which to build comprehensive literacy teaching. A comprehensive literacy classroom ensures that this infrastructure is inclusive, extensive, far reaching, and wide ranging in the content of literacy. Literacy involves all aspects of reading, writing, listening, viewing, and speaking. It is the thread within all content areas. Weaving curriculum, assessment, and instruction daily in a comprehensive literacy classroom is crucial for student achievement. If our ultimate goal, as educators, is for students to exhibit a wide mental grasp of all aspects of literacy, then teachers must be knowledgeable about how to teach and reach the "whole child." By the whole child, I am referring to the developmental domains of the student's cognitive growth, mental and physical health, and social and emotional welfare. In a comprehensive literacy classroom, the whole child or comprehensive learner is at the center of all areas of curriculum, assessment, and instruction. Figure 1 illustrates the composition of a comprehensive learner that helps to shape the whole child or 21st-century learner: These aspects include being a critical thinker, creative learner, cooperative worker, effective and active leader, and more. In this chapter, I provide an overview of the CAI cycle, and I provide detail on how to best meet the needs of comprehensive learners.

C = Curriculum

The first aspect of the CAI comprehensive literacy classroom is curriculum. Using a standards-based curriculum is the initial step for teachers to be aware of what they want their students to know and be able to do. By aligning lessons with current standards, teachers can express a specific purpose for what they want students to learn and apply. It is vital that the standards are useful in the classrooms and can be measured (Marzano & Haystead, 2008). The five components of reading identified by the NRP's report (NICHD, 2000)—phonemic awareness, phonics, fluency, vocabulary, and comprehension—are embedded within current U.S. state standards, benchmarks, and grade-level expectations. Phonemic awareness is the ability to orally compose a sequence of sounds and manipulate these sounds to form words. Phonics is the ability to recognize the relation between written

FIGURE 1. The Whole Child/21st-Century Learner

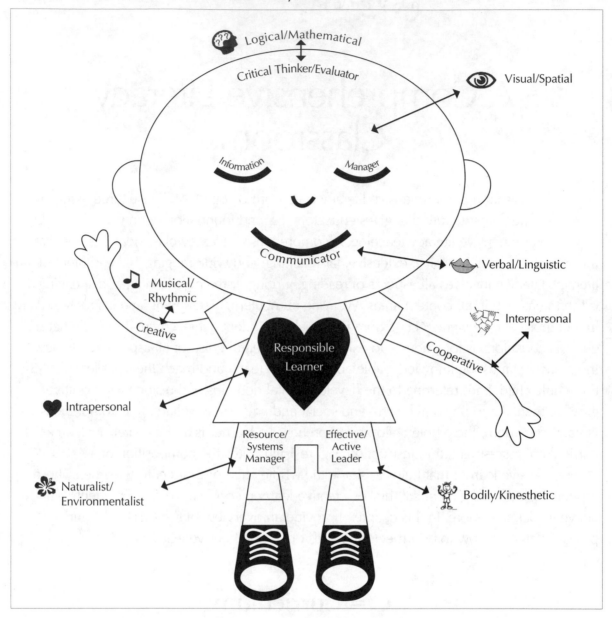

language (letters) and spoken language (sounds). Fluency is the ability to read orally with speed and accuracy and is the bridge between word recognition and comprehension. Vocabulary is the ability to use words orally and in written communication by applying word meaning effectively. Comprehension is the ability to apply meaning to what is read. It is imperative that teachers and students gain a firm understanding of these five components and their corresponding strategies, which represent what strategic readers "do."

Table 2 identifies the strategies within the five components highlighted in Chapters 2–6. Applying strategies in a standards-based curriculum involves bringing the students to a metacognitive level within the curriculum. When students reflect on the purpose of the

TABLE 2. Strategies Within the Five Essential Reading Components

Phonemic Awareness	Phonics	Fluency	Vocabulary	Comprehension
Rhyming	Synthesizing	Phrasing	Associating	Previewing
Isolating and Identifying Phonemes	Analyzing	Assisted Reading	Contextualizing	Activating and Building Background Knowledge
Blending Phonemes	Contextualizing	Rereading	Categorizing	Predicting
Segmenting Phonemes	Patterning	Expressing	Visual Imaging	Questioning
Manipulating Phonemes	Spelling	Pacing	Analyzing	Visualizing and Sensory Imaging
	Recognizing	Wide Reading	Word Awareness	Inferring and Drawing Conclusions
		Accuracy	Wide Reading	Summarizing
			Referencing	Determining Importance
				Synthesizing

lesson by answering the question "Why are we doing this?" after a lesson, they begin to regulate, evaluate, and monitor their thinking. Effective learners can describe what they are learning, not just what they are doing (Marzano, 2007). Metacognitive thinking causes students to be conscious of their learning processes and reinforces their understanding of the purpose of the lesson. They are then able to make conscious choices about what they need to do to learn the standards, and they are able to effectively apply strategies to achieve a level of success as readers and writers. Knowing which strategy to use provides students with the control to comprehend—and demonstrate their wide mental grasp of—the curriculum. Chapters 2–6 outline the strategies proficient readers apply independently and at times simultaneously, as needed, to acquire meaning from the text.

Literacy is the basis for all other content area learning. If students cannot read and write proficiently through various modes of meaning, their resulting inability to acquire necessary academic achievements in other areas becomes a deficit for learning. Content area literacy involves students reading and writing about multiple forms of texts (Readence, Bean, & Baldwin, 2007). The literacy communalities of reading, writing, and thinking still underpin these content areas, even with a variety of text formats. According to Shanahan and Shanahan (2008), "the different disciplines result in unique challenges for readers" (p. 53). Multimodal learning is necessary in helping students meet the challenges of multiple forms of text in today's society across content areas (Jewitt & Kress, 2003; Thompson, 2008; Unsworth & Heberle, 2009). These various modes of text representations (e.g., digital media, artistic designs, symbols) support the learners' meaning making process. Teachers who are serious about their commitment to developing a comprehensive literacy classroom must put this commitment into practice with a daily schedule that devotes a substantial portion of the day to a comprehensive literacy curriculum throughout all content areas. Integrating with the content areas of science, social studies, and even portions of the mathematics curriculum standards is the key to sound and relevant learning. Several important factors that support high-quality literacy learning instruction include maximizing the time students spend on reading, blending reading and writing into every subject area, explicitly instructing students about how to construct meaning from texts, applying critical literacy, and providing students with many opportunities to discuss what they are reading and to share from different points of view (Behrman, 2006; Hall & Piazza, 2008; Knapp, 1995; Lenz, 2006).

Teachers' ultimate goal should be to provide real and relevant learning opportunities for students to apply the curriculum, make connections, and explore meaning before, during, and after reading strategically.

A = Assessment

The next component of the CAI comprehensive literacy classroom is assessment. Assessments are windows into the learner's knowledge, beliefs, and attitudes. There are numerous purposes for gathering information about students. Educators assess to determine the progress of students' cognitive development, inform instruction, demonstrate teacher and school accountability, motivate and encourage students, and aid in educating and assessing the whole child. Students and teachers should utilize a variety of assessment tools such as oral reading records, observations, surveys, interviews, conferences, portfolios, anecdotal notes, developmental checklists, and commercial assessments to accommodate these assessment purposes (Afflerbach, 2007; Beaver, 2006; Edwards, Turner, & Mokhtari, 2008). As teachers collect these artifacts, it is imperative that the assessments are used for learning about the whole child and to inform instruction.

Using Assessment for Learning and Evaluation for Informing

Assessment results reveal the students' current knowledge base (i.e., strengths) and their need for future growth (i.e., weaknesses). Once the evidence is formulated, it is recorded as "raw-score" data. If educators just record this data (e.g., a level 24 or 89%, interpersonal) and continue to cover the curriculum without feedback or using the data to inform instruction, students may fall into a cycle of failure. With this method, teachers are assessing "for recording" not for learning. Ultimately, assessment for learning "keeps students and their teachers in touch with understanding and achievement on a continuous basis, allowing them to know what specific actions they can take to improve learning every day" (Stiggins & Chappuis, 2008, p. 44). Assessment collaboration between student and teacher allows students to know themselves and gives voice to students' learning.

The data from these assessments must then be evaluated, which means "making judgments about the effectiveness of teaching for learning on the basis of credible objective assessment" (Traill, 1995, p. 5). Once the teacher evaluates the assessment, he or she must map out any changes in students' behavior as the students continue to develop as readers, collaborating and planning instruction with students accordingly (Davis, 2003; Fountas &

Pinnell, 1999; Stiggins & Chappuis, 2008). This allows teachers to differentiate instruction based on the specific needs of the students.

Types of Assessments: Screening, Diagnostic, Progress Monitoring

Teachers use a screening assessment to determine whether there are any specific deficits in the students' performances. Literacy screening assessments are brief, informal or formal assessments that identify students who are likely to need extra or alternative forms of instruction. If screening results indicate proficiency, then initial instruction continues. However, if concerns arise based on the evaluation from the screening results, further diagnosis is necessary. The teacher then administers a diagnostic assessment to determine their strengths and weaknesses. In the classroom, teachers need to select a diagnostic that best assesses the problem area identified through the screening. The results of the diagnostic will then indicate the type of instruction needed for immediate and intense intervention. Teachers must give periodic, ongoing monitoring assessments for all students to evaluate student progress after instruction. This helps to decide whether instruction has been effective and should continue or if it should be revised. The assessment data dictates what instruction is appropriate to meet differing student needs. Instruction should be driven by the appropriate data. This data can range from very specific objectives to a wide range of information that informs classroom practice and leads to better application of materials and curriculum goals, making student success possible and pursuable rather than impossible and improbable (Tierney & Readence, 2005).

Developmental Stages or Levels of Reading

Knowing students' reading abilities is essential for teachers. Skillful teachers strategically observe their students' reading and writing behaviors and identify the specific characteristics each student is exhibiting as a literacy learner. As students develop into strategic readers, they gradually move through four stages or levels of reading: emergent, early, transitional, and fluent. These stages will be explained in more detail throughout this section. Teachers can identify points along this gradual process toward strategic reading through the behaviors the readers demonstrate. Observation of learners at work provides "information needed to design sound instruction" (Clay, 2002, p. 11). Today's classrooms have a variety of these leveled learners regardless of the grade. Therefore, it is important for teachers to be familiar with the characteristics within all the levels to reach all readers.

When teachers are able to see their students in light of students' individual reading behaviors, they begin to recognize how they can support their students as readers. For example, if a student has the characteristics of an early reader, the teacher can then decide how to best support that student's further developmental progress in reading. The teacher uses this interaction to help propel the student into the next stage, that of a transitional reader. Therefore, it is vital that teachers gain a keen insight into these stages. This knowledge will assist educators in deciding what types of assessments and instructional strategies and techniques are suitable for their students' specific reading needs.

Within each developmental stage there is a corresponding table that highlights instructional techniques presented in this book, grouped by the five components of reading. Teachers may use these charts as resources when choosing a component to teach their readers. The techniques are categorized according to when they are best used for effective instruction: before, during, or after reading of a particular text.

I also created developmental reader assessments for each of the developmental stages (see CD ⊙). These rubric scale assessments help teachers determine more specifically the developmental level of an emergent, early, transitional, or fluent reader's reading behaviors. Teachers align instruction with the appropriate area of reading that best supports identified behaviors. Teachers observe students with appropriate level text and mark and date the indicator box (Never, Rarely, Often, Always) that best reflects students' behavior. Next, teachers analyze the rubric scale to determine areas of strength and weakness for individual students. Then, teachers guide instruction based on the needs of the student. The goal, of course, is to help the student to progress to the next level of reading. When 8 out of 10 boxes are marked "Always," the student is considered a solid reader at that level.

EMERGENT STAGE. The emergent stage of reading is a time when students begin to make correlations among oral, written, and printed stimuli. These readers enjoy listening to stories, and they understand that print conveys a message. They are acquiring the ability to apply concepts about print to support their development as readers. Their understanding of the direct link of sounds to letters, pictures to words, and speech to sentences clarifies this concept. Through the repetitive use of language and illustrations, these students are able to glean the contextual meaning of written words. The Emergent Reader Assessment (see CD ⊙) identifies these behaviors. Logographic and environmental information (e.g., stop signs) assists emergent readers in approximating meanings of words. Emergent readers benefit from books with short and simple text and with pictures that directly connect to a specific word. The texts should use natural language that has familiar concepts and objects that allow the emergent reader to make connections. There is a consistent format with well-spaced regular print.

Table 3 highlights emergent instructional techniques presented in this book, grouped by the five components of reading.

EARLY STAGE. In the early stage of reading, students have mastered emergent reading behaviors and are becoming more comfortable with the basic concepts about print. They are reading and writing stories at an increasingly higher level of complexity. By using problem-solving skills (e.g., checking and confirming), the early stage reader collects clues about meaning from the letters, words, and illustrations in unfamiliar text. Early stage readers begin to discuss what they are reading with others. These readers are less dependent on rhyme, repetition, and patterns within text and also are beginning to phrase words more

TABLE 3. Emergent Reader Techniques

	Phonemic Awareness	Phonics	Fluency	Vocabulary	Comprehension
Before Reading	Musical Rhyme Rhyming Jar Mirror/Mirror Draw It	Stir It Up Star Search Blinders Predict/Preview/ Polish/Produce Word Walls Letter Recognition High-Frequency Words Irregular and Sight Words	ABC Punctuation Style Book Baskets/ Browsing Boxes	Move to the Meaning Interactive Word Walls Picture and Word Sorts Alphaboxes* Charades Read-Alouds	What I Know… What I Wonder… Book Introduction Text Traits: Getting to Know the Text Anticipation/ Reaction Guides* Picture Walk Story Impression
During Reading	Chime With Rimes		Shared Book Experience Echo Reading Choral Readers Express Yourself* Commercial Programs	Playing With Plurals Read-Alouds	Connect and Reflect Ripple Effect Wordless Picture Books Sensory Impressions*
After Reading		Letter–Sound Magnetic Connection Onset and Rimes		Collaborate and Elaborate* Museum Walk Word Jars Journal Circles* Read-Alouds Resource Buddies	Sketch to Stretch Frame This Detail/Retell Picture This

*Adaptation portion of that particular technique.

fluently. "Their eyes are beginning to control the process of reading, so they do some of their reading without pointing" (Fountas & Pinnell, 1999, p. 5). The Early Reader Assessment (see CD 🄯) provides a quick reference to these behaviors. Although repetitive patterns are still present in the texts early readers are reading, variations in sentence length and language are common; sentences include core high-frequency words that these students can read automatically. The texts selected for early readers should contain simple concepts and story lines that are familiar to students and that relate to real-world experiences. They may have some dialogue among characters. The illustrations should support big concepts rather than specific words. Story lines tend to have a beginning, middle, and end. The text may look easy but ideas require more control of aspects of print.

Table 4 highlights early instructional techniques presented in this book, grouped by the five components of reading.

TRANSITIONAL STAGE. Students in the transitional stage of reading are able to make sense of longer and more complex texts. Transitional stage students easily adapt strategies to support reading for meaning. They use all available clues to find meaning, and these

TABLE 4. Early Reader Techniques

	Phonemic Awareness	Phonics	Fluency	Vocabulary	Comprehension
Before Reading	Musical Rhyme* Mirror/Mirror* Graphing Phonemes Silly Segmenting Bingo/Bongo Colored Cubes	Stir It Up* Letterboxes Stretch It Star Search* Predict/Preview/ Polish/Produce* If I Can Spell Word Walls Look/Say/Cover/ Write/Check* Irregular and Sight Words*	Eye–Voice Span Express Yourself Selecting "Just-Right" Books	Semantic Feature Analysis* Interactive Word Walls Picture and Word Sorts List/Group/Label Read-Alouds*	Book Introduction Text Traits: Getting to Know the Text Skim and Scan Tapping 'N To Reading Journaling Wordless Picture Books* Chapter Tours
During Reading	Draw a Rhyme	Chant/Challenge/ Chart Vowel Patterns Jingles Working With Words	Choral Readers Read-Alongs Listen to Me Punctuation Police Commercial Programs Beam Reading Tempo Time	Cloze Passages With Semantic Gradients	Skim and Scan Connect and Reflect Interpreting Text Journaling or Group Chart Somebody/ Wanted/But/ So*
After Reading	Pair–Share Match Alliteration Activation Hot Seat Body Blending Syllable Giving Egg-Cited About Phonemes Say It Again	Letter–Sound Magnetic Connection* Chant/Challenge/ Chart Onset and Rimes Pattern Sort Brain Tricks Creating Words	Phrase Strips Listen to Me Dramatic Sentences	Collaborate and Elaborate* Alphaboxes Museum Walk* Four Corners Vocabulary Tree Notebook Word Jars Journal Circles Glossary Use	Drama Sensory Impressions Interpreting Text Detail/Retell Summary Ball Main Idea Wheel* Creating a Play

*Adaptation portion of that particular technique.

students can efficiently self-correct to maintain the contextual intent. They are using informational systems (e.g., semantic-meaning, syntactic-structure and grammar, and graphophonics-visual) to self-monitor and to assist in achieving reading independence across the content areas (e.g., math, science, social studies). Transitional readers need relevancy of textual situations to build vocabulary, simple elements (e.g., plot, character, setting, and dialogue), and fluency. They begin to use more verbal expressions as they read, and they self-monitor as needed to maintain meaning from the text. The Transitional Reader Assessment (see CD 🔘) provides a quick reference to these behaviors. Appropriate texts for the transitional reader have more complex language structures (e.g., similes, metaphors) and less emphasis on patterned text. They have more sophisticated and complex themes, with multiple characters providing a variety of perspectives to follow.

Table 5 highlights transitional instructional techniques presented in this book, grouped by the five components of reading.

TABLE 5. Transitional Reader Techniques

	Phonemic Awareness	Phonics	Fluency	Vocabulary	Comprehension
Before Reading	Think Sounds Body Blending* Graphing Phonemes* Silly Segmenting* Colored Cubes*	Word Walls Look/Say/Cover/ Write/Check Irregular and Sight Words*	Phrase Strips Totally Tonality Book Clubs	Compare 'n Share Contextual Redefinition What Do You Mean? Interactive Word Walls Picture and Word Sorts List/Group/ Label* Four Corners* Eye Spy With My Eye Knowledge Rating Read-Alouds* Author Study	Book Introduction Text Traits: Getting to Know the Text Skim and Scan Anticipation/ Reaction Guides Think Sheet Question– Answer Relationships
During Reading		Word Detectives Vowel Pattern Jingles Working With Words	Pausing With Punctuation Choral Readers Repeated Reading/ One-Minute Reads Recorded Reading: Record/ Check/Chart Multimedia Reading Commercial Programs Time/Record/ Check/Chart	Author Study	Connect and Reflect Question Logs: 3Rs Somebody/ Wanted/But/ So Highlighting
After Reading	Rhyming Jar* Draw a Rhyme* Pair–Share Match* Mirror/Mirror* Alliteration Activation* Bingo/Bongo* Syllable Segmentation	Roll-Read- Record Brain Tricks* Creating Words*	Eye–Voice Span* Recorded Reading: Record/ Check/Chart Time/Record/ Check/Chart	Reflection Connection Semantic Feature Analysis Collaborate and Elaborate* Contextual Redefinition Flip-a-Chip Word Jars Quick Writes Author Study Book Talks Thesaurus Use	Save the Last Word for Me Talk Show Detail/Retell Narrative Pyramid Somebody/ Wanted/But/ So Main Idea Wheel Mind Mapping Rewriting a Story Say Something

*Adaptation portion of that particular technique.

FLUENT STAGE. Increasingly heavy reliance on the text, with less reliance on illustrations, indicates a reader's progression into the fluent stage of reading. The illustrations are now only of limited support and more often merely assist in extending the text. Fluent readers can comfortably read independently for extended periods. They recognize many words by sight, and reading happens with automaticity. Prosodic features are evident in their reading through use of intonation, expressions, and accents, and they adjust their pacing according to the purpose and difficulty of the text. Fluent readers have a plethora of strategies for decoding unknown words. These students have become accustomed to challenging vocabulary and become deeply involved with conceptual points of stories. Comprehension occurs at a sophisticated level (i.e., synthesizing and interpreting) more frequently. The Fluent Reader Assessment (see CD 🔘) provides a quick reference to these behaviors. The focus in this fluent stage should be a greater immersion into wide reading. These readers are familiar with complex sentence structures, sophisticated story concepts, and a variety of literary genres. The font size is small and there is minimum picture support in the text. Many new, multisyllable words are embedded within the text for the fluent reader to read and interpret for meaning.

Table 6 highlights fluent instructional techniques presented in this book, grouped by the five components of reading.

Assessing the Whole Child = Creating a Strategic Reader

As educators strive toward creating strategic readers, it is important to get to know the whole child. Effective whole-child assessments are interdependent and can occur simultaneously as they address the developmental domains of students' cognitive growth, mental health and physical well-being, social and emotional welfare, and learning approaches (Coffield, Mosely, Hall, & Ecclestone, 2004; Gardner, 1993; Hodgkinson, 2006; Kohn, 2005; Levine, 2002; Maslow, 1943; O'Connor & Jackson, 2008; Zigler & Finn-Stevenson, 2007; Zigler, Singer, & Bishop-Josef, 2004). There is not one magical assessment that will evaluate the whole child; it is important to recognize that different learners learn best at different times with different contents and in different contexts. Therefore, a one-size-fits-all, "high-stakes" achievement test may still leave educators and students motivated by the score and not the process of learning.

With each educational initiative, we should be able to gain clearer insight on how to reach and teach students. We should be evaluating what was effective within the initiative, and what did not have major impact on student achievement. Although NCLB has its challenges, we still need to continue using the cognitive, scientifically based knowledge gleaned from NCLB along with the focus on the artistic standards incorporated in Goals 2000 and the multitude of current theories available that strive to successfully propel our learners in the 21st century. It is possible "to learn by making sense of experience, gain deep understanding, pick things up from the context, get a feel for things, engage in creative problem solving, master self-regulation and take charge of one's own learning" (Caine &

TABLE 6. Fluent Reader Techniques

	Phonemic Awareness	Phonics	Fluency	Vocabulary	Comprehension
Before Reading		Word Walls Irregular and Sight Words*		Compare 'n Share* Reflection Connection* Context Complex Clues Interactive Word Walls Picture and Word Sorts Read-Alouds* Genre Study	Book Introduction Text Traits: Getting to Know the Text Skim and Scan Story Impressions* Two-Column Note Prediction Survey, Question, Read, Recite, Review
During Reading		Working With Words	Eye 2 Eye Choral Readers Interpretation/ Character Analysis Commercial Programs Digital Portfolio for Oral Reading	Genre Study	Connect and Reflect Survey, Question, Read, Recite, Review Scenarios With T-Charts Highlighting*
After Reading	Think Sounds* Syllable Segmentation* Word Changers	DISSECT Calculating Cues Dancing With Diphthongs Brain Tricks		Move to the Meaning* Collaborate and Elaborate Flip-a-Chip* Root Words Word Jars	Survey, Question, Read, Recite, Review Detail/Retell Synthesizing Target

*Adaptation portion of that particular technique.

Caine, 2007, p. 2). Assessments are a window into the learner's knowledge, beliefs, and attitudes.

Research in learning styles and intelligences indicates that there are multiple individual styles that teachers can identify and use to select specific instructional strategies to support students' strengths (Gardner, 1983; Levine, 2002). Gardner's (1983, 1993) theory of multiple intelligences suggests that there are a number of distinct forms of intelligence that each individual possesses to some degree. These intelligences are included as indicators to consider when assessing and informing instruction that is individualized to meet the needs of the learners. Table 7 aligns the multiple intelligences and whole-child standards to ways a 21st-century child experiences learning, types of techniques, levels of teacher talk, and alternative forms of assessments. The techniques in this book incorporate and note these intelligences and standards. Aligning the multiple individual styles that focus on proven research-based practices with instructional techniques ensures success for both educators and comprehensive learners. Research suggests that the brain is a pattern detector and

TABLE 7. Comprehensive Learner Matrix

Whole Child/ 21st-Century Learners	Abilities (What they are able to do)	Interests (What they like to do)	Motivation Tools (How to enthuse them)	Cognition (How they actively think)	Teacher Talk (How to communicate with them)	Assessment Tools (How to know if they can do it)
Visual/Spatial (Information Managers)	Perceive the visual, locate and organize relevant information, relate to size, area, or position	Design Draw Observe Doodle Paint	Cartoons Images Multimedia Visual aids Virtual reality games Collages	In pictures: Mental images Graphic organizers Spatial orientation	Visualizing in their mind's eye Illustrating Interpreting Representing	Visual metaphors and analogies Checklists Graphs Rubric
Verbal/Linguistic (Communicators)	Communicate for a given purpose, subject matter, and audience, story teller	Read Write Format stories Write in a diary Debate Tell stories	Bestselling books Word games Wikis/Blogs Peer counseling Humor Dialogue	With words: Elaborative Expressive Symbolism	Convincing Describing Explaining Translating Identifying Listing	Surveys Interviews Word associations Linguistic humor
Logical/ Mathematical (Critical Thinkers/ Evaluators)	Use reason and identify problems that need new and different solutions	Experiment Puzzles Brain teasers Analyze abstract relationships	Graphing Evaluation Calculating Exploring Research	Reasoning, inductive and deductive Quantifying Critically Logically	Analyzing Calculating Distinguishing Verifying Comparing and contrasting	Strategic games Matrices Mnemonics Spreadsheets Problem solving
Musical/ Rhythmic (Creative Learners)	Create, understand, and communicate intuitively	Sing and hum Listen to music jingles and raps Improvise Compose	Audio taping Rhythms Choral reading Musical instruments	By melody or rhythm patterns	Creating Demonstrating Expressing Performing	Tonal patterns Musical performances Checklists Compositions
Bodily/ Kinesthetic (Effective/Active Leaders)	Control body movements, handle objects, multitask	Sports Dance Work with hands Create things	Acting Field trips Active learning Role-playing	Movement sensations Global collaborators	Acting out Constructing Creating Dramatizing	Projects Interviews Dramatizations
Interpersonal (Cooperative Workers)	Recognize and respond to others moods, motivations, and desires	Spend time helping others E-mail, texting Community events	Reporting Dialogue Debate Peer teaching	Communicating Self-reflecting Metacognitively Simulations	Brainstorming Role-playing Sharing Collaborating	Group projects Discussions Paraphrasing Buzz sessions
Intrapersonal (Responsible Learners)	Self-reflect and have awareness of one's own strengths and weaknesses	Plan Imagine Think time Problem solve	Journaling Learning logs Independent learning Goal setting	In relation to their self Reflection Imagery	Concentrating Imagining Self-reflecting Rehearsing "I statements"	Self-assessments Independent contracts Portfolios
Naturalist/ Environmentalist (Resource/System Managers)	Distinguish among features of environment	Backpack Nature walks Visit zoos	Interacting with plants, animals, and other objects of nature	Systematic Orderly Environmental	Classifying Analyzing Investigating	Charts Graphs Systems Scavenger hunt lists Classification graphic organizers

Note. I've adapted Gardner's designation of naturalist to also include environmentalist; this term helps to reflect a focus on conservation and improving the environment.

needs multiple experiences and instructional methods that are congruent in order for the brain to seek and make connections for understanding (Jensen, 2005; Lyons, 2003). For this reason, it is necessary for you to know your students as readers and writers and to know the strategies, techniques, and teacher talk that are important for the students' success as literacy learners. Building, or scaffolding, upon what the students are able to do and guiding them to new understandings are the keys to creating a comprehensive literacy.

Assessing Through Conversational Coaching: Teacher Talk

To bring your students to a metacognitive level with their reading strategies, you will need to be highly aware of the questions, statements, and prompts you are using to support learning. You can use this type of teacher talk as a tool embedded into your conversations as you coach your students to process and think strategically. "In our brains, processing turns data into stored knowledge, meaning, experiences, or feelings" (Jensen & Nickelsen, 2008, p. 105). Your teacher talk should ask questions (e.g., "What words or phrases did the author use to help you create an image in your mind?"), make statements (e.g., "Try to picture in your mind someone who would remind you of a character in the story."), or say prompts (e.g., "I can image what it is like to....") that bring readers to process the information. Students who are exposed to higher order thinking and questioning comprehend more than students who are passively asked lower order questions (Amer, 2006; Anderson & Krathwohl, 2001; Bloom & Krathwohl, 1956; Eber, 2007; Kunen, Cohen, & Solman, 1981; Redfield & Rousseau, 1981; Taylor, 2008). Teacher talk is the link to scaffolding instruction to help students be aware of their use of strategies and to think about the processes that are occurring to apply a particular strategy. This is the metacognitive awareness that is imperative for readers to develop into strategic readers. Chapters 2–6 incorporate a variety of teacher talk with each of the strategies.

I = Instruction

Instruction is the final aspect of a CAI comprehensive literacy classroom. Instruction is an "act" that supports active learning. The instructor "can have a profound influence on student learning" (Marzano, Pickering, & Pollock, 2001 p. 3). The initial instruction needs to be clear, concise, and meaningful to engage the learners. An instructional framework begins with establishing a physical environment and a classroom community that is conducive to learning. Teachers should have knowledge of the whole reader as they scaffold their instruction systematically. Using the scaffolding model, teachers gradually release instruction through literacy approaches (read-aloud, modeled writing, shared literacy, guided reading and writing, and independent literacy). As teachers align instruction with the needs of students, they may need to respond to intervention through differentiating their techniques.

Effective instruction considers the conditions for optimal learning and then actively strives to combine the art and science of teaching to create strategic readers.

Conditions for Optimal Learning

Expectations, procedures, and an environment conducive to learning all need to be determined and in place for a comprehensive literacy classroom to be successful. Cambourne's (1995) conditions for learning is one model to help teachers implement the conditions that should be in place for optimal learning. In all their literacy endeavors, teachers should examine these nine conditions and the literacy approaches that align with them, remembering their ultimate goal being superlative learning. Table 8 defines each condition and shows the alignment of the condition with a comprehensive literacy classroom.

Gradual Release Through Scaffolding = I → We → You

Scaffolding instruction is a concept that focuses on how individuals learn (Collins, Brown, & Newman, 1989; Vygotsky, 1978) and provides support in the development of their learning. The support is given "to students within their zone of proximal development enabling them to develop understandings that they would have not been capable of understanding independently" (Many, Taylor, Wang, Sachs, & Schreiber, 2007, p. 19). Pearson and Gallagher (1983) further developed the scaffolding research with their concept about the gradual release of responsibility (GRR). GRR calls for support to be given by the teacher while the students are learning a new concept, skill, or strategy; that support then slowly diminishes as the students gain responsibility for their own learning. The GRR framework gradually moves from the teacher modeling ("*I* do it") through collaboration by sharing and guiding ("*We* do it") to a state of self-sufficiency ("*You* do it!").

Modeling by the teacher occurs with every new learning experience and is imperative before the student can be expected to attempt the unknown. Initially, the teacher models what he or she wants the students to be able to do (e.g., a strategy within one of the five components of reading). Teachers should demonstrate these strategies in a metacognitive manner. For example, if the teacher wants to concentrate on the summarizing strategy, he or she will be the doer and thinker in front of the students. After reading from a selection of text, the teacher begins to think aloud the objective: "I just read a part from this story, and I want to see if I can focus on the key elements of what I am reading, because that is what good readers do. So now I am going to think of a way to show how I can summarize it." The teacher then selects a technique (e.g., Narrative Pyramid) that supports the modeled strategy, and he or she thinks aloud the process of the strategy: First, the teacher demonstrates setting up the pyramid by saying, "I am going to draw some lines in a pyramid format. The top of the pyramid only has one line for one character. I will need to think of a character that was very important in the story and write only that character's name on the first line." This process of thinking aloud demonstrates examples of what happens in the mind of a reader. In effective instruction, this modeling is necessary and is the basis for optimal learning.

TABLE 8. Conditions for Optimal Learning

Condition	Description (Adapted from Cambourne, 1995)	Comprehensive Literacy Classroom	Stations (Adapted from Nations & Alonso, 2001)
Immersion	To be exposed to an environment rich in spoken and written language	Provides multiple opportunities for reading, writing, listening, speaking, and viewing using a wide variety of materials All literacy approaches Community building	Provides a print-rich environment with words and labels around stations Immerses students with books and book talk Encourages students to talk to one another as they develop skills and strategies
Demonstration	To observe models of proficient, strategic reading and writing	Models what the students' need to know and be able to do, be explicit, and deliberate during initial instruction Read-alouds and modeled writing	Models for students before any activity is placed in a station Explains the what, why, and how of each task Models process as well as product Revisits demonstrations as needed
Expectation	To believe that literacy strategies and skills can and will be acquired	Identifies and posts reasonable expectations and procedures with students Ongoing informal and formal assessments	Teaches and models expectations for station use Sets up stations in a supportive yet challenging manner
Engagement	To want to try authentic reading and writing strategies and techniques To be confident about support	Interacts in experiences of successful readers and writers Focuses on tasks responsive to literacy Participates in shared literacy Provides cooperative learning experiences	Connects minilessons to the station experiences in the classroom Gives students many opportunities to practice and apply skills and strategies Shares the purpose of each activity with purpose cards at stations
Use	To apply authentic reading and writing throughout daily life	Integrates with other content areas Is relevant to life application Participates in guided/small groups and independent literacy	Gives students many opportunities to practice and apply skills and strategies at stations
Approximations	To be free to explore and make attempts at what proficient, strategic readers and writers can do	Promotes risk taking and supports instruction at the learner's need level Builds trust and positive social skills Participates in guided literacy and critical literacy	Provides many opportunities in stations without mastery expected all the time Values the process, not just the finished product Places examples in stations to support student learning

(continued)

TABLE 8. Conditions for Optimal Learning *(continued)*

Condition	Description (Adapted from Cambourne, 1995)	Comprehensive Literacy Classroom	Stations (Adapted from Nations & Alonso, 2001)
Response	To receive feedback on attempts to read and write strategically	Gives specific, timely, and relevant feedback Gives voice to students Includes conferences, small groups, and journal responses	Invites students to positively respond to the work of peers Encourages and informs students about their progress Responds supportively and constructively
Responsibility	To be able to make choices and decisions To be engaged rather than observing	Provides opportunities to make choices Allows for student ownership and self-regulation Participates in independent literacy	Sets up stations so the learner can make meaningful decisions about reading and writing Allows for choice within stations

Teachers should continue to utilize GRR throughout their instruction of the curriculum. After teacher modeling of each strategy, students need time to interact with the teacher to gain further understanding. When the students begin to try the strategy on their own, the teacher should be there to guide them. The final phase of this scaffolding process is for the student to apply the strategy independently. According to Routman (2003), "When teachers understand and internalize this model, teaching and learning become more effective, efficient, and enjoyable" (p. 43). Comprehensive literacy classrooms are conducive to this maturation of learning because students have the opportunity to become proficient strategic readers and writers in a supportive, risk-free environment.

Figure 2 shows the GRR concept. The "solid-core" instruction is at the center of the target, and instruction gradually moves outside the center for the student to gain independence. Teachers and students can move within the zones as needed throughout the day.

Instructing the Whole Child = Creating a Strategic Reader

In order for students to become responsible for their learning, educators need to empower them to be intrinsically motivated, strategic, and able to direct their own learning. This form of self-regulation is the ultimate design of a strategic reader (Hilden & Pressley, 2007; Horner & O'Connor, 2007; Paris, Wasik, & Turner, 1991; Parsons, 2008; Perry, Hutchinson, & Thauberger, 2007). When designing instruction, teachers reflect and utilize the data gained through assessing the whole child (i.e., interests, motivation, levels, styles). Instructing the whole child involves tapping into the interests and motivations of the learner. Igniting this aspect of the whole learner will inspire effort and bring forth engagement on the part of the student, ultimately increasing student achievement (Brophy, 1983; Dewey, 1913; Fink & Samuels, 2008; Harackiewicz, Durik, Barron, Linnenbrink-Garcia, & Tauer, 2008; Jang, 2008; Jensen, 2005; Kohn, 1993; Lavoie, 2007; Skinner & Belmont, 1993). Table 9 highlights the concepts of motivation, engagement, and interest. The techniques in this book incorporate these concepts through the process of creating strategic readers.

FIGURE 2. Gradual Release of Responsibility

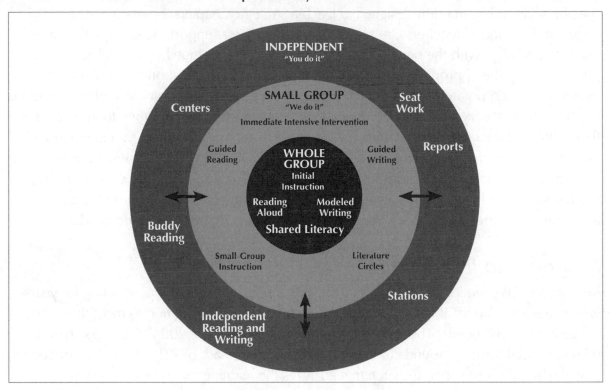

TABLE 9. Interest, Motivation, and Engagement

Interest	Motivation	Engagement
The awareness in which the student is aroused, demonstrates curiosity about, and shows drive and passion toward the task.	The factors that stimulate and give incentive (intrinsic and extrinsic); reason, action, and desire that causes a certain behavior.	The degree to which the student is actively and passionately connected to the learning experience.
What are the student's passions? What is the student doing after school or in his or her free time? What does the student talk about/express most? What are the characteristics of his or her appearance (i.e., clothes, hair)?	Why did he or she do what was done? Does the student initiate action when given the opportunity? Is the student exerting intense effort in the learning tasks? Is the student demonstrating enthusiasm and curiosity toward the given learning experience?	Is the student willingly participating? Does the student genuinely care about the learning experience? Is the student actively involved in the outcome of the experience? Does the student share in the responsibility of their learning?

The process of planning this type of instruction begins with the end in mind (Covey, 1989, 2006; Tomlinson & McTighe, 2006; Wiggins & McTighe, 2005). Educators need to think similar to designers and ask questions like, "What would be an interesting and engaging activity to support the students to uncover the main purpose of the lesson?" Instructing the whole child requires teachers to be knowledgeable of the strategies (curriculum), the learner (assessment), and the techniques (instruction). Techniques are the specific skills and instruction designed to teach a strategy. Chapters 2–6 incorporate a variety of techniques; teachers can select the ones that best support the strategy they are teaching and align with the needs of their students. Each technique begins with stating the purpose (why), the appropriate developmental level, and the corresponding multiple intelligences incorporated to instruct the whole child. It is essential that the students have the opportunity to observe the teacher modeling the initial instruction and then to interact as they emulate the strategy the technique is designed to support. Teachers should begin with high-quality, effective instruction to reach the whole child. However, if a student becomes weakened in an area and demonstrates a need for additional support, it is critical for the teacher to respond with immediate intense instructional intervention. This response accelerates the "mending and repairing to whole" process of the fragmented child.

Response to Intervention

Response to intervention (RTI) is what effective teachers have been implementing for years with struggling readers. It is the act of providing high-quality instruction to meet the struggling readers' needs. The Individuals with Disabilities Act of 2004 (IDEA) combined with the NCLB form the foundation for the "official" trademark of RTI. RTI is an instructional practice based on scientific research that analyzes the learning rate over time to make important educational decisions about students with learning disabilities (Allington & Walmsley, 2007; Batsche et al., 2005; Reutebuch, 2008). It recommends a multi-tiered intervention approach based on progress monitoring of the instructional practice in general and special favoring for small-group and individualized tutoring (Allington, 2008; Fuchs & Fuchs, 2008; Vaughn, Linan-Thompson, & Hickman, 2003). Figure 3 identifies the Three Tier

FIGURE 3. Three Tier Model of Intervention

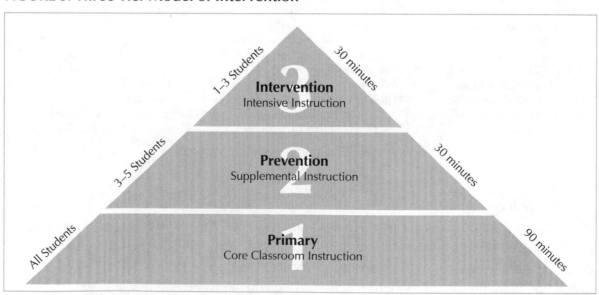

Model of Intervention being implemented throughout U.S. schools. The techniques presented in this book support strategies that are research proven to create strategic readers as you respond to the individual needs of the learners throughout the tiers.

Comprehensive Literacy Approaches

The comprehensive literacy classroom uses this same process of gradual release to implement the literacy approaches: reading aloud, modeled writing, shared literacy, guided reading and writing, and independent literacy. These literacy approaches are the basis for a comprehensive literacy block that teachers can utilize to effectively implement the components of reading, writing, listening, viewing, and speaking within the curriculum. Table 10 is a comprehensive literacy tool that highlights the characteristics of each of the

TABLE 10. Characteristics of Literacy Approaches in a Comprehensive Classroom

I/Model (focuses on demonstration)
- ☐ Selections should be challenging, build background knowledge, and appeal to students' interests or topic of study
- ☐ Uses a variety of genres
- ☐ Teacher demonstrates explicit, deliberate, and meaningful initial instruction
- ☐ Teacher models daily reading and writing strategies through "think alouds"
- ☐ Teacher explains and models the what, how, and why of each task prior to any independent task
- ☐ Purpose for reading or writing is established with specific strategy
- ☐ Familiarizes students with vocabulary and language being used
- ☐ Builds a classroom environment that captures the essence of reading
- ☐ Fosters a community of readers

We/Shared Model (focuses on engagement and approximation)
- ☐ All students have access to the text
- ☐ Initial instruction for a specific skill or strategy occurs
- ☐ Instruction is explicit, systematic, collaborate, and integrated intricately with reading and writing
- ☐ Emphasizes the reading–writing reciprocal relationship
- ☐ Teachers and students interact with the text
- ☐ Uses a variety techniques and emphasizes learning styles
- ☐ Students demonstrate active engagement which begins to foster independence
- ☐ Students gain confidence with support
- ☐ Builds a community of readers and writers

We/Guided Model (focuses on use, approximation, and response)
- ☐ Teacher arranges small, flexible groups
- ☐ Groups have similar needs (prevention or intervention) or interests determined by assessment
- ☐ Teacher selects text based on development level
- ☐ Teacher observes, assesses, and guides students' use of reading and writing skill and strategies
- ☐ Students read text independently, practicing previously introduced teaching points
- ☐ Teacher and student return to text for a teaching point after reading
- ☐ Purpose and teaching points are clear and evident to students

You/Independent Model (responsibility and employment)
- ☐ Students self-select appropriate "just right" books
- ☐ Students process information at their individual pace and practice reading and writing strategies
- ☐ Provides opportunities to engage and explore language
- ☐ Teacher conferring with students one to one
- ☐ Students respond to text by making connections and exploring meaning
- ☐ Students share book recommendations
- ☐ Students use a variety of genres
- ☐ Students self-regulate

TABLE 11. Comprehensive Literacy Block

Segment (Approach)	Who	Duration	Difficulty of Text	Grouping	Resources/Application	Content Area
Reading Aloud (Modeling, Demonstrating, Thinking Aloud) "I" Model	Teacher	10–15 minutes	High (Challenge)	Whole class	Picture books, short stories, chapter books, student-generated stories, variety of genres, connections, think-aloud	Language arts, science, social studies, health, mathematics
Modeled Writing (Modeling, Demonstrating) "I" Model	Teacher	10–15 minutes		Whole class	Part of a writing workshop or the literacy workshop minilesson, morning message, language experiences, creative writing, lists, think-aloud	
Shared Literacy (Interacting, Engagement, Approximation) "We" Model	Teacher, Student	30–45 minutes	Moderate–High (Instructional)	Whole class or small groups	Big Books, short stories, excerpts from stories, chapter books, poetry, chants, sentence strips, magazines, newspapers, student-generated writing, minilesson reading/writing workshop	
Guided Reading* Small-Group Instruction (Guiding, Supporting, Scaffolding, Differentiating) "You more than I" Model	Student, Teacher	40–60 minutes	Moderate–Easy (Instructional/Independent)	Small groups or independent, same-level groups, interest groups, literature groups, targeted strategy/skill-based groups, individual conferences	Leveled text, magnetic letters, dry-erase boards or plastic plates, flashlights, mirrors, stretch it strips, learning logs, sticky notes	
Guided Writing* (Guiding, Supporting, Scaffolding, Differentiating) "You more than I" Model	Student, Teacher				Brainstorming, peer talk, writing folders, conferencing, author study and texts	
Independent Literacy* (Independent, Responsible, Employment) "You" Model	Student†		Easy (Independent)		Journals, literacy response logs, observation notebooks, research projects, literacy stations, silent reading, literature circles, commercial programs, browsing boxes with "just right" text	

*These approaches may be occurring simultaneously.
†All students participate in a small group 2–4 times per week based on student needs (struggling readers meet more frequently).

literacy approaches. Educators can use this comprehensive literacy tool as a form of self-assessment of indicators for a professional development plan or as an observation checklist for reading coaches or administrators.

Comprehensive Literacy Block

The comprehensive literacy block is a teaching framework for which teachers should use, at a minimum, a 120-minute block of instructional time. This block of time includes a 90-minute uninterrupted reading block and additional writing instruction time. Table 11 details a sample comprehensive literacy block and shows the approaches and the skills each segment of the block teaches (i.e., who is involved, how long it lasts, what type of text is used, and what type of grouping and resources are needed). This table will assist teachers in planning their own comprehensive literacy blocks.

This literacy schedule allows flexibility in the order and sequence of the specific literacy approaches used. For example, the teacher first selects teaching content from the area of language arts (e.g., comprehension, one of the five components of reading, and the strategy of summarizing). Next, the teacher selects a technique within the strategy (e.g., Narrative Pyramid within the strategy of summarizing in Chapter 6) and incorporates specific teacher talk to support the thinking process of the strategy. If this is the first time teaching this technique, the teacher will need to use the approach of modeling the technique and thinking aloud the thought process for the technique. Teachers may prefer to implement a unit of study on a specific concept or strategy using a variety of techniques that support it. Concentrating on this specific strategy for several weeks is powerful for the learner because there is time for modeling, practical application, and chances for multiple attempts. Table 12 lists literacy station ideas to support independent literacy within the comprehensive literacy block.

The Challenge

The CAI cycle continues throughout the learning process. All three components need to be present in a comprehensive, systematic, explicit approach to meet the multiple needs and diverse learning styles within today's classrooms. Figure 4 shows the student as the core of a comprehensive literacy classroom. It is imperative to keep the student at the center of all decisions on curriculum, assessment, and instruction; the Venn diagram depicts how CAI intersects and allows flexibility for the teacher (e.g., the teacher may assess and then analyze the data to determine the need for immediate, intense intervention in one or more of the five components with specificity in an identified strategy). Curriculum, assessment, and instruction are the infrastructure that, when aligned, create a powerful comprehensive literacy classroom.

I challenge you, the educator, to identify the characteristics of your readers: know your reader. Know what motivates them and how to engage them in their learning process. You

TABLE 12. Literacy Station Ideas

Sample Stations	Sample Materials	Example Techniques
Word Work: To explore letters and words (PA, P, V)	Bingo chips Dry-erase boards and pens Highlighting tape Letters and stamps Letter boxes Overhead projector Picture cards and stickers Pipe cleaners Play dough Pocket chart Shaving cream Sentence strips Transparencies	Alphaboxes Brain Tricks Chant/Challenge/Chart Colored Cubes Egg-Cited About Phonemes Graphing Phonemes Hot Seats (with cups) If I Can Spell Letterboxes Letter–Sound Magnetic Connection Mirror/Mirror Pattern Sort Onset and Rimes Reflection Connection Roll-Read-Record Silly Segmenting Vowel Pattern Jingles Word Detectives
Right On Writing: To explore, compose, and publish written work (PA, P, V, C)	Binding materials Class message board Computers Emotions chart Journal Markers and highlighters Mirrors Pencils and pens Props Student mailboxes Thesaurus and dictionaries Variety of genres Variety of paper Writing folders	Alliteration Activation Express Yourself High-Frequency Words If I Can Spell Irregular and Sight Words Journaling Mind Mapping Mirror/Mirror Museum Walk Narrative Pyramid Onset and Rimes Pattern Sort Punctuation Police Quick Writes Rewriting a Story Sketch to Stretch Totally Tonality
Literally Listening: To listen to readings and read along to use and analyze strategies (F, V, C)	Books on tape CD or tape player Drawing boards Flashlights Headphones Listening logs Prerecorded stories Variety of texts	Draw a Rhyme Draw It Choral Readers Listen to Me Read-Alongs Say It Again Recorded Reading: Record/Check/Chart Time/Record/Chart/Check
Reader's Book Nook: To practice reading strategies (F, V, C)	Comfortable environment (couch, comfy chair, lamps) Flashlights Leveled text Reading log Student published books Stuffed animals Tour hats Variety of genres and formats	Beam Reading Book Baskets/Browsing Boxes Book Clubs Chapter Tours Choral Readers Selecting "Just Right" Books Wordless Picture Books

(continued)

TABLE 12. Literacy Station Ideas *(continued)*

Sample Stations	Sample Materials	Example Techniques
Creative Arts: To use props or role play, dramatize, or retell stories (F, V, C)	Costumes Masks Materials for story props Puppet theater Texts Variety of puppets	Charades Choral Readers Creating a Play Detail/Retell Drama Express Yourself Interpretation/Character Analysis Interpreting Text Sensory Impressions Talk Show Totally Tonality
Poet-Tree: To read, write, or make illustrations of poems (PA, P, F, V, C)	Anthology of poems, variety of different forms of poetry Cut out of a tree Dry-erase board Pocket chart Poetry books and large white paper for charts Poetry notebooks Sentence strips	Chime With Rimes Choral Readers Interpretation/Character Analysis Listen to Me Onset and Rimes Say Something Sensory Impressions Stretch It Vocabulary Tree Notebook

Note. PA = Phonemic awareness, P = Phonics, F = Fluency, V = Vocabulary, C = Comprehension

FIGURE 4. The CAI Cycle

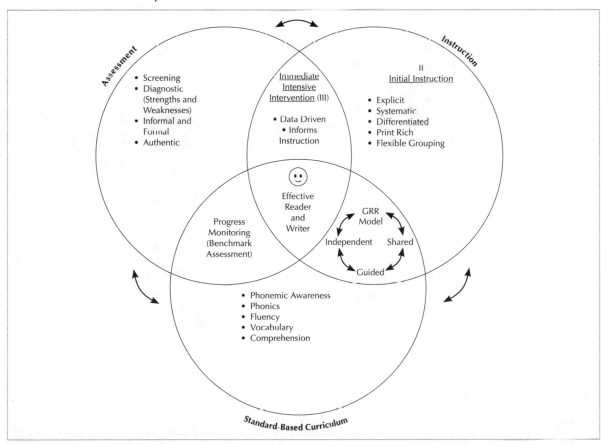

will be empowered when you know your students' developmental stages (emergent, early, transitional, or fluent). Once you identify these reading stages through appropriate assessments, it is then necessary to align strategies and techniques in all five components of reading instruction at a suitable level for the students as needed. It is my hope that you will be encouraged to have a repertoire of strategies, techniques, and teacher talk to meet the individual needs of the diverse learners within your classroom. You may apply the strategies, techniques, and teacher talk presented in this book in any order according to the needs of your students.

My final challenge is for you to consider reading as an art and yourself as an artist. Imagine your students' minds as canvases, just waiting and inviting you to give color and meaning to their learning so you can create the ultimate masterpiece—strategic readers!

Phonemic Awareness

Segmenting Phonemes with **Silly Segmenting** technique

Blending Phonemes with **Body Blending** technique

Isolating and Identifying Phonemes with the **Mirror/ Mirror** technique

Phonemic awareness is a vital link to the success of every reader. To support students in becoming proficient readers, it is important to understand what phonemic awareness is, why it is essential, what strategies and techniques to implement, and how to talk to students so they will think strategically. Phonemic awareness is the understanding that speech is composed of a sequence of sounds combined to form words, and it is the main component of phonological awareness. Students need to have a certain level of phonological awareness to benefit from formal reading instruction.

According to the International Reading Association (IRA; 1998), phonological awareness encompasses larger units of sound, whereas phonemic awareness stems from this concept but refers to smaller units of sound. These small units of speech correspond to letters of an alphabetic writing system; these sounds are called phonemes and can make a difference in a word's meaning. For example, the word *met* has three phonemes, /m/, /e/, /t/. By changing the first phoneme to /j/, we can produce a new word, *jet*, with a completely different meaning.

A student's awareness of phonemes has been shown through extensive research to hold singular predictive power, accounting for as much as 50% of the difference in their reading proficiency at the end of first grade (Cunningham & Stanovich, 1998; Juel, 1988; Menzies, Mahdavi, & Lewis, 2008; NICHD, 2000; Snow, Burns, & Griffin, 1998; Wagner, Torgesen, & Rashotte, 1994). With this kind of evolving research, educators are looking more closely at how phonemic awareness affects reading achievement. This relationship between phonemic awareness and learning to read is most likely one of reciprocal causation (Perfetti, Beck, Bell, & Hughes, 1987; Shaywitz & Shaywitz, 2007). The goal is for students to become familiar with the sounds (phonemes) that letters (graphemes) represent and to become familiar with hearing those sounds within words.

Being phonologically aware means knowing ways in which oral language is divided into smaller components and is manipulated (Chard & Dickson, 1999). Phonological awareness develops in a continuum of listening to sounds, word awareness, rhyming, syllable awareness, and phonemic awareness (being able to isolate, identify, categorize, blend, segment, delete, add, and substitute phonemes). It is important to note that phonemic awareness is included in the larger component of phonological awareness, and that phonological awareness is not the same as phonics. Phonics refers to the relation between phonemes and graphemes. Too often, educators interchange phonological awareness, phonemic awareness, and phonics. Table 13 and Figure 5 help to illustrate the relations among phonological awareness, phonemic awareness, and phonics using a nature metaphor.

This chapter highlights phonemic awareness in the context of phonological awareness. The strategies and their corresponding techniques detailed in this chapter include the following:

- Rhyming: Musical Rhyme, Rhyming Jar, Draw a Rhyme, and Pair–Share Match

- Isolating and Identifying Phonemes: Mirror/Mirror, Alliteration Activation, Hot Seat, and Think Sounds

- Blending Phonemes: Draw It, Chime With Rimes, Body Blending, and Syllable Giving

- Segmenting Phonemes: Egg-Cited About Phonemes, Graphing Phonemes, Silly Segmenting, and Syllable Segmentation

- Manipulating Phonemes: Bingo/Bongo, Colored Cubes, Say It Again, and Word Changers

The phonemic awareness matrix in Table 14 (page 35) matches the techniques in this chapter to the developmental levels from Chapter 1 (emergent, early, transitional, and fluent). To be effective when using the strategies and techniques presented in this chapter,

TABLE 13. Descriptions of Phonological Awareness, Phonemic Awareness, and Phonics

Terminology	Definition	Metaphor Description
Phonology	The study of the unconscious rules governing speech and sound production. The linguistic component of language	Sky—Governing the big picture
Phonological Awareness	The awareness of sound structure. The ability to notice, think about, or manipulate the larger unit of sound auditorally and orally.	Clouds—Look up and become aware of the cloud(s) in the sky
Word Awareness	The ability to recognize that spoken language is made up of individual words and that words form sentences.	Raindrop—Comes out of the cloud (a component of phonological awareness)
Rhyming Awareness	The ability to recognize, isolate, and generate corresponding sounds, especially ending sounds.	Raindrop—Comes out of the cloud (a component of phonological awareness; hair, care)
Syllable Awareness	The ability to identify syllables (i.e., the smallest unit of speech with a vowel sound), distinguish between one and two syllables, and count, blend, and segment syllables in words and sentences.	Raindrop—Comes out of the cloud (a component of phonological awareness; /wa/ /ter/)
Phonemic Awareness	The awareness that spoken language consists of a sequence of phonemes (i.e., the smallest unit of sound).	Hail—Also comes out of cloud but contains a combination of particles (onset and rimes, blending, segmenting, manipulating phonemes)
Phonics	The system by which symbols represent sounds in an alphabet writing system. The relationship between spelling patterns and sound patterns.	Ground—Foundation; Rain hits the ground intermittently, helping to make the ground fertile (products of phonological awareness)
Metalinguistic	The ability to think about and reflect upon one's language.	Seed—Planting a seed after making the connection between water and the ground (recognizing the connection among phonological awareness, phonemic awareness, phonics)
Orthography	The method of representing the spoken language with written symbols.	Roots—Branching off from seed (punctuation, stages of spelling)
Graphemes	The written symbol used to represent a phoneme.	Stems—The parts you see (letters)
Morphemes	The structure of meaningful language units.	Leaves—Parts of a plant (prefixes, suffixes)
Decode and Write Words	The ability to derive a pronunciation for a printed sequence of letters based on knowledge of spelling and sound correspondence.	Flower—The product of rain and good soil (reading and writing)

FIGURE 5. Illustration of Relationship Among Phonological Awareness, Phonemic Awareness, and Phonics

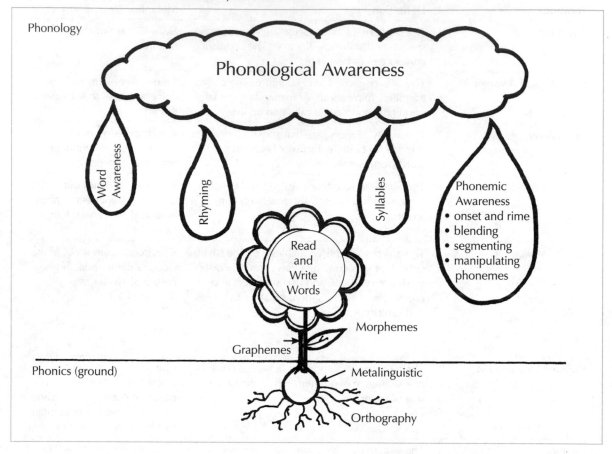

teachers should allow ample time for teacher modeling and student application long before independent application is expected. Teachers should select and model reading aloud of appropriate text to apply the techniques in a meaningful manner, which supports authentic learning for strategic reading. By using this process, students are able to see first the whole text (i.e., appropriate text), then see the parts systematically (i.e., strategies and techniques), and finally, apply the parts back to the whole (i.e., become metacognitively aware of strategies while reading text). Using quality literature and promoting language development throughout the techniques will help to enhance students' development of the strategies. In addition, teachers can use the motivation and engagement feature within many techniques as an additional means (i.e., multiple intelligence, standard) of motivating the whole child and creating 21st-century learners (refer to Chapter 1 for a description of the whole child and Figure 1, page 8, for an illustration). This allows for differentiation within the technique as needed to educate the whole child.

TABLE 14. Phonemic Awareness Techniques

	Emergent	Early	Transitional	Fluent
Before Reading	Musical Rhyme (R) Rhyming Jar (R) Mirror/Mirror[†] (I) Draw It (B)	May include all Emergent techniques Musical Rhyme* (R) Mirror/Mirror* (I) Graphing Phonemes (S) Silly Segmenting (S) Bingo/Bongo (M) Colored Cubes (M)	May include all Emergent and Early techniques Think Sounds[†] (I) Body Blending* (B) Graphing Phonemes* (S) Silly Segmenting* (S) Colored Cubes* (M)	May include all Emergent, Early, and Transitional techniques
During Reading	Chime With Rimes (B)	Draw a Rhyme (R)		
After Reading		Pair–Share Match (R) Alliteration Activation (I) Hot Seat[†] (I) Body Blending[†] (B) Syllable Giving (B) Egg-Cited About Phonemes[†] (S) Say It Again (M)	Rhyming Jar* (R) Draw a Rhyme* (R) Pair–Share Match* (R) Mirror/Mirror* (I) Alliteration Activation* (I) Bingo/Bongo* (M) Syllable Segmentation (S)	Think Sounds*[†] (I) Syllable Segmentation* (S) Word Changers (M)

*Adaptation portion of the technique.
[†]Technique is illustrated on Creating Strategic Readers DVD series.
Note. The developmental levels are shown across the top of the table horizontally. Down the left side of the matrix are the suggested times when these techniques are most effective—before, during, and after reading. This matrix is a guide and is by no means an exhaustive list.
(R) Rhyming; (I) Isolating and identifying phonemes; (B) Blending phonemes; (S) Segmenting phonemes; (M) Manipulating phonemes

Phonemic Awareness Strategy: Rhyming

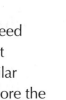

Rhyming provides students with an opportunity to begin developing an awareness of sounds, and it is one of the early phases of phonemic awareness. Emergent readers need many opportunities to hear and identify rhymes (end parts that sound alike but do not necessarily look alike) and to repeat the ending sounds by generating words with similar sound groups (Runge & Watkins, 2006). Providing students with opportunities to explore the similarities and differences in the sounds of words helps them to have an insight that language has not only meaning and message but also physical form (Adams, 1990).

Appropriate text that best supports the application of the rhyming strategy has a variety of words in the text that rhyme.

Rhyming Text Examples:

Dealey, E. (2002). *Goldie Locks has Chicken Pox*. New York: Aladdin Paperbacks.

Raffi. (1990). *Down by the Bay*. New York: Crown.

Silverstein, S. (1974). *Where the Sidewalk Ends*. New York: HarperCollins

Teacher Talk: Statements, Questions, and Prompts for Rhyming

Following is a list of suggested teacher talk that encourages readers to think strategically as they employ the rhyming technique. Try using some of these statements, questions, and prompts with your students as you work through the techniques in the following section.

- How do you know that your words rhyme?

- Draw what rhymes with _____. How did you know what to draw?

- Explain how these two words are alike.

- What sounds do you hear at the end of these two words: _____ and _____?

- What part of the word makes the rhyme or rime and explain the difference?

- Have you ever heard a nonsense rhyme in a story? Give an example.

- Say a word that sounds like _____.

- Which two words rhyme (say three words, such as *cat, bat, fish*)? Why did you pick the two words you did? Can you think of another word that would rhyme with these words?

- Which two pictures rhyme? Why did you pick those pictures?

As you implement the various techniques that support this strategy, use the following behaviors as a guide as you assess students' ability to rhyme. Do students exhibit these behaviors never, rarely, often, always?

- ☐ Hearing and recognizing rhymes

- ☐ Repeating ending sounds and generating new words with similar sounds

- ☐ Applying rhyme in context for meaning

Techniques for Rhyming

Musical Rhyme

Phonemic Awareness: Rhyming

Purpose: To identify and generate rhyming words

Level: Emergent (Adaptation for Early)

ELL Technique: Yes

Multiple Intelligences: Visual/spatial, verbal/linguistic, musical /rhythmic, bodily/kinesthetic, interpersonal, intrapersonal

Materials: Musical Rhyme Pictures (see CD ◉), music that has a fun beat—preferably without words—like the Rockin' Rhymin' Teddy Bear song (Hartmann, 2001); For Adaptation: stuffed animal such as a teddy bear

Procedure:

1. Select pictures that correspond with rhyming words you are studying (multiple rhyming cards are permissible).

2. Make a large circle on the floor with the picture cards and have each child stand behind one of the cards.

3. Select music that has a fun beat, preferably without words, to start and stop along the way like musical chairs, or use Jack Hartmann's CD (2001) and follow along with the CD to Rockin' Rhymin' Teddy Bear song.

4. Start the music and have the students begin walking around the picture circle. Intermittently pause the music and have the students stop in front of a card. Call out a word and have the students check to see if the picture they are standing in front of rhymes with the stated word. Suggested teacher talk might be, "Try to hear the ending sounds from these two words _____ and _____."

5. Have the student(s) with the rhyming picture jump into the middle of the circle and say aloud their rhyming word(s) (i.e., the name of the item on their picture card). Suggested teacher talk could be, "What part of the word makes the rhyme?" Have the remaining students use a predetermined signal (e.g., thumbs up) to assess if the student inside the circle has rhymed with the indicated word. If a student has rhymed successfully, they stay inside the circle. Continue this process several times until the majority of the students have joined the "rhyming" group.

Motivation/Engagement: Prior to playing Musical Rhyme, think about the students' names and create words that rhyme to use when the music stops. Students listen for the word and determine if they are the match. When they hear their rhyming match, they jump inside the circle and identify themselves as the rhyming partner and think of more words that rhyme with their name. Read a poem from a content area, theme, or use clapping games such as "Miss Mary Mack." Choose a body signal (e.g., hands up or down; sway to right or left) to identify the initial rhyming word and demonstrate the rhythm of the poem. Have the students analyze movements and determine the pattern of the body signal. Read aloud poetry such as "Teddy Bear, Teddy Bear, Turn Around." Have partners dramatize the poem and then create new rhyming segments to the selected poem.

Adaptation for Early Readers: The students can also stay in one place and pass the teddy bear around like a "hot potato" and when the music stops whoever is holding the stuffed animal generates a rhyming word that corresponds with a given word.

Rhyming Jar

Purpose: To generate a rhyming word that completes the sentence for meaning

Level: Emergent (Adaptation for Transitional)

ELL Technique: No

Multiple Intelligences: Verbal/linguistic, bodily/kinesthetic, interpersonal

Materials: Rhyming Jar Sentences (see CD), jar, strips of paper, chart paper

Procedure:

1. Write or copy Rhyming Jar Sentences on strips of paper, omitting the final rhyming word (e.g., I want a new bed, and I will paint it _____ [red]; Look next to the rake, there is a big _____ [snake]). Place the strips into a jar.

2. Select a strip from the jar and read it aloud, emphasizing the first rhyming word (e.g., whisper the word bed in the first sentence above). This first word becomes the rhyme of the day. Leave out the rhyming word at the end of the sentence.

3. Have students work in pairs to generate rhyming words to complete the sentence. Suggested teacher talk for this technique might be, "Does your rhyming word at the end of the sentence make sense? Why or why not?"

4. Have students be "detectives," looking for other oral and written words that rhyme with the word of the day. Suggested teacher talk could be, "Explain how your words rhyme."

5. Add the discovered rhyming words that make sense in the sentence to a posted class-generated list. Categorize rhyming words according to a unit of study (e.g., animals, color words, sports).

Motivation/Engagement: Give the initial sound for the omitted rhyming word. Ask students to listen to the rhyming sentence and then act out the sentence.

Adaptation for Transitional Readers: Have students create the rhyming sentence strips to place in the Rhyming Jar that correspond with a concept you are studying.

Draw a Rhyme

Purpose: To determine a rhyming word that makes sense in a story in order to complete a sentence and to create a visual representation of the rhyme

Level: Early (Adaptation for Transitional)

ELL Technique: Yes

Multiple Intelligences: Visual/spatial, verbal/linguistic, logical/mathematical, bodily/kinesthetic, intrapersonal

Materials: Draw a Rhyme (see CD 💿), rhyming poems, drawing paper or dry erase boards, electronic play-a-sound books, scissors, felt, foam board

Procedure:

1. Select a rhyming poem and read it aloud to the students, omitting the ending rhyming words. Suggested teacher talk might be, "Draw what rhymes with _____."

2. Have students fill in each missing word by drawing on drawing paper or dry erase boards their proposed rhyming word. Suggested teacher talk could be, "How do you know what to draw?"

3. Have students share their drawings after reading aloud the entire poem and compare their results with others.

Motivation/Engagement: Use interactive electronic play-a-sound books and have the students match or touch the picture that best goes along with the story. Provide the mouth gesture of the initial sound or make the initial sound of the omitted rhyming word. Record some poems for use with this technique and place them at the listening center. Have students listen to the poems on their own and draw the rhyming words or have precut shapes from felt or foam board that represent the desired rhymes. Have students put together the felt or foam pieces to "build a rhyme." Use the Draw a Rhyme reproducible as a premade activity: Omit the rhyming words shown along the right side and have students illustrate.

Adaptation for Transitional Readers: Have students design their own Draw a Rhyme (i.e., create it themselves from an object or an animal). Compare Draw a Rhyme to a rebus story. Read *I Love You: A Rebus Poem* (Marzollos, 2000) and have students create their own rebus stories.

Note: Adapted from Fitzpatrick (1997), Hamner (n.d.)

Pair–Share Match

Purpose: To hear, match, and communicate rhyming words

Level: Early (Adaptation for Transitional)

ELL Technique: Yes

Multiple Intelligences: Visual/spatial, bodily/kinesthetic, interpersonal, intrapersonal

Materials: Musical Rhyme Pictures and Pair–Share Match (see CD 💿), rhyming words from text

Procedure:

1. Select a number of rhyming words from a text recently read in class or from the Musical Rhyme Pictures.

2. Copy the Pair–Share Match reproducible and cut apart the eggs and nests. Attach the rhyming pictures to the matching egg and nest pattern cutouts (e.g., dog on an egg, and fog on the nest).

3. Distribute to each student either an egg or a nest cutout. Have students "fly" around the room to find the partner who has their rhyme match. Suggested teacher talk could be, "How are your rhymes alike?"

4. Have the newly formed pairs generate other rhyming words to match their words. Suggested teacher talk might be, "Can you think of another word that rhymes with _____?" and "What sounds do you hear at the end of each of your words?"

5. Have partners share their match with the class.

6. Reread the text, noting rhymes in the text by whispering them when you encounter them as you are reading.

Adaptation for Transitional Readers: Provide blank cutout eggs for students to record their new Pair–Share rhyming words. This phase of the technique combines phonics with phonological awareness. Place eggs and nests at a center and have students determine which match. Add symbols on the back for self-checking. Have students locate words or pictures in texts that rhyme with the pictures or words on cutouts.

Note: Adapted from Fredericks (2001)

Phonemic Awareness Strategy: Isolating and Identifying Phonemes

Isolating phonemes is a strategy that allows the students to recognize individual sounds in a word. Attending to these phonemes increases students' awareness that words are made up of individual sounds that connect together to form a word. When students apply this strategy, they are demonstrating their ability to think about and separate individual sounds from one another within a word (e.g., the first sound in *dog* is /d/, the medial sound in *wet* is /e/, and the final sound in *like* is /k/). Students need to explore the articulation of these sounds with techniques that support the correct positioning of their mouths. "This type of explicit attention to vocal gestures can be helpful at the beginning of phonemic awareness instruction" (Manyak, 2008, p. 659). Positioning of the lips and tongue is vital to articulating sounds correctly and has a positive effect on the students' word reading (Castiglioni-Spalten & Ehri, 2003).

Identifying phonemes is a strategy in which students focus on separate distinctions of initial, medial, and final sounds in words to recognize their similarities and differences. Students who can use this strategy are able to think about and notice that two or more words may have the same initial sound (e.g., *ball*, *bat*, and *balloon*), medial sound (e.g., *met*, *Greg*, and *tell*), or final sound (e.g., *call*, *pool*, and *doll*). Identifying these sounds is important as students move through the developmental stages of reading, and it provides students with a tool for reading as well as writing.

Appropriate text that best supports the application of the isolating and identifying phonemes strategy has a variety of words highlighting specific sounds.

Isolating and Identifying Phonemes Text Examples:

dePaola, T. (1973). *Andy: That's My Name*. New York: Prentice Hall.

Martin, B., Jr, & Archambault, J. (1989). *Chicka Chicka Boom Boom*. New York: Scholastic.

Obligato, L. (1986). *Faint Frogs Feeling Feverish and Other Terrifically Tantalizing Tongue Twisters*. New York: Vikings Children's Books.

Teacher Talk: Statements, Questions, and Prompts for Isolating and Identifying Phonemes

Following is a list of suggested teacher talk that encourages readers to think strategically as they isolate and identify phonemes. Try using some of these statements, questions, and prompts with your students as you work through the techniques in the following section.

- Describe how you position your lips and teeth when you say the _____ sound?
- Think of words that begin with the same sound as _____.
- What other words start the same as the word _____?
- Where do you hear the _____ sound in the word?
- What sound do you hear at the end of the word _____?
- What is the difference between the sound and the letter?
- Try to get your mouth ready to make the _____ sound.
- How do you position your mouth when you start that word?
- How do you make that sound?
- Is the sound _____ in that word closer to the beginning or ending sound?

As you implement the various techniques that support this strategy, use the following behaviors as a guide as you assess students' ability to isolate and identify phonemes. Do students exhibit these behaviors never, rarely, often, always?

- ☐ Identifying and separating individual sounds by positioning the mouth, lips, teeth, and tongue to correspond with appropriate sound
- ☐ Distinguishing similarities and differences in beginning sounds (e.g., *cup, car, ball*)
- ☐ Distinguishing similarities and differences in medial sounds (e.g., *cup, cap, copp*)
- ☐ Distinguishing similarities and differences in ending sounds (e.g., *pan, pal, pad*)

Mirror/Mirror

This technique is highlighted on the Creating Strategic Readers DVD/VHS series.

Purpose: To identify and demonstrate positioning of the mouth, lips, and teeth with isolated sounds

Level: Emergent (Adaptations for Early and Transitional)

ELL Technique: Yes

Multiple Intelligences: Visual/spatial, verbal/linguistic, logical/mathematical, bodily/kinesthetic, interpersonal, intrapersonal

Materials: Text, hand-held mirrors; For Adaptation: camera, objects, basket

Procedure:

1. Select a word from a text and say it, isolating the beginning sound. With hand-held mirrors, have students practice positioning their mouths to say the sound you isolated. Suggested teacher talk might be, "How do you position your mouth when you start the word _____?"

2. Have partners describe to each other what they notice happening to their mouths when they say a certain sound. Suggested teacher talk could be, "Describe the position of your mouth for that sound."

Adaptation for Early Readers: Take and print close-up pictures of students' positioning their mouths for a variety of sounds. Place several of the highlighted pictures at a center. Collect items that correlate with the sounds in a basket. Have the students select an item, check the position of their mouth in the mirror, then place an object under a corresponding picture to create a graph.

Adaptation for Transitional Readers: Students use mirrors to check the positioning of their mouth for vowels as they reread their own writing. For example, use the word *penguin* and have the students reflect on the syllables in the word. Have them determine what vowel sound they hear in the first syllable and note the position of their mouth in the mirror. The short vowel *i* in the word *penguin* has more of a smile position than the first syllable short vowel *e* in penguin, which drops the chin a little more than the *i* vowel position. Have students place their hand under their chin while looking in their mirror to feel and see the difference between the two vowels as they say them.

Alliteration Activation

This technique is highlighted on the Creating Strategic Readers DVD/VHS series.

Purpose: To identify beginning sounds and create additional words that begin with the same sounds

Level: Early

ELL Technique: Yes

Multiple Intelligences: Visual/spatial, verbal/linguistic, logical/mathematical, intrapersonal

Materials: Text, small objects, bucket or bag, chart paper

Procedure:

1. Place a few chosen objects in a bucket or bag. Have students take turns choosing a small object from the bucket or bag, saying the name of the object, and then thinking of an associated word beginning with the same sound as the object. For example, a student could take a pencil out of the bag and say, "pretty pencil." Suggested teacher talk might be, "Think of words that begin with the same sound as _____."

2. Continue to pass the bucket or bag around the room and have students generate alliterations for the objects. Suggested teacher talk could be, "What other words start the same as _____?"

3. List students' responses on chart paper and read or reread a chosen text, noting alliterative words.

Motivation/Engagement: Have students introduce themselves by using a verb after their name that has the same beginning sound as their name (e.g., Derek dreams, Jacey jumps, Brooke bounces). Have students create tongue twisters with their names (e.g., Bailey bakes biscuits before breakfast).

Note: Adapted from Love & Reilly (1996)

Hot Seat

Phonemic Awareness: Isolating and Identifying Phonemes

This technique is highlighted on the Creating Strategic Readers DVD/VHS series.

Purpose: To recognize and dramatize positioning of isolated sounds

Level: Early

ELL Technique: Yes

Multiple Intelligences: Visual/spatial, verbal/linguistic, bodily/kinesthetic, intrapersonal

Materials: Text, chairs or hula hoops, three marked cups, marble, three cards each with one letter—*B* (beginning sound), *M* (middle sound), and *E* (ending sound)

Procedure:

1. Line up three chairs in the front of the room. Attach one card to each chair and explain that these are the hot seats. You also can substitute hula hoops in place of the chairs by placing the hoops on the floor and letting students stand inside the circles.

2. Have students line up and take turns sitting in the hot seats.

3. Ask questions about words the class is studying or words from a text you are reading and have the students demonstrate their responses by sitting in the chair with the card matching their answer. For example, if the word is *cat*, you could ask, "Where do you hear the /t/ sound in the word *cat*?" The student would move to the last chair labeled *E* and sit in it, representing the ending sound.

4. Reread the text you are studying and note beginning or ending sounds in words from the text.

5. Choose a word with more than three sounds. Ask, for example, "Where do you hear the /a/ sound in *table*?" Once the student is sitting in the middle hot seat, ask, "Is the /a/ sound closer to the beginning of the word or closer to the end of the word?" Have the student lean toward the chair that represents the answer.

Motivation/Engagement: In small groups, have students line up labeled cups (*B, M, E*) and choose challenge words from their leveled texts to have them demonstrate positioning of the sounds by placing a marble in the correct cup that represents the isolated sound and then defend decision.

Think Sounds

Phonemic Awareness: Isolating and Identifying Phonemes

This technique is highlighted on the Creating Strategic Readers DVD/VHS series.

Purpose: To isolate, identify, and match beginning and ending sounds in words

Level: Transitional (Adaptation for Fluent)

ELL Technique: Yes

Multiple Intelligences: Visual/spatial, verbal/linguistic, logical/mathematical, interpersonal

Materials: Think Sounds reproducible (see CD ⊙), objects; For Adaptation: vocabulary journal or chart paper

Procedure:

1. Form a small group of students to sit in a circle. Provide these students with a starter word (e.g., *soap*). Suggested teacher talk might be, "Think about the word *soap*. What sound do you hear at the end of the word?"

2. Select a student to start the group "Think Sound Train" by thinking of a word that begins with the final sound in the word that you say (e.g., *soap* ends in /p/, so the student could say *pan*). Suggested teacher talk could be, "What sound do you hear at the end of the word ____? Now, try to think of a word that begins with that sound."

3. Have the next student say a word that begins with the ending sound of the last word created (e.g., *pan* ends in /n/, so the student could say *name*). Remind the students to pay

attention to the final sound, not the final letter, when creating a new word (e.g., in *name*, /m/ is the final sound, not the letter *e*).

4. Have the group continue adding to their Think Sound Train. If a team member cannot add a word to the group train, then the student will need to start over with a new word to create a new train.

Motivation/Engagement: Use objects or the pictures from the Think Sounds reproducible and have students match and create a Think Sound Train.

Adaptation for Fluent Readers: Create teams and use content area concepts, such as matter in science (i.e., molecule-liquids-solid-definite-temperature-reaction-number), or use a fiction book that the class is reading and the students have to come up with characters, setting, emotions, and so forth from the story to create their train . Have students capture words created from their team train on chart or in vocabulary journals to share and use as a review of unit.

Note: Adapted from Zgonc (1999)

Phonemic Awareness Strategy: Blending Phonemes

Blending phonemes is a strategy that involves listening to a sequence of separately spoken sounds and then combining the sounds to form a whole word. This synthesis approach gives the students an opportunity to hear individual sounds in words and blend them into a meaningful whole. Techniques should be provided for students to blend by syllable (e.g., /gar/-/den/), onset or initial sound (e.g., the /b/ in *bike*), rime (the vowel and the letters that follow it in a syllable, e.g., the /ike/ in *bike*), and individual phonemes (e.g., /c/-/a/-/t/). According to the NRP report (NICHD, 2000), blending instruction benefits reading acquisition, and it yields even more effect when representing these combined sounds with letters. This combination of connecting phonemes and graphemes helps the students associate phonemic awareness with application to reading and writing in a synthetic approach (Allor, Gansle, & Denny, 2006; Edelen-Smith, 1997; Lundberg, Frost, & Petersen, 1988).

Appropriate text that best supports the application of the blending strategy has a variety of words for combining sounds.

Blending Phonemes Text Examples:

Rovetch, L. (2001). *Ook the Book*. San Francisco: Chronicle.

Seuss, Dr. (1963). *Hop on Pop*. Boston: Houghton Mifflin.

Taback, S. (1997). *There Was an Old Lady Who Swallowed a Fly*. New York: Viking.

Teacher Talk: Statements, Questions, and Prompts for Blending Phonemes

Following is a list of suggested teacher talk that encourages readers to think strategically as they blend phonemes. Try using some of these statements, questions, and prompts with your students as you work through the techniques in the following section.

- Try to listen to the sounds I say and put them together to make a word.
- What object do you see in your mind when you blend the sounds together?
- Explain how hearing each individual sound slowly helps you to form a word.
- What word do you form when you blend these sounds together?
- Think about the sounds you hear and combine them together to form a word.
- What are you doing with the word part sounds to form the word?
- What sounds did you blend to form the word?
- How does hearing the onset and then the rime help you to form the word?

As you implement the various techniques that support this strategy, use the following behaviors as a guide as you assess students' ability to blend phonemes. Do students exhibit these behaviors never, rarely, often, always?

- ☐ Listening to a sequence of sounds and then combining onset and rimes to form a word
- ☐ Identifying and blending the syllables of a word together
- ☐ Identifying and blending the isolated phonemes into a word

Techniques for Blending Phonemes

Draw It

Phonemic Awareness: Blending Phonemes

Purpose: To integrate phonemes to form a word and to draw a picture of the word

Level: Emergent

ELL Technique: Yes

Multiple Intelligences: Visual/spatial, verbal/linguistic, logical/mathematical

Materials: Text, paper, pencil or crayons, pictures of objects

Procedure:

1. Have students fold a sheet of paper into fourths and listen as you pronounce the names of four objects. The objects you select need to be easy items for the students to draw and should preferably be from the text your class is reading.

2. As you say the name of an object, segment the name either by syllables (/pen/-/cil/), onset and rimes (/r/-/ake/), or phonemes (/d/-/e/-/s/-/k/). Suggested teacher talk might be, "Try to listen to the sounds I say and put them together to make a word."

3. Have students blend the sounds you say orally and then draw a picture to represent each word they form. Suggested teacher talk might be, "What object do you see in your mind when you blend the sounds together?"

Motivation/Engagement: Place several pictures in front of students, segment a word, and allow students to choose the picture that correlates with sounds in the word. Have students say the word by blending all the sounds that represent the picture.

Note: Adapted from Blevins (1997)

Chime With Rimes

Phonemic Awareness: Blending Phonemes

Purpose: To hear the onset and rime of a word and blend them together to form the word

Level: Emergent

ELL Technique: Yes

Multiple Intelligences: Verbal/linguistic, musical/rhythmic, interpersonal, intrapersonal

Materials: Text, word list from text with onsets and rimes, puppet

Procedure:

1. Use a puppet to represent one of the characters in a story you are reading (e.g., the old lady who swallowed a fly). Have the puppet model blending by chanting the jingle, "It starts with /l/ and it ends with /ike/, put it together and it says *like*."

2. After the puppet models blending, select a volunteer to listen to the puppet say the onset and have the volunteer create a rime that would make a new word.

3. Have the puppet say a sentence in a rhythmic or chanting manner and encourage students to clap their hands and follow along with the puppet.

4. Have them fill in the word at the end of the sentence. For example, "I know a word, it ends with /eek/ and starts with /p/. The word is _____ [peek]." Suggested teacher talk might be, "How does hearing the onset and rime help you form the word?"

5. Continue this process using different onsets and rimes (/ot/ + /p/ = pot; /elt/ + /m/ = melt). Suggested teacher talk could be, "What word do you form when you blend these sounds together?"

Motivation/Engagement: Have the students introduce themselves to the puppet by using their names to create an onset and rime blend. "Hi, my name starts with /N/ and it ends with /ick/, put it together and you just met Nick."

Note: Adapted from Yopp (1992), Zgonc (1999)

Body Blending

Phonemic Awareness: Blending Phonemes

This technique is highlighted on the Creating Strategic Readers DVD/VHS series.

Purpose: To hear the individual units of sound in a word and act out the blending of the phonemes to form the word

Level: Early (Adaptation for Transitional)

ELL Technique: Yes

Multiple Intelligences: Verbal/linguistic, logical/mathematical, bodily/kinesthetic, interpersonal

Materials: Text, hula hoops; For Adaptation: Note cards

Procedure:

1. Place one hula hoop on the ground for each phoneme represented in a chosen word (e.g., *met* would have three hoops).

2. Select the proper number of students to each "be a phoneme" in the word, and have each student stand in a hoop.

3. Have one student begin by saying the first sound while simultaneously linking arms with the next student. The next student says the second sound. Suggested teacher talk might be, "Think about the sounds you hear, and combine them to form a word."

4. Continue until all the students standing in the hoops have said their sounds and linked arms to form a word.

5. Have all the linked students take one step forward out of their hula hoops and pronounce the entire word in unison. Suggested teacher talk could be, "How does slowly hearing each individual sound help you when forming a word?" Have the students who physically blended the word search and find that word in the text.

Adaptation for Transitional Readers: Using spelling words, write the letters on a note card that represents a unit of sound (this incorporates phonics into the lesson). Mix up the letter cards representing the spelling word and pass them out to each team. Have the teams work to unscramble the letters and then perform their word not by showing their letter card, but by saying the sound and forming the word. The rest of the class listens to the sounds and tries to discover the word and record it.

Syllable Giving

Phonemic Awareness: Blending Phonemes

Purpose: To blend together smaller parts of words (i.e., syllables) to form a word

Level: Early

ELL Technique: Yes

Multiple Intelligences: Verbal/linguistic, musical/rhythmic, bodily/kinesthetic, interpersonal

Materials: Text, wrapped box with a rock inside

Procedure:

1. Circulate the room and select a student. Give the student a box wrapped to look like a present, but that has a rock inside. Say, "I will give you a clue as to what is inside the box." Then, pronounce the name of an object syllable by syllable, placing a long pause on each syllable (e.g., /vi/-/de/-/o/, /car/-/pet/, /dish/-/wash/-/er/, /gui/-/tar/). Suggested teacher talk might be, "What are you doing with the word part sounds in order to form the word?"

2. Shake the box once as you say each syllable. The rock inside will shake to represent the number of individual sounds you hear.

3. When the student correctly blends together the syllables, he or she becomes the next one to present the gift to another student. Suggested teacher talk might be, "What sounds did you blend in order to form the word?"

4. The "gift-giving" student thinks of a word to blend orally by syllables and says the parts of the word for all to hear.

Motivation/Engagement: Have students participate in singing with syllables the song "If You Think You Know This Word" to the tune of "If You're Happy and You Know It, Clap Your Hands."

> If you think you know this word, whisper it now!
>
> If you think you know this word, whisper it now!
>
> If you think you know this word,
>
> Then tell us what you heard,
>
> If you think you know this word, whisper it now!

Say a segmented word such as /pen/-/cil/, and have the student respond by saying the blended word. Alternative actions: shout, sing, clap, jump.

Note: Adapted from Adams, Foorman, Lundberg, & Beeler (1997); Yopp (1992)

Phonemic Awareness Strategy: Segmenting Phonemes

Segmenting phonemes is a strategy that incorporates hearing a word and then breaking it into its separate parts. Research shows that phoneme segmentation contributes to students' ability to read and spell words (Allor et al., 2006; Ball & Blachman, 1991). There are many techniques that support students in segmenting phonemes. For example, students can segment sentences to words (e.g., "The dog barks" into /the/, /dog/, /barks/), words to syllables (e.g., *garden* into /gar/-/den/), words to onset and rime (e.g., *bike* into /b/-/ike/), and words to individual phonemes (e.g., *cat* into /c/-/a/-/t/). Tangible objects (e.g., buttons, paper clips, or other counters) representing sounds serve as visual support for students, and these objects can then be replaced by letters when segmentation is done in written form such as phonics (Newbury, 2007).

Appropriate text that best supports the strategy of segmenting phonemes has a variety of words that are appropriate for breaking apart the sounds.

Segmenting Phonemes Text Examples:

Martin, B., Jr (1974). *Sounds of a Powwow*. New York: Holt, Rinehart, and Winston.

Showers, P. (1991). *The Listening Walk*. New York: HarperCollins.

Vaughan, M. (1995). *Tingo Tango Mango Tree*. Morristown, NJ: Silver Burdett.

Teacher Talk: Statements, Questions, and Prompts for Segmenting Phonemes

Following is a list of suggested teacher talk that encourages readers to think strategically as they segment phonemes. Try using some of these statements, questions, and prompts with your students as you work through the techniques in the following section.

- How many counters did you place inside your container? Try to shake out each sound you hear in the word _____.
- How many sounds do you hear in the word _____? What are the sounds?
- What is the difference between the word _____ and the word _____?
- Try to "push" the number of sounds you hear in the word.
- Count the number of parts you hear in the word.
- How does stretching out the word help you?
- What happens when you stretch the word?
- Try to say the word slowly to hear the individual sounds in the word.
- Demonstrate how many syllables you hear in the word.
- How many words do you hear in the sentence?

As you implement the various techniques that support this strategy, use the following behaviors as a guide as you assess students' ability to segment phonemes. Do students exhibit these behaviors never, rarely, often, always?

- ☐ Identifying and separating a sentence to individual words
- ☐ Identifying and separating individual words to syllables
- ☐ Identifying and separating words to onset and rime
- ☐ Identifying and separating individual units of sound in a word

Egg-Cited About Phonemes

This technique is highlighted on the Creating Strategic Readers DVD/VHS series.

Purpose: To hear individual units of sound in words and shake out the sounds

Level: Early

ELL Technique: Yes

Multiple Intelligences: Verbal/linguistic, musical/rhythmic, bodily/kinesthetic

Materials: Text, plastic eggs, objects for counters like colored candies or paper clips

Procedure:

1. Select words from a text you are reading in class.

2. Give each student a plastic egg and some counters.

3. Pronounce a word and have the students decide how many phonemes are in the word. While saying each phoneme, have students insert the appropriate number of counters into the egg. Suggested teacher talk might be, "How many counters did you place inside your egg? Why?" Have students close the eggs and use them to shake out each individual sound they hear. Suggested teacher talk could be, "Try to shake out how many sounds you hear in the word _____ using your egg."

Motivation/Engagement: Sing to the tune of Bingo "There was a teacher who had a word and _____ was its name-o." Have students use their eggs to shake out the sounds that represent the letters in the word presented or have them shake only when the sound is omitted.

Phonemic
Awareness:
Segmenting
Phonemes

Graphing Phonemes

Purpose: To identify phonemes and determine the number of phonemes in a word.

Level: Early (Adaptation for Transitional)

ELL Technique: No

Multiple Intelligences: Visual/spatial, verbal/linguistic, logical/mathematical, interpersonal

Materials: Graphing Phonemes reproducible and Graphing Phonemes Answer Key Chart (see CD 💿), text, magazines

Procedure:

1. Copy and cut out the picture cards from the Graphing Phonemes reproducible. Distribute a set of picture cards to teams of students.

Phonemic
Awareness:
Segmenting
Phonemes

2. Have students take turns saying the name of the object in a picture and determining how many phonemes they hear in that word. Suggested teacher talk might be, "How many sounds do you hear in the word _____?"

3. Have students sort their picture cards by the number of phonemes in each word. Then, have teams discuss and depict their findings on the Graphing Phonemes Answer Key Chart and write the total number of phonemes in the space provided. Suggested teacher talk might be, "What is the difference between the word _____ and the word _____?"

Motivation/Engagement: Have students select pictures from magazines and sort them by number of phonemes.

Adaptation for Transitional Readers: Using their spelling words, have students say the word to a partner and have the other student determine the number of sounds or syllables in the word and create a graph with spelling words. This combines phonemic awareness and phonics.

Note: Adapted from Blevins (1997)

Silly Segmenting

Phonemic Awareness: Segmenting Phonemes

This technique is highlighted on the Creating Strategic Readers DVD/VHS series.

Purpose: To separate individual units of sounds in a word and demonstrate sounds through a tangible representation

Level: Early (Adaptation for Transitional)

ELL Technique: Yes

Multiple Intelligences: Visual/spatial, verbal/linguistic, logical/mathematical, bodily/kinesthetic

Materials: Text, clay

Procedure:

1. Give students small balls of clay and ask them to shape their clay into snakes (long, rolled-up strips of clay).

2. Pronounce a word from a text you are reading and have students separate their snakes into a corresponding number of segments, with each segment representing a phoneme. Suggested teacher talk might be, "Demonstrate how many sounds you hear in the word."

3. Have students point to each section of their snakes and say the sounds separately.

4. Ask students to pick up each individual segment while pronouncing the corresponding phoneme and place it into the palms of their hands, reforming the word. Suggested teacher talk could be, "What sounds do you hear in the word?"

5. Repeat the process with a new word from the text you are reading.

Motivation/Engagement: Instead of breaking the snake apart, have students stretch the clay as they pronounce the individual sounds. The students can place the stretched snake on their desks and repeat the process with a new word and a new ball of clay to compare the lengths of the words.

Adaptation for Transitional Readers: Substitute phonemes for syllables and ask what letter or letters represent the syllable section. Have students reflect on the vowel(s) within the snake section. Give clues for the students to demonstrate a word that would best complete a mystery word. For example, "I am thinking of a four syllable word—it is a book of words and their definitions" (/dic/-/tion/-/ar/-/y).

Syllable Segmentation

Purpose: To differentiate syllables in a word and examine various ways to segment syllables

Level: Transitional (Adaptation for Fluent)

ELL Technique: Yes

Multiple Intelligences: Visual/spatial, verbal/linguistic, logical/mathematical, bodily/kinesthetic, naturalist/environmentalist

Materials: Text, picture cards, sticky notes, overhead projector, paper plates, ball, Syllable Clap song (Whyte & Record, 2008); For Adaptation: examples of cinquains and haikus

Procedure:

1. Review common syllable spelling patterns (e.g., closed syllable, open syllables, consonant + *le*).

2. Select words from a text you are studying and say a word so that students can listen, examine sounds, and determine how many syllables are in the word. You can also show a picture card of the word.

3. Display sticky notes to denote each syllable in the example word. Glide your hand under each syllable sticky note as you repeat the word, counting the number of syllables. You can break each syllable into individual phonemes by putting a tally mark on the syllable sticky note to denote the number of phonemes in each syllable.

Motivation/Engagement: Sing the Syllable Clap song and show pictures of a two-, three-, and four-syllable word. Use sound boxes, paper plates, a student's hand, or a ball to have students demonstrate segmenting.

Sound boxes—Draw boxes on an overhead projector to represent the syllables in a word.

Paper plate push—Have students line up paper or plastic plates in a horizontal row and then push each plate forward while saying the sound or syllable.

Hand—Have students segment sounds by using their left palms as phoneme "push mats."

Ball—Using a ball, have students bounce the number of sounds or syllables in a word.

Adaptation for Fluent Readers: Read books of poetry and have students notice that poets arrange words in lines. Have the students create cinquains and haikus.

Cinquain

Line 1—Title (2 syllables)

Line 2—Describe (4 syllables)

Line 3—Action (6 syllables)

Line 4—Feeling or effect (8 syllables)

Line 5—Synonym for initial noun (2 syllables)

Haiku

Line 1—5 syllables

Line 2—7 syllables

Line 3—5 syllables

Phonemic Awareness Strategy: Manipulating Phonemes

In order for students to manipulate sounds strategically, first they will need to be able to blend and segment phonemes. Manipulating phonemes involves adding, deleting, and substituting phonemes in words, and it is the most difficult area of phonological awareness (Ben-Dror, Frost, & Bentin, 1996; Love & Reilly, 1996; Manyak, 2008). Students can make new words by adding a phoneme to an existing word (e.g., /p/ + /art/ forms the word part), removing a phoneme to create another recognizable word (e.g., removing the /c/ from *call* makes the new word *all*), or substituting one phoneme with another to make a new word (e.g., changing the /a/ in *mat* to /e/ forms the new word *met*).

Students should have many opportunities to manipulate phonemes orally as well as in written work, and they should do so progressively, beginning with the initial phoneme, final phoneme, and then the medial phonemes. Instruction that emphasizes phoneme manipulation with letters supports students' ability to acquire phonemic awareness skills better than instruction without letters (NICHD, 2000).

Appropriate text that best supports the application of the manipulating phonemes strategy has a variety of words suitable for word play.

Manipulating Phonemes Text Examples:

Most, B. (1996). *Cock-a-Doodle-Moo*. San Diego, CA: Harcourt Brace.

Plater, I. (1998). *Jolly Olly*. Crystal Lakes, IL: Rigby.

Seuss, Dr. (1974). *There's a Wocket in My Pocket*. Boston: Houghton Mifflin.

Teacher Talk: Statements, Questions, and Prompts for Manipulating Phonemes

Following is a list of suggested teacher talk that encourages readers to think strategically as they manipulate phonemes. Try using some of these statements, questions, and prompts with your students as you work through the techniques in the following section.

- What sounds are added or deleted to make the new word?
- How did this activity help you think about the sounds in the words?
- How did you change the word to make a new word?
- What was the original word? What is the new word? How are they different?
- What did you have to do to make the new word?
- What sound do you hear the first time?
- Listen to these words and determine which word is the "odd man out."
- What word would be created if /m/ was removed from the word *mat*?
- What sound do you hear in the word *hair* that is missing in *air*?

As you implement the various techniques that support this strategy, use the following behaviors as a guide as you assess students' ability to manipulate phonemes. Do students exhibit these behaviors never, rarely, often, always?

- ☐ Adding a phoneme to an existing word to create a new word
- ☐ Deleting a phoneme word to create a new word
- ☐ Substituting a phoneme word to create a new word

Techniques for Manipulating Phonemes

Bingo/Bongo

Phonemic
Awareness:
Manipulating
Phonemes

Purpose: To listen to and identify manipulated sounds

Level: Early (Adaptation for Transitional)

ELL Technique: Yes

Multiple Intelligences: Visual/spatial, verbal/linguistic, musical/rhythmic, interpersonal

Materials: Bingo/Bongo materials (see CD ●), bingo markers

Procedure:

1. Copy and distribute bongo cards with pictures representing words that students will manipulate. Give directions for students to listen to the word you say, followed by the

sound that needs to be substituted. Suggested teacher talk could be, "The bingo word is *dog*. Place a marker on the bongo word that is the same as dog with the initial sound changed to /l/."

2. Have the students select the picture that represents the bongo word (changed word) and place a marker on the bongo card. Suggested teacher talk might be, "Explain how you found your picture."

Motivation/Engagement: Create bongo boards using the vowel picture examples provided to identify the initial vowel substitute.

Adaptation for Transitional Readers: Have students create bongo words from their spelling words.

Colored Cubes

Purpose: To represent phonemes with objects and to identify the sound of the object by adding, deleting, or substituting phonemes

Level: Early (Adaptation for Transitional)

ELL Technique: Yes

Multiple Intelligences: Visual/spatial, verbal/linguistic, bodily/kinesthetic

Materials: Text, colored cubes or paper cutouts, note cards

Procedure:

1. Select words from a text you are reading in class. Give each student two red, two blue, two green, and two yellow square cutouts (or colored block cubes).

2. Pronounce a word (e.g., *at*) and have the students select two different-colored squares to represent the phonemes in the word. Suggested teacher talk could be, "Why are the cubes different colors? What do they represent?"

3. Next, have the students point out which color represents the /a/ sound and which one represents the /t/ sound (like colors represent like sounds). Then ask the students to show you the word *cat*. (The students should choose a different-colored square to represent the /c/ sound.)

4. Have students make *sat* by changing the /c/ square to a different color for the /s/ sound. Ask the students to change the vowel from /a/ to /i/ to form a new word, again using different colored squares for the sounds. Suggested teacher talk might be, "If that says *cat*, show me *cut*. Show me the word *me*, now show me *em*. What did you do to the cubes to make the new word or nonsense word?"

Motivation/Engagement: To move from phonemic awareness into phonics, substitute letter tiles (i.e., letters on note cards) for the colored squares or write the letters directly on the squares after manipulating the sounds.

Adaptation for Transitional Readers: To add additional challenges, have the students change the order of the sounds or duplicate a sound that already appears elsewhere in the word.

Note: Adapted from Blevins (1997)

Say It Again

Purpose: To substitute phonemes to make new words

Level: Early

ELL Technique: No

Multiple Intelligences: Verbal/linguistic, bodily/kinesthetic, interpersonal, intrapersonal

Materials: Text, chart

Procedure:

1. Say a word from the text and have the students repeat the word, adding and deleting sounds to begin creating new words. For example, you could say the word *cat* and ask the students to change the /c/ to /b/ and say it again, forming the new word *bat*. Another example is to have the students say the word *milk* and then say it again without the /l/ sound. It is acceptable if the newly formed word is a nonsense word. Suggested teacher talk might be, "How did you change the word to make a new word?"

2. Record newly created words on a chart so students can see how they manipulated the sounds. Suggested teacher talk could be, "What was the original word? What is the new word? How are they different?"

Motivation/Engagement: Use the student's name by removing the first sound of the name. For example, change Brandon to Trandon. Have the students listen as you change the name and stand when they identify themselves. Next, have the identified student introduce himself or herself as, "I am Brandon, Trandon" and then add one more name change (e.g., Landon). Have the other students listen and identify the substitution.

Word Changers

Purpose: To apply the meaning from one word to another and substitute the vowel to make a new word that correlates with the clue word

Level: Fluent

ELL Technique: No

Multiple Intelligences: Verbal/linguistic, logical/mathematical, interpersonal

Materials: Word Changers (see CD 🔘), text, clue words

Procedure:

1. Select words to manipulate from the text or content area of study.

2. Ask students to listen to words you call out and to think about the meaning of the word or clue phrase you give. For example, "Listen to your first word: *nine*. Now think of the meaning of the word *zero*. Use the word *nine* and change out the vowel to make a new word that means *zero*."

3. Have students either say the new word, share with partners what they did to change the word, or have them record the new vowel that made the word change meaning.

Motivation/Engagement: Give table groups word cards and word phrases to match up and complete the word changer. Have teams present their word changers and describe what they had to do to make the new word match the meaning of the clue word or phrase.

Phonemic Awareness Wrap-Up

Phonemic awareness, one of the five areas identified in the NRP report (NICHD, 2000), shows a strong relation to success in the acquisition of reading. "Teachers should recognize that acquiring phonemic awareness is a means rather than an end. PA is not acquired for its own sake, but rather for its value in helping learners understand the alphabetic system to read and write" (NICHD, 2000, p. 2-6). The strategies, techniques, and teacher talk presented in this chapter support teachers in maximizing their students' potential in becoming strategic readers. When teachers stroke their brushes (techniques and teacher talk to build phonemic awareness) across their canvases, they are adding another dimension to their masterpieces—strategic readers.

Chapter 3

Phonics

Synthesizing with **Stretch It** technique

Spelling with **Working With Words** technique

Analyzing syllables with **Roll-Read-Record** technique

Phonics is a component of reading and writing that involves the reader's ability to synthesize, analyze, contextualize, pattern, spell, and recognize words. Being able to read, pronounce, and write words by associating letters with sounds represents the basis for the alphabetic principle. Coupling this part of the phonics process with the brain's capacity to make connections allows phonics to be a support in the reading process and makes phonics one of the means to a very important end—that is, meaningful reading.

Phonics is part of the graphophonic cueing system that demonstrates the relationship between sounds in speech and letters in print. Proficient strategic readers use the graphophonic cueing system to demonstrate their awareness of graphemes (the visual representations of phonemes), sound–symbol associations, and the structural analysis of a word. This ability to decode unknown words simultaneously using a semantic cueing system (reading for meaning) and a syntactic cueing system (using grammatical structure and word order) supports reading fluently with comprehension and aids in becoming a strategic reader.

Research by neuroscientists and cognitive scientists suggests that the most effective phonics instruction is planned, sequential, explicit, systematic, multisensory, and, most important, meaningful (Campbell, Helf, & Cooke, 2008; Herron, 2008; NICHD, 2000; Stahl, Duffy-Hester, & Stahl, 1998). Therefore, teaching phonics in a comprehensive literacy program allows for specific, focused instruction within the confines of purposeful teaching. "In teaching phonics explicitly and systematically, several instructional approaches have been used. These approaches include synthetic phonics, analytic phonics, embedded phonics, analogy phonics, onset-rime phonics, and phonics through spelling" (NICHD, 2000, p. 2-89). Teachers need to identify the effective strategies within these approaches and "make a conscious effort to examine and reflect upon the strategies they use for teaching phonics in order to select the best type of experiences for the children they teach" (Morrow & Tracey, 1997, p. 651). Systematic phonics instruction should be integrated with the other components of reading instruction (phonemic awareness, fluency, vocabulary, and comprehension) to create a comprehensive literacy classroom. It is important that there is a form of balance among all the components and not to judge reading competence on phonics skills alone.

This chapter highlights the strategies embedded within phonics approaches and defines the approaches in a strategic manner. Teachers need to determine which strategy best supports the instructional purpose for the specific lesson. This allows teachers to teach phonics strategies explicitly and systematically while being responsive to the needs and readiness level of each student, using a variety of techniques rather than just one phonics approach. Table 15 defines the phonics strategies and aligns each strategy to standards. Teachers should determine daily which strategies, techniques, and teacher talk best correlate with the individual needs of the learners in their classrooms. The strategies and techniques in this chapter include the following:

- Synthesizing: Stir It Up, Letter–Sound Magnetic Connection, Letterboxes, and Stretch It

- Analyzing: Star Search, Chant/Challenge/Chart, Roll-Read-Record, and DISSECT

- Contextualizing: Blinders, Predict/Preview/Polish/Produce, Word Detectives, and Calculating Cues

- Patterning: Onset and Rimes, Pattern Sort, Vowel Pattern Jingles, and Dancing With Diphthongs

- Spelling: Word Walls, Working With Words, Brain Tricks, If I Can Spell, Creating Words, and Look/Say/Cover/Write/Check

- Recognizing: Letter Recognition, High-Frequency Words, and Irregular and Sight Words

Table 16 matches the techniques in this chapter to the developmental levels from Chapter 1 (emergent, early, transitional, and fluent). To be effective, when using the

TABLE 15. Definitions of Phonics Strategies

Strategies	Definition	Standards
Synthesizing	Combine parts or elements to form a whole Letter + sound = word	✓ Blend sounds orally to make words ✓ Understand that letters represent sounds ✓ Blend sounds to make word parts & words ✓ Blend beginning, middle, and ending sounds to recognize/read words
Analyzing	Read the whole word and then "take it apart" to investigate word parts	✓ Recognize rhyming words ✓ Use word patterns ✓ Use knowledge of consonants, blends, and common vowel patterns ✓ Use knowledge of less common vowel patterns
Contextualizing	Uses context clues to form words by applying several cueing systems	✓ Explain that printed materials provide information ✓ Use knowledge of the story and topic ✓ Use knowledge of sentence structure to read words ✓ Use information in the story to read words ✓ Apply meaning clues, language structure, and phonetic strategies
Patterning	Recognizes parts of unknown word and compares with similar pattern from known words	✓ Recognize rhyming words ✓ Use word patterns ✓ Use knowledge of common vowel patterns ✓ Use knowledge of less common vowel patterns and homophones
Spelling	Transforms sounds into letters and letters into written word form	✓ Draw pictures and/or use letters and phonetically spelled words ✓ Use correct spelling for frequently used words and phonetically regular words in final copies ✓ Use correct spelling for frequently used words ✓ Edit final copies for spelling
Recognizing	Identifies words quickly and automatically	✓ Recognize rhyming words ✓ Identify words ✓ Read with accuracy

strategies and techniques presented in this chapter, teachers should allow ample time for teacher modeling and student application long before independent application is expected. Teachers should select and model reading aloud of appropriate text to apply the techniques in a meaningful manner, which supports authentic learning for strategic reading. By using this process, students are able to see first the whole text (i.e., appropriate literature), then see the parts systematically (i.e., strategies and techniques), and finally, apply the parts back to the whole (i.e., become metacognitively aware of strategies while reading appropriate literature). Using quality literature and promoting language development throughout the techniques will help to enhance students' development of the strategies. In addition, teachers can use the motivation and engagement feature within many techniques as an additional means (i.e., multiple intelligence, standard) of motivating the whole child and creating 21st-century learners (refer to Chapter 1 for a description of the whole child and

TABLE 16. Phonics Techniques

	Emergent	Early	Transitional	Fluent
Before Reading	Stir It Up (Sy) Star Search (A) Blinders (C) Predict/Preview/Polish/ Produce (C) Word Walls (Sp) Letter Recognition (R) High-Frequency Words (R) Irregular and Sight Words (R)	May include all Emergent techniques Stir It Up* (Sy) Letterboxes (Sy) Stretch It† (Sy) Star Search* (A) Predict/Preview/Polish/ Produce* (C) If I Can Spell (Sp) Word Walls (Sp) Look/Say/Cover/Write/ Check* (Sp) Irregular and Sight Words* (R)	May include all Emergent and Early techniques Word Walls (Sp) Look/Say/Cover/ Write/Check (Sp) Irregular and Sight Words* (R)	May include all Emergent, Early, and Transitional techniques Word Walls (Sp) Irregular and Sight Words* (R)
During Reading		Chant/Challenge/Chart (A) Vowel Pattern Jingles (P) Working With Words (Sp)	Word Detectives (C) Vowel Pattern Jingles (P) Working With Words (Sp)	Working With Words (Sp)
After Reading	Letter–Sound Magnetic Connection† (Sy) Onset and Rimes (P)	Letter–Sound Magnetic Connection* (Sy) Chant/Challenge/Chart (A) Onset and Rimes (P) Pattern Sort (P) Brain Tricks (Sp) Creating Words (Sp)	Roll-Read-Record† (A) Brain Tricks* (Sp)	DISSECT (A) Calculating Cues (C) Dancing with Diphthongs (P) Brain Tricks (Sp)

*Adaptation portion of the technique.
†Technique is illustrated on Creating Strategic Readers DVD series.
Note. The developmental levels are shown across the top of the table horizontally. Down the left side of the matrix are the suggested times when these techniques are most effective—before, during, and after reading. This matrix is a guide and is by no means an exhaustive list.
(Sy) Synthesizing; (A) Analyzing; (C) Contextualizing; (P) Patterning; (Sp) Spelling; (R) Recognizing

Figure 1, page 8, for an illustration). This allows for differentiation within the technique as needed to educate the whole child.

Phonics Strategy: Synthesizing

Students apply the strategy of phonetic synthesizing by converting letters (i.e., graphemes) into sounds (i.e., phonemes) and by then combining those sounds to create a word. *Synthesizing* means to combine parts or elements to form a whole. This strategy mirrors the synthetic approach described in the NRP report (NICHD, 2000, p. 2-89). Some educators use the term *synthetic* with the term *explicit* when referring to phonics due to the precise way letters and sounds are associated and then blended together through decoding. Adams (1990) defines explicit phonics as "the provision of systematic instruction or the relation of letter sounds to words" (p. 49). This provision is necessary for students who have little prerequisite knowledge about print and phonemic awareness.

The phonemic awareness strategy of isolating and identifying sounds in Chapter 2, combined with the ability to associate those sounds with the represented letter or letters, is the foundation for synthesizing. "The more students pay attention to what their mouths do when they make a speech sound, the more likely they are to remember the association of sound to letter" (Herron, 2008, p. 80). Implementing the synthesizing strategy systematically enhances the identification and blending of phonemes by providing opportunities to merge sounds in succession. Incorporating instructional techniques that support these associations enables students to become independent strategic readers.

Appropriate text that best supports the application of the synthesizing strategy has a variety of words suitable for combining parts of a word to form the whole word.

Synthesizing Text Examples:

Clinton, C., & Quails, S. (2008). *Phillis's Big Test*. New York: Houghton Mifflin.

Cowley, J. (1996). *Annabel*. Bothell, WA: Wright Group.

Prelutsky, J. (1982). *The Baby Uggs Are Hatching*. New York: Greenwillow.

Teacher Talk: Statements, Questions, and Prompts for Synthesizing

Following is a list of suggested teacher talk that encourages readers to think strategically as they synthesize. Try using some of these statements, questions, and prompts with your students as you work through the techniques in the following section.

- Say the word (e.g., *table*) and feel what your mouth does after you say the sounds.
- Look at the letters and think about the sounds that they make to blend the word.
- Visualize the letters coming together with their sounds to form the word.
- How does slowly hearing the sounds help you form a word?
- What word do you see after you record the sounds?
- What word do you form when you blend these letters together?
- How many sounds do you hear in the word _____?
- When you stretch the word, what is happening?

As you implement the various techniques that support this strategy, use the following behaviors as a guide as you assess students' ability to synthesize. Do students exhibit these behaviors never, rarely, often, always?

- ☐ Recognizing that sounds can be associated with letters
- ☐ Combining parts (sounds) to form a whole (word) by decoding
- ☐ Blending sounds with body movements and associating movements to letters

Stir It Up

Phonics: Synthesizing

Purpose: To listen and identify sounds and letters in words and generate additional words that have the same identified letter–sound correlations

Level: Emergent (Adaptation for Early)

ELL Technique: Yes

Multiple Intelligences: Visual/spatial, verbal/linguistic, logical/mathematical, musical/rhythmic, bodily/kinesthetic, interpersonal

Materials: Text, ABC card set, chef hat, music like the "Special Soup" song (Hartmann, 2002b); For Adaptation: Magnetic letters, large bowl, large spoon, graph, cookie sheet

Procedure:

1. Place ABC cards in a circle or oval shape on the floor and have students stand on the outside of the circle beside the cards.

2. Turn on music or use the song "Special Soup" and have the students begin to march around the cards like a game of musical chairs until you turn off the music.

3. When you stop the music, have the students turn and look down at their position. Call out a letter or make the sound and have the students determine if they are the selected student by where they are standing when the music stopped. The selected student then jumps into the circle, puts on the chef hat, and orally adds to the pretend class soup a food object that begins with the sound or letter you called.

4. If the added ingredient matches, the rest of the students say, "Stir it up, stir it up," while they are making a stirring motion. If the ingredient does not match the students say, "take it out, take it out," while making a motion that pretends to be pulling it out and throwing it over their heads.

5. Additional cooks (i.e., students with ingredients they think should be added for the selected letter or sound) can jump into the pot and share their "ingredient" for the soup.

Adaptation for Early Readers: Place a magnetic letter on each of the ABC cards and have the student who adds an ingredient to the soup place their magnetic letter in a large bowl in the middle of the circle. After several students have added to the soup bowl, use a large spoon to "stir it up." Pour the letters out on a magnetic cookie sheet and have the students use the letters to try to make words. Make a graph of words using the number of letters or the number of words in the created word list. A graph can also be made to accompany the soup items that were given to determine how many sounds or letters are in the ingredients presented.

Letter–Sound Magnetic Connection

This technique is highlighted on the Creating Strategic Readers DVD/VHS series.

Purpose: To recognize and show that letters have names and that sounds can be associated with letters

Level: Emergent (Adaptation for Early)

ELL Technique: Yes

Multiple Intelligences: Visual/spatial, verbal/linguistic, logical/mathematical, bodily/kinesthetic, interpersonal

Materials: Text, magnetic letters, magnetic board, dry-erase marker

Procedure:

1. Use magnetic letters to practice connecting sounds in chosen words. As you say each sound, place the magnetic letters next to each other. Suggested teacher talk might be, "How does slowly hearing the sounds help you form a word?"

2. Pronounce a specific sound (i.e., phoneme).

3. Have a student volunteer choose the letter that matches that sound and place it on the magnetic board. Continue this process until you form a word. Suggested teacher talk could be, "What word do you form when you blend these letters together?"

4. Have students position the letters close to one another, then blend and pronounce the sounds a little faster to "read" the word.

5. Reread the text you are studying, noting words from the technique that you modeled.

Adaptation for Early Readers: In a small group, give each student some magnetic letters. Call out a sound (e.g., /c/) and have the student with that letter place it on the magnetic white board. Ask the student to come up with a word that begins with that letter or sound. Once the child says a word (e.g., *candle*), draw the number of sound boxes to correspond with the word given with a dry-erase marker. A picture can also be illustrated by the sound boxes for deepening understanding of the word. Have the selected student put the word in a sentence that makes sense. Work the rest of the sounds in the word, having the students with the represented letter connect them to the others on the magnetic board to form the word.

Letterboxes

Purpose: To hear sounds in words, associate letters to represent the sounds, and blend sounds together to form words

Level: Early

ELL Technique: Yes

Multiple Intelligences: Visual/spatial, verbal/linguistic, logical/mathematical, bodily/kinesthetic, intrapersonal

Materials: Letterboxes reproducible (see CD), text, letter sets, straws (mirrors), Optional: Dry-erase markers

Procedure:

1. Give each student his or her own set of letters to manipulate, Letterboxes reproducible, and a small straw to wave as a wand. An alternative to using individual sets of letters is to use laminated letterboxes and let students use dry-erase markers to write the letters.

2. Choose words that have between two and six phonemes. Call out words for students to listen to, pronouncing the words slowly so that the students can hear the phonemes. Have students write the words in the appropriate letterboxes, depending on how many phonemes each word has. Have the students write the letters in the boxes as they hear the sounds in the words. Suggested teacher talk could be, "How does slowly hearing the sounds help you to form a word?"

3. Have students wave their wands over a word from left to right as they say its sounds, carefully blending all the sounds together. Tell students that the key is to blend the letter being said with the pronunciations of the subsequent letter(s). Suggested teacher talk might be, "What word do you see after you note the sounds? Read it slowly to hear the sounds in the word you noted."

4. Reread the text you are studying, noting the words you modeled.

Motivation/Engagement: In a small group, have students hold a handheld mirror and say the sounds from the letter boxes, thinking about the way their mouth is positioning for each box (see Mirror/Mirror technique in Chapter 2 for more details). Have the students describe the position of their mouth when they make the sound and which letter or letters did they record to represent the sound(s). Ask the students to compare and contrast the sound and mouth position to the letters presented.

Note: Adapted from Cunningham (2000), Murray & Lesniak (1999)

Stretch It

Phonics: Synthesizing

This technique is highlighted on the Creating Strategic Readers DVD/VHS series.

Purpose: To recognize and demonstrate that letters have names and that sounds can be associated with letters

Level: Early

ELL Technique: Yes

Multiple Intelligences: Visual/spatial, verbal/linguistic, logical/mathematical, musical/rhythmic, bodily/kinesthetic

Materials: Text, 8 × 10 and 2 × 2 laminated squares with white construction paper, elastic strips, stapler, dry-erase marker, "Do the Word Stretch" from *Shake, Rattle 'N Read* CD (Hartmann, 2002a), audio recorder

Procedure:

1. Model for students how to make stretch-it strips by doing a class demonstration using 8 × 10 laminated white construction paper stapled to a large elastic strip. Select several words to synthesize from a text you are reading in class.

2. Make small 2 × 2 stretch-it strips for students by stapling at least two laminated paper squares each onto a group of elastic strips for a visual representation.

3. Play the song "Do the Word Stretch" and have students pretend they are holding rubber bands and stretching the words.

4. Using a dry-erase marker, have students write the letters of a word on the squares. Each square should represent the letter(s) associated with the individual sound in the word. Suggested teacher talk might be, "How many sounds do you hear in the word _____?"

5. Have students stretch the elastic word and then slowly bring the word back together while merging the sounds. Suggested teacher talk might be, "When you stretch the word, what is happening?"

6. Reread the text, using the word the students stretched.

Motivation/Engagement: Place several different sizes of the stretch-it elastic strips and a dry-erase marker at the listening center. Record some words on audio recorder and have students select the appropriate stretch-it strip according to how many sounds they hear in each word on the recording. Then, students write the sounds on the strips and check their work with an answer key for feedback. Finally, wipe off students' responses and reuse the strip as you repeat the process.

Phonics Strategy: Analyzing

Analyzing a word requires the students to take an identified word and examine its parts. This strategy encourages students to explore the letter–sound relation while analyzing the word structure. Students use the analyzing strategy to read a whole word and then "take it apart" to investigate how the word works. This strategy aligns with the concepts of the analytic phonics approach. "Analytic programs begin by teaching children some words and then helping children to analyze those words and learn phonics rules and generalizations based on those words" (Cunningham, 2000, p. 184). According to the NRP report, "analytic phonics avoids having children pronounce sounds in isolation to figure out words. Rather, children are taught to analyze letter–sound relationship once the word is identified" (NICHD, 2000, p. 2-99). Students discover implicitly the intricacies of word power when they utilize phonetic analyzing as a strategy in reading with meaning.

Appropriate text that best supports the application of the analyzing strategy has a variety of words suitable for investigating a specific skill.

Analyzing Text Examples:

Carle, E. (2002). *"Slowly, Slowly, Slowly," Said the Sloth*. New York: Penguin.

Langstaff, J. (1989). *Oh, A-Hunting We Will Go*. Boston: D.C. Heath.

Rayevsky, K., & Rayevsky, R. (2006). *Antonyms, Synonyms, and Homonyms*. New York: Holiday House.

Teacher Talk: Statements, Questions, and Prompts for Analyzing

Following is a list of suggested teacher talk that encourages readers to think strategically as they analyze. Try using some of these statements, questions, and prompts with your students as you work through the techniques in the following section.

- What features of the words are alike?

- What patterns do these words have?

- What sound occurs in all these words?

- What characteristics are similar among these words?

- Explain rules or generalizations you see in these words?

- Describe how studying the word helps you?

- Look at your word and think about how the word is designed. Push out the parts of the word.

- What specific skill can you teach us using your name?

- What do you notice about the word?

As you implement the various techniques that support this strategy, use the following behaviors as a guide as you assess students' ability to analyze. Do students exhibit these behaviors never, rarely, often, always?

☐ Focusing on the whole word and then identifying specific aspects within the word

☐ Explaining parts and patterns within words

☐ Examining and describing if a phonetic rule aligns with the word or not

Star Search

Purpose: To focus on students' names as the whole part and analyze for the specific aspects

Level: Emergent (Adaptation for Early)

ELL Technique: Yes

Multiple Intelligences: Visual/spatial, verbal/linguistic, bodily/kinesthetic, interpersonal, intrapersonal

Materials: Text, name cards for each student, board or chart; For Adaptation: Scissors

Procedure:

1. Give each student a card with his or her name written on it or have the students write their name on the card.

2. Encourage students to admire their names, analyzing them for a specific aspect (e.g., number of syllables, graphemes, or phonemes; letter formation; letter–sound connections). Suggested teacher talk could be, "What can you teach us from your name?"

3. Write the students' names on a name board or chart and continue analyzing the various concepts within the names. Suggested teacher talk might be, "Tell me something special about your name."

Adaptation for Early Readers: Cut apart the letters on a name card and pass them out to student volunteers. Have these students come to the front of the group, holding up the letters. Have them line up and ask the class to try to read the name. The class can also put the name into a cheer ("Give me a _____ ... what does it spell?"). Have the students add movement as they connect the letters to their sounds. The students crouch low to the ground and slowly rise up to "peak" in volume at the vowel sound(s) in their names.

Note: Adapted from Bear, Invernizzi, Templeton, & Johnston (2008); Calkins (2001); Cunningham (2000)

Chant/Challenge/Chart

Purpose: To identify and describe patterns within words using a closed or open word sort

Level: Early

ELL Technique: No

Multiple Intelligences: Visual/spatial, verbal/linguistic

Materials: Text, highlighting tape, chart paper

FIGURE 6. Sample Words We Have Analyzed

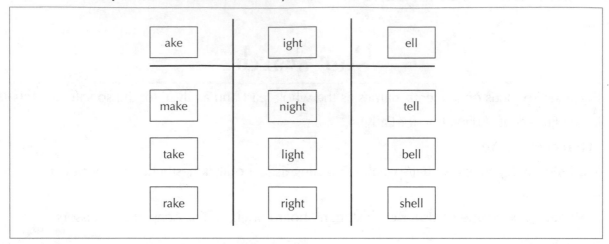

Procedure:

1. Display a selected poem, chant, or story that coordinates with a particular theme of study.

2. Use highlighting tape to "capture" several words within the text that illustrate the concept being taught (e.g., words that have the same beginning sounds, words with the same inflectional endings, or words that rhyme).

3. Have students chant the text with a partner, in small groups, or with the whole group.

4. Challenge the students to examine the highlighted words and determine how the words are alike. Suggested teacher talk might be, "What features of the words are alike?"

5. Have students sort the words according to a variety of categories (e.g., beginning sounds, vowel patterns, syllable stress or syllable structure, and roots and stems) and record their findings on a class chart entitled "Words We Have Analyzed." Suggested teacher talk could be, "What pattern do these words have?" (See Word Sorts technique in Chapter 5 for a description of open and closed sorts.) See Figure 6 for an example.

6. Have students discuss the characteristics of each of the words they sorted. Suggested teacher talk could be, "What characteristics are similar among these words?"

Roll-Read-Record (RRR)

Phonics: Analyzing

This technique is highlighted on the Creating Strategic Readers DVD/VHS series.

Purpose: To focus on a word and analyze it for the specific parts within the word

Level: Transitional

ELL Technique: Yes

Multiple Intelligences: Visual/spatial, verbal/linguistic, bodily/kinesthetic, interpersonal

Materials: Roll-Read-Record reproducible (see CD 💿), text, large and small number cubes (e.g., dice)

Procedure:

1. After reading a text, have students roll a number cube and then search for a word within the text that has the same number of phonemes, syllables, and so forth as the number on the cube.

2. Students can use the hand push technique described in Chapter 2 to push out the analyzed parts as they determine the placement of their word on the graph and record it on the Roll-Read-Record reproducible. Suggested teacher talk, "Look at your word and think about how the word is designed. Push out the parts of the word."

Motivation/Engagement: Students work with partners to roll, read, and record their vocabulary or spelling words on the reproducible and explain why they placed their words under the specific columns. Students can also take home a small number cube to analyze their weekly words as homework or search for words in newspapers or magazines to record.

DISSECT

Purpose: To examine a word by breaking the word into its parts, use other resources to read the word successfully, and describe this process

Phonics: Analyzing

Level: Fluent

ELL Technique: Yes

Multiple Intelligences: Visual/spatial, verbal/linguistic, logical/mathematical

Materials: DISSECT reproducible (see CD 🖴), text, dictionary

Procedure:

1. **Discover:** Have the student discover the context by examining syntactic and semantic cues when reading. If the student comes to an unknown word, they skip the word and read to the end of the sentence. Then using the context of the sentence, the student predicts the unknown word. If the prediction does not match, have the student analyze the word.

2. **Isolate:** The student isolates the prefix by dividing it from the root. Have the student look at the first part of the word and try to pronounce the phoneme/prefix. If a prefix is determined, the student can draw a box around it to "isolate the prefix."

3. **Separate:** Next, have the student separate the suffix by dividing it from the root.

4. **Say:** Have the student attempt to pronounce or say the stem by reading what is left of the word. If the stem is recognized, the student can read the prefix, stem, and suffix together. If the stem is not named, have the student examine the stem.

5. **Examine:** The student examines the stem by dividing the letters and applying knowledge of phonics rules. Suggested teacher talk might be, "Explain what rule or generalization you see in the word?" Have the students write their findings in their learning logs. The student

can divide the stem into small, pronounceable word parts. They can apply the three rules of phonics below if needed. Although strategic readers do not necessarily consult rules when reading, knowing the rules can help them to analyze words and to compare an unknown word to known words with similarities. Suggested teacher talk could be, "How does studying the word help you?"

The following are 3 rules of phonics:

> Rule 1: If the stem or part of the stem begins with a vowel, separate the first two letters. If it begins with a consonant, separate the first three letters and pronounce the rest. Follow through with Rule 1 until the stem is reached.
>
> Rule 2: If the student cannot make sense of the stem after using Rule 1, take off the first letter of the stem and use the rule again.
>
> Rule 3: The student can check the hints for pronunciation when two different vowels are together.

6. **Check** and **Try**: If the student is unable to read the unknown word after the first five steps, then have him or her check with someone, or try the dictionary to identify the word. After recording their findings, ask students to work with a partner and share their discovery.

Motivation/Engagement: Use an object to dissect and describe how each of the parts create the whole (e.g., a plastic toy frog with dissectible parts, a remote control car). For graphic support, have the students use the DISSECT reproducible to follow step by step as they dissect the unknown word.

Note: Adapted from Lenz & Hughes (1990)

Phonics Strategy: Contextualizing

In contextualizing, students use letter–sound correspondences and integrate this association with context clues to form a word. Context clues are hints within the text that help students decode unknown words. Phonetic contextualizing is a strategy that helps students assume responsibility for applying several cueing systems. Acquiring this strategy empowers students with another way to identify unfamiliar words they encounter as they engage in ongoing reading and writing. "If, as reading detectives, children are clued up on clues, they can achieve success with unknown words and gradually internalize strategies to help them in the future" (Farrington, 2007, p. 9). Students use whole, meaningful text (semantic cues), an awareness of letter–sound association (graphophonic cues), and their understanding and probability of the language (syntactic and collocation cues) to support contextual reading.

> [Students' understanding of] the context in which a word occurs can help to emphasize or boost the activation of contextually relevant components of the word's meaning, to select alternative interpretations of ambiguous words, and even to create a meaning for the word where there otherwise might be none. (Adams, 1990, p. 175)

The teacher may employ the whole-part-whole approach of teaching "with, through, and about whole written texts," breaking a section of the text into a specific part and then embedding the part "within the context of meaningful reading and writing" (Strickland, 1998, p. 43). This embedded approach, identified in the NRP report (NICHD, 2000, p.2-89), allows students an opportunity to apply the phonic contextualizing strategy to solve unknown words encountered in text.

Appropriate text that best supports the application of the contextualizing strategy has a variety of words that are supported by surrounding words.

Contextualizing Text Examples

Martin, A. (2005). *A Dog's Life: The Autobiography of a Stray.* New York: Scholastic.

Miranda, A. (1997). *To Market, to Market.* Orlando, FL: Harcourt.

Taback, S. (1997). *There Was an Old Lady Who Swallowed a Fly.* New York: Viking.

Teacher Talk: Statements, Questions, and Prompts for Contextualizing

Following is a list of suggested teacher talk that encourages readers to think strategically as they contextualize. Try using some of these statements, questions, and prompts with your students as you work through the techniques in the following section.

- What happens when you read with blinders?
- What will make sense here and match the beginning letter of this covered word?
- How does using your peripheral vision help you?
- After seeing the onset, what word would make sense and visually match the part shown?
- Try to use the letter–sound clues to help you figure out the unknown words.
- What questions did you ask yourself that helped you to figure out the unknown word?
- How do the words around the unknown word help you?
- What words were easy for you to predict? Why?
- Explain how you make predictions for unknown words.

As you implement the various techniques that support this strategy, use the following behaviors as a guide as you assess students' ability to contextualize. Do students exhibit these behaviors never, rarely, often, always?

- ☐ Recognizing and describing the use of peripheral vision
- ☐ Predicting words using surrounding text for meaning
- ☐ Applying the structural cues of the unknown word based on the meaning of the surrounding words

Blinders

Purpose: To recognize and use peripheral vision when attempting to read unknown words

Level: Emergent

ELL Technique: Yes

Multiple Intelligences: Visual/spatial, bodily/kinesthetic

Materials: Books

Procedure:

1. Have students hold a book on each side of their faces to block their peripheral vision and have them attempt to walk around the room without bumping into one another. Suggested teacher talk could be, "How does using your peripheral vision help you?"

2. Next, have students remove the books and walk around the room again.

3. Discuss with the class how this analogy is similar to reading—that is, students only look at one word at a time to figure out unknown words. Point out that they have "blinders" on when they are only attending to a particular word. Tell them that when they take in all the surrounding words (i.e., use their peripheral vision), they are able to use them to support the strategy of contextualizing. Suggested teacher talk might be, "What happens when you read with blinders?"

Predict/Preview/Polish/Produce

Purpose: To predict words that would make sense in the text by using the surrounding words

Level: Emergent (Adaptation for Early)

ELL Technique: Yes

Multiple Intelligences: Visual/spatial, verbal/linguistic, logical/mathematical, intrapersonal

Materials: Text, sticky notes or highlighting tape, dry-erase boards, overhead projector; For Adaptation: Bag

Procedure:

1. Read a section from the text and omit words by covering them with a sticky note or highlighting tape, saying the word *blank* for each omitted word.

2. **Predict**: Have students turn to a partner and predict what they think are the omitted words. The students also can write their predictions on dry-erase boards, or the teacher

may chart some students' predictions on the overhead projector. Have students discuss with their partners why they chose their predicted words.

3. **Preview**: Preview the first letter of the omitted word by pulling back the sticky note or tape to expose only the first letter (or instead of first letter, cover the ending letters or vowels). Suggested teacher talk might be, "What would make sense here and match the beginning letter of this covered word?"

4. **Polish**: Have students polish their predictions by checking their previous predictions for the omitted word with the preview you have just given them. Suggested teacher talk could be, "After seeing the onset, what word would best make sense and visually match the part shown?"

5. **Produce**: Reveal the other letters to produce the omitted word.

Adaptation for Early Readers: Place the letters from the word in a bag. Pull a letter out and have the students begin to confirm or change predictions based on the letter choices. At a literacy station, write four to five sentences for students to view, and cover one word in each sentence. Have the sentences follow a similar word pattern (e.g., covering the final word, covering the digraph words, covering the words with blends). The students "Guess the Covered Word" (Cunningham, 2000), record the words, and list how they discovered the covered word.

Word Detectives

Purpose: To use context clues to figure out unknown words

Level: Transitional

ELL Technique: Yes

Multiple Intelligences: Visual/spatial, interpersonal, intrapersonal

Materials: Word Detectives reproducible badge (see CD 🔘), texts, highlighting tape

Procedure:

1. While reading a text selection, have students use highlighting tape to mark words that are unknown to them.

2. After reading, ask students to return to the highlighted words and become "word detectives." Have students use the Word Detectives reproducible badge to support their strategic word solving. Each point of the star has one instruction. Suggested teacher talk might be, "What questions did you ask yourself that helped you figure out the unknown word? How do the words around the unknown word help you?"

3. To report their findings, have students meet with the "sheriff" (a designated word-solving helper). The sheriff can give the students feedback and support as needed.

Calculating Cues

Purpose: To determine the unknown word by the polarity of the word and the probability the word will be next to the other words presented

Level: Fluent

ELL Technique: Yes

Multiple Intelligences: Visual/spatial, verbal/linguistic, logical/mathematical, interpersonal

Materials: Calculating Cues reproducible (see CD), texts, collocation phrases

Procedure:

1. Read a well-known phrase or idiom and omit a word within that phrase.

2. Have the students use the probability of the choice of word to complete or finish the phrase (e.g., once upon a _____ [time]; [par] _____ for the course).

3. Ask students to search for the phrase in other texts or in their writing folders. They can examine how the word was used in context.

Motivation/Engagement: Copy idiom cards from the Calculating Cues reproducible and distribute them to partners. Have one partner read the idiom and omit the underlined word. The other partner determines the omitted word based on the familiarity with and understanding of the phrase. Students then compare and contrast the discovered word for its positive or negative meaning. Have students record their explanations or their definitions on the cards. Together the partners create sentences to describe meaning of the idiom and justify their placement of the phrase.

Note: Adapted from Baron & Hirst (2004), Farrington (2007)

Phonics Strategy: Patterning

Proficient strategic readers use patterning as a strategy to identify unknown words. With this strategy, the reader recognizes parts of the unknown word and compares these with a similar pattern from a known word. Parts can be the beginning letter(s) that precedes the vowel (onset) and the rhyming pattern that follows the onset (rime). "Sets of words with matching rimes, such as bell, tell, sell are nothing more or less than phonograms or word families" (Adams, 1990, p. 139). In fact, Wylie and Durell (1970) point out that nearly 500 words can be derived from only 37 rimes. Readers can decode and encode these words by dividing them between the onset and rime and then blending these two parts together (e.g., /b/-/ike/ blended together is *bike*). To use this patterning strategy, the reader may need to apply his or her prior knowledge of a part of the word (e.g., the /ike/ rime from the name *Mike* can help identify *bike*).

The patterning strategy corresponds with the analogy approach. In this approach, students access parts of the word they already know to figure out unfamiliar words (NICHD, 2000; White, 2005). White (2005) states,

> Analogy based phonics is strategic when, through teacher modeling, children learn that when they are reading and come to a word they do not know, they can try to "think of a word they do know" (i.e., a word with the same spelling pattern). (p. 234)

Students use their prior knowledge to seek the pattern in an unknown word to generate pronunciation to form the new word. According to Cunningham (2000), our brain is a pattern detector, and we should give it every opportunity to investigate and organize patterns. Working with patterns can reinforce letter–sound combinations and students' ability to merge these combinations together to read words accurately. The techniques presented in this section help students acquire the patterning strategy.

Appropriate text that best supports the application of the patterning strategy has a variety of words that share common patterns.

Patterning Text Examples:

Martin, B., Jr, & Archambault, J. (1988). *Barn Dance*. New York: Holt.

Shihab Nye, N. (2008). *Honeybee: Poems and Prose*. New York: HarperCollins.

Wood, A. (1984). *The Napping House*. New York: Harcourt Brace.

Teacher Talk: Statements, Questions, and Prompts for Patterning

Following is a list of suggested teacher talk that encourages readers to think strategically as they examine patterns. Try using some of these statements, questions, and prompts with your students as you work through the techniques in the following section.

- How are these words similar or different in their vowel pattern?
- Why did you classify these words together?
- Explain how these words are similar.
- If you take the first letter away and add this beginning sound, what new word would you have?
- How do you know that this is a pattern?
- Compare this word to other words you know.
- Describe what parts are similar.
- Is there another word that you know that has the same "chunk" in it? Explain how knowing that word helps you with this word.
- Try to find words that have this phonogram somewhere in the word.

- How does this word fit the pattern in the other words?
- If this is _____ (point and say the word), what word might this be? Why?

As you implement the various techniques that support this strategy, use the following behaviors as a guide as you assess students' ability to pattern. Do students exhibit these behaviors never, rarely, often, always?

☐ Identifying parts within words

☐ Sorting words according to common patterns

☐ Developing new words with similar patterns

Techniques for Patterning

Onset and Rimes

(Note: This technique has four different methods: Whole-Part-Whole, Part-to-Whole, Whole-to-Part, and Cloze.)

Purpose: To recognize patterns within words and to form new words with similar patterns

Level: Emergent–Early

ELL Technique: Yes

Multiple Intelligences: Verbal/linguistic, bodily/kinesthetic, interpersonal

Whole-Part-Whole Materials: Onset and Rimes reproducible (see CD ●), text, markers, notebooks, online program like Construct a Word (www.readwritethink.org/materials/construct)

Whole-Part-Whole Method Procedure:

1. After reading a sentence from a selected text, present students with a word from the text. Read the word to the students, noting the particular rime sound you are studying (e.g., *night*).

2. Use two different colored markers (one color for the onset *n* and the other color for the rime *ight*) to highlight the word for all the students to see; record the word on a chart.

3. Have students generate other words they can make by changing the onset but keeping the rime (e.g., *sight, fight*). Record their newly formed words underneath the highlighted word. Suggested teacher talk might be, "Explain how these words are similar."

4. Return to the text and have a student reread the sentence containing the highlighted word.

5. Ask students to record the original word and the newly generated list of words in a notebook, which will become their "Rime Time" journal of words.

Motivation/Engagement: Allow students to work with a computer-assisted program like Construct a Word from the ReadWriteThink website (www.readwritethink.org/materials/construct). Construct a Word provides a simple, engaging way for students to generate dozens of different words by first choosing an ending or rime (for example -*at, -op*) and then adding a beginning letter or blend. When a correct word is created, the word is stored in a word bank where students can read and review their words. It uses animation and sound to guide students through the steps of creating words, and it employs prompts that are clear and easy to master.

Part-to-Whole Materials: Onset and Rimes reproducible (see CD ⊙), hula hoops or large construction paper, note cards

Part-to-Whole Method Procedure:

1. Write some onsets and rimes on note cards and put them in two stacks at the front of the room. You can use the Onset and Rimes reproducible for a list of rimes to help you get started. Lay out three hula hoops or three large pieces of construction paper on the floor.

2. Have students take turns stepping up to the "Rime Time" area and selecting one onset card and one rime card from the stacks.

3. Ask students to hop into the first hula hoop or onto the paper and pronounce the onset. Then, have students hop into the next hula hoop or piece of paper and say the rime.

4. Finally, have students hop into the third hula hoop or onto the third piece of paper and pronounce the blended word. Continue this process, with several students selecting onsets and rimes to "hop out." Suggested teacher talk could be, "When you hop out the word, what are you doing to the word?

Motivation/Engagement: Create a matching game using two different color cards (one color for a variety of onsets and the other for examples of rimes). Students play the game by taking turns turning over the displayed cards and trying to form a word from the text that was read.

Whole-to-Part Materials: Note cards, bookmaking software such as Easy Book

Whole-to-Part Method Procedure:

1. Present students with a list of several sets of words that have the same rime but different onsets.

2. Ask students to examine the words in small groups and discuss how the words are the same and how they are different.

3. Have students write down the words, underlining the onsets and circling the rimes in each set. Then, have students create other words that would match the rime sets and add them to their lists. Suggested teacher talk could be, "What pattern do you find in these words?"

Motivation/Engagement: Students can use bookmaking software such as Easy Book or a word processing document to create a class word pattern book. Partners can work together on pairing onsets and rimes) to create a list of words sharing the same pattern. Collect the patterns to make a class book or add to a word wall. (This idea was contributed by classroom teacher Shannon McCoy.)

Cloze Materials: Sentence strips, note cards

Cloze Procedure:

1. Select a phonogram or rime (e.g., -*ab*), and list several words on note cards that are formed using this phonogram (e.g., *lab, grab, cabin, crab*).

2. Record sentences on sentence strips that use the words in context, omitting the phonogram word from each sentence.

3. Have students read the sentences and determine which word card would complete each sentence.

4. Discuss how changing the onset completely changes the meaning of a word. Suggested teacher talk could be, "If you take away the first letter and add this beginning sound, what new word would you have now?"

Pattern Sort

Purpose: To sort words according to their common patterns

Level: Early

ELL Technique: Yes

Multiple Intelligences: Visual/spatial, logical/mathematical, bodily/kinesthetic

Materials: Text; note cards, chart, board, or overhead projector; pipe cleaners, computer programs or websites to sort words (www.readwritethink.org/materials/wordfamily)

Procedure:

1. List a variety of words sharing common patterns in a place where all students can see them, such as on note cards, a chart, the board, or the overhead projector. Suggested teacher talk could be, "What vowel pattern do you notice in these words?"

2. Have students sort the words according to their patterns. For an open sort, have students sort the words into groups according to their own judgment, which makes students attend to the connections in the words. Then, students can give a title or label to the patterns they noted from the words. With a closed sort, you select the categories the students will use. Suggested teacher talk might be, "How do you know that this is a pattern?"

Motivation/Engagement: Use pipe cleaners to create a circle around the words in the text. Continue reading until there are six or seven sets of rhyming words. Write the words on note cards. Pass out the cards to students, reread the text, and have volunteers hold up a rhyme card when they hear the corresponding rhyme. Identify the patterns within the words on the cards and discuss the pattern these words have in common. Discuss any words that have spelling patterns different from the main pattern being discussed. Suggested teacher talk might be, "Why did you classify these word cards together?" Place several of the word cards that have the same spelling pattern together, and have students underline the letters that represent the pattern. Students also may use computer programs or sites like ReadWriteThink's Word Family Sort (www.readwritethink.org/materials/wordfamily) to sort words at a station independently.

Note: Adapted from Bear et al. (2008), Gillet & Kita (1979)

Vowel Pattern Jingles

Purpose: To identify and examine vowel patterns, unlocking the alphabetic code, shifting vowel sounds, and reading with accuracy and fluency

Level: Early–Transitional

ELL Technique: No

Multiple Intelligences: Verbal/linguistic, musical/rhythmic, intrapersonal

Materials: Vowel Pattern Jingles (see CD ⊙), texts

Procedure:

1. Select a vowel pattern to highlight and choose a text that supports that pattern.

2. Copy the Vowel Pattern Jingles reproducible and distribute to each student or make it into a poster. Sing or say the jingle for the pattern you are using.

   - The closed vowel pattern is a word or syllable that contains only one vowel and is followed by one or more consonants (e.g., *cat, went, lunch*). The jingle that supports this pattern is, "One lonely vowel squished in the middle says its special sound just a little."

   - The open vowel pattern has one vowel at the end of the word that says its letter name to represent the long vowel sound (e.g., *we, no, fly*). The open vowel pattern jingle is, "If one vowel at the end is free, it pops way up and says its name to me."

   - The silent *e* pattern demonstrates words or syllables that end in *e*. These words contain one consonant before the final *e* and one vowel before that consonant. The vowel sound says its name to represent the long vowel sound (e.g., *take, rope*, and *bike*). The jingle for this pattern is, "When the *e* is at the end, the sound is gone; it makes the other vowel in the word say its name long."

   - The two-vowel pattern refers to vowel digraphs and vowel diphthongs. Vowel digraphs are known as the "double vowel talkers"; they are syllables containing two adjacent vowels in which the first vowel is long (e.g., *play, tree, seat*). The vowel digraph jingle is, "When two vowels go walking, the first one does the talking and says its name." Vowel diphthongs are syllables that contain two adjacent vowels in which the vowels say neither their long nor their short sounds but instead make a "whine" sound (e.g., drew, book, boy). The jingle for this pattern is, "Sometimes when two vowels are together they make a whine sound, like when you fall down and want to be found—ow, aw, oy, and boo-hoo."

- The bossy *r* pattern is a word or syllable containing one vowel followed by the letter *r* (e.g., *star*, *girl*, *water*). The jingle for this pattern is, "When the vowel is followed by the letter *r*, the vowel has to let the *r* be the star."

- The *c* + *-le* pattern, which occurs in two-syllable words, has a consonant immediately before an ending *-le* (e.g., *whistle*, *apple*, *purple*). The consonant before the *-le* is included in the syllable break with the *-le*. The jingle for this pattern is, "The *-le* grabs the consonant right before it, and it makes a clean syllable break to form the split."

3. Have students list words from the text that follow the vowel pattern. Suggested teacher talk could be, "How do you know that this is a pattern? What vowel pattern is within the word?"

Motivation/Engagement: Invite students to create their own jingles as ways they may remember patterns that occur in some words.

Note: Adapted from Cheyney & Cohen (1998)

Dancing With Diphthongs

Phonics: Patterning

Purpose: To examine and create a representation of various vowel diphthongs

Level: Fluent

ELL Technique: Yes

Multiple Intelligences: Visual/spatial, bodily/kinesthetic, interpersonal

Materials: Text, music, digital camera, chart paper, note cards, *Adaptive Dance and Rhythms for All Ages with Basic Lesson Plans* (Kramer, 2008)

Procedure:

1. Describe vowel diphthongs as the gliding vowels, which move continuously from an initial vowel position to a final position. Compare the description to dancing and discuss the types of ball-room dance steps and other dance steps that have a gliding movement.

2. Distribute to partners note cards listing a vowel diphthong and have partners generate words to correspond with their diphthong (e.g., *ou*: *sound*, *mouth*, *blouse*).

3. Partners use the sound of their diphthong and listen to music to create a dance step (like a dip or a turn) to demonstrate their sound. Instead of the dance count 1, 2, 3, 4 they would substitute the counting for the spelling of the word (*s-ou-n-d*) with each word having the same dance step to represent their diphthong.

Motivation/Engagement: Take a digital picture of each dance step and create a vowel diphthong chart. In addition, use Adaptive Dance and Rhythms for All Ages with Basic

Lesson Plans (Kramer, 2008) to help you create opportunities to highlight the strategy in creative and artistic ways. The lessons in the book provide explicit procedure for utilizing music and rhythms to provide inspiration for right and left brain development and expressive movement.

Phonics Strategy: Spelling

Spelling as a strategy helps readers transform sounds into letters and letters into written word form. Proficient strategic readers use their phonics knowledge to enable them to read and write words (Cunningham & Allington, 2007; Gentry, 2006). Reading and spelling are interdependent; students need many opportunities to explore sound and letter relationships in real text, manipulate letters to form words, search for patterns within words, and sometimes decode words sequentially. It is through reading that students visually store shapes of words so that, when writing, they can recall how the words looked when they were read. "When students decide that a word doesn't look right, they rewrite the word several different ways using their knowledge of spellings patterns" (Tompkins, 2001, p. 114). Guiding students through using their visual memory of the word is one technique teachers use, rather than always asking students to sound out words when they are trying to spell a word (Conrad, 2008; Moustafa, 1997).

When students view spelling strategically, they are able to evolve through the developmental stages and "attack" the thinking process that occurs as they gain word power. Explicit spelling instruction does allow students to transfer word knowledge over time into independent composing (Amtmann, Abbott, & Berninger, 2008; Liow & Lau, 2006). Gaining word power requires students to process spelling through word studies that enable them to explore, inspect, visualize, chunk, sound out, approximate, and use memory devices, patterns, and their multiple senses (i.e., hearing, seeing, and feeling). Strategic readers and writers think of spelling as a strategic tool on their quest to gain word power. Keeping the formal procedures and routines of word study as simple and predictable as possible allows students to become inventors, choreographers, and word explorers (Calkins, 2001).

Many studies have noted the various spelling stages and their characteristics (Freeman, 1995; Gentry, 1989; Gentry & Gillet, 1992; Graves, 1982; Pinnell & Fountas, 1998; Sharp, Sinatra, & Reynolds, 2008; Tompkins, 2000; Vacca, Vacca, & Gove, 1995). Following are the stages and some suggested approaches to support the growth of the speller within each stage. Note that researchers and practitioners use multiple names when referring to the same spelling stages.

Prephonetic/Precommunicative/Emergent Stage—Students in this initial stage are not yet connecting letters with the words they are writing to convey a message; they are using scribbles and letter-like forms to represent a message. Their messages may be randomly arranged on the pages (e.g., right to left, top to bottom, left to right, or all over) or may be in a nonsense form and often cannot be read by others. Approaches to support students who are trying to develop at this stage of spelling include listening to pattern books, identifying words within the text, matching initial and final consonants with sounds, playing with the sounds in words, drawing pictures and then writing about their drawings, dictating stories, and exploring directionality.

Semiphonetic/Early Phonetic/Early Letter Name/Alphabetic Stage—Students demonstrate the early signs of connecting letters and sounds in writing and reading. Their spelling includes single letters to represent words, sounds, and syllables. Students at this stage omit vowels most of the time. Approaches for this stage are using word walls for names, high-frequency words, and easy word patterns; language experiences (i.e., writing personal experiences with teacher support to connect written form with oral language); sorting words according to the initial or final consonant sounds; and changing the onsets of words to form a new word.

Phonetic/Early/Within Word Pattern Stage—Students in this stage spell words the way they hear them and, at times, by patterns they see from other words. Vowels, consonants, and some blends and digraphs may appear in their writing of words, but they may be inconsistent. This stage is important because it represents the beginning use of word segmentation in students' writing. Approaches that support phonetic spellers include using word walls; reading texts with reasonable picture support, appropriate level high-frequency words, and patterned words that can be decoded with ease; exploring long and short vowel sound relationships; using rhyming words; and incorporating phonemic awareness activities.

Structural/Syllables and Affixes/Transitional Stage—Students at this stage demonstrate the use of structural elements (e.g., syllables, inflectional endings, affixes) in their writing. They are consistent in using a vowel in every syllable and are beginning to use the morphemic relationships of words (e.g., happy, happier, happiest, unhappily, happiness, happily). Their spelling is moving from a dependence on phonology (sound) to relying more on visual representations and structures of words. Approaches for this stage are using word studies on more complex spelling patterns and structural elements, using a word wall, reading more complex text with less picture support, practicing solving multisyllabic and irregular technical words, and proofreading.

Conventional/Meaning/Derivational/Advanced/Correct/Fluent Stage—In this last stage, students are spelling the majority of the words correctly in their writing. Students are aware of and use a variety of rules and generalizations of the orthographic (written) system and know how to use historical roots to derive meaning. Approaches that support this advanced speller are using word studies on root words and their meanings, examining vowel alterations in derivationally related pairs, and reading complex text with specialized content vocabulary and many multisyllabic words.

Appropriate text that best supports the application of the spelling strategy has a variety of words suitable for the students' specific stage of spelling.

Spelling Text Examples:

Benjamin, A. (1987). *Rat-a-Tat, Pitter Pat.* New York: HarperCollins.

Burt, A., & Vandyck, W. (2005). *Spelling Repair Kit: Improve Your Spelling Skills.* London: Hodder and Stoughton.

Prelutsky, J. (1983). *The Random House Book of Poetry for Children.* New York: Random House.

Teacher Talk: Statements, Questions, and Prompts for Spelling

Following is a list of suggested teacher talk that encourages readers to think strategically as they spell. Try using some of these statements, questions, and prompts with your students as you work through the techniques in the following section.

- What words can you make from these letters?
- What is the secret word that uses all of these letters?
- What are ways you can "think out" how to write the word?
- Try to visualize the word in your mind. Paint the word on the inside of your eyelids.
- Look at the word you wrote. Does the word look right? Why or why not?
- Visualize the word in your mind, and "take a picture" of it.
- How does knowing how to spell _____ help you spell _____?
- How does the word wall help you?
- Describe other words that sound almost the same.
- What categories would you sort your words into, based on the patterns you see within the words?
- What patterns do you see in these words?
- Try to think about other "chunks" that are within the word to help you.
- Name the letters with your inside-your-mind voice.
- Do you remember seeing that word somewhere else? If so, where?

As you implement the various techniques that support this strategy, use the following behaviors as a guide as you assess students' ability to spell. Do students exhibit these behaviors never, rarely, often, always?

- ☐ Creating associations to remember how to spell words
- ☐ Connecting words by spelling patterns
- ☐ Manipulating letters to discover letter–sound relationship

Word Walls

Phonics: Spelling

Purpose: To interact with words and identify letters needed when spelling

Level: Emergent–Fluent

ELL Technique: Yes

Multiple Intelligence: Visual/Spatial, musical/rhythmic, bodily/kinesthetic

Materials: Text, words for wall, space on wall or board, different colors of construction paper, scissors, spiral notebooks or file folders

Procedure:

1. Select four or five words each week to add to a class word wall (i.e., a designated section on a wall to display words). These words are ones that students need often for their reading and writing, and these words are the ones often confused with other words.

2. Write words on different colors of construction paper and cut around the configuration.

3. Place the words on the wall alphabetically by the first letter. There may also be word walls that highlight certain features (e.g., themes, contractions, and compounds). Complete minilessons with the word wall words, allowing the students to interact and use the wall as a resource for word study.

Motivation/Engagement: Students can interact with the words on the word wall by clapping, chanting, and writing the words; reviewing skills; discovering words by clues given; playing word games; writing the word in sentences; and doing word sorts. Suggested teacher talk could be, "How does the word wall help you? Try to check the word wall to see how _____ is spelled." Students can make individual portable word walls in spiral notebooks or on file folders.

Note: Adapted from Hoyt & Therriault (2008)

Working With Words

Phonics: Spelling

This technique is highlighted on the Creating Strategic Readers DVD/VHS series.

Purpose: To explore, inspect, visualize, chunk, sound out, approximate, and use memory devices, patterns, and multiple senses (i.e., hearing, seeing, and feeling)

Level: Early–Fluent

ELL Technique: No

Multiple Intelligences: Visual/spatial, verbal/linguistics, logical/mathematical, bodily/kinesthetic, interpersonal

Materials: Working With Words reproducible (see CD 💿), *Words Their Way* (Bear et al., 2008)

Procedure:

1. Present a word to the students and have them say it aloud. (The word is _____.)

2. Encourage students to stretch the word like a rubber band or use Stretch It strips (see synthesizing strategy, this chapter). Compare the word to other words that are about the same length in sound. (Say the word slowly.)

3. Have students use their hand and do the hand push technique in Chapter 2. (I hear _____ sounds).

4. Display the word to the students to look at it and then have them record the word. (Write the word down.)

5. Have students tap out the letters in the word on their hands or desk. (The word has _____ letters, and because it has _____ sounds, there will or will not be one sound for each letter.)

6. Investigate the word for any spelling patterns and highlight them. (The spelling pattern is _____.)

7. Report the investigation findings about the words. (This is what I know about the vowels in the word _____.)

8. Use the Word Wall technique or other resources to compare and contrast the word with other words on the word wall. (Another word on the word wall with the same vowel sound is _____. The spelling patterns are the same or different because _____.)

Motivation/Engagement: Assign students to groups according to their spelling development based on the *Words Their Way* (Bear et al., 2008) assessment. Each week give teams a list of developmental spelling words to "work" on using a laminated Working With Words reproducible. Students can have their own Working With Words form to practice working with words.

Note: Adapted from Gaskins, Ehri, Cress, O'Hara, & Donnelly (1996/1997)

Brain Tricks

(Note: This technique has three different methods: Mnemonics, Making Connections, and Visualization.)

Purpose: To create associations to remember how to spell words

Level: Early–Fluent

ELL Technique: No

Multiple Intelligences: Visual/spatial, verbal/linguistics, logical/mathematical, bodily/kinesthetic, interpersonal

Materials: Brain Tricks reproducibles (see CD 💿), chart paper

Mnemonics Procedure:

1. Have students create associations to remember spellings of certain words. For example, to remember how to spell the word *friend*, say "I'll see my friend at the end of the week on Friday." Suggested teacher talk might be, "What are some ways you try to 'think out' how to spell a word?"

Making Connections Procedure:

1. Copy and distribute the Brain Tricks: Making Connections reproducible. Have students write the words they are studying at the top of the form in the puzzle pieces.

2. Ask students to take each word and record connections they can make about the word (e.g., rhymes with, starts like, goes with, and means).

3. Continue steps 1 and 2 for all chosen words.

4. Have students share and discuss the connections with a partner.

Visualization Procedure:

1. Copy and distribute the Brain Tricks: Visualize reproducible. Have students pretend they are taking a picture of a word. Suggested teacher talk could be, "Try to visualize the word in your mind and 'take a picture' of it."

2. Have students hold up their hands and "click" the word as if they are using a camera to take a picture of the word presented.

3. Ask students to close their eyes and try to see the word, putting a frame around the picture they took.

4. When the students open their eyes, have them write the word in a picture frame on the reproducible.

Motivation/Engagement: Play the Wheel game (Cunningham, 2000), based on the game show *Wheel of Fortune*, in which students are contestants trying to figure out a hidden word from the text being read. Write a category to which the word belongs on chart paper and then under the category draw blanks for each letter in the word(s). Ask the contestants (i.e., students) for a specific vowel or consonant, "Is there a ___?" If the student guesses a correct letter, the letter is written on the line. If the guess is incorrect, the student loses a turn and the next contestant continues to figure out the hidden word. If a student knows the hidden word, they must continue to spell it out completely before stating the word.

Note: Adapted from Cunningham (2000), Pinnell & Fountas (1998)

If I Can Spell

Purpose: To connect words according to their spelling patterns

Level: Early

ELL Technique: Yes

Multiple Intelligences: Visual/spatial, logical/mathematical, bodily/kinesthetic, interpersonal, intrapersonal

Materials: If I Can Spell reproducible (see CD), text, magnetic letters

Procedure:

1. Copy and distribute the If I Can Spell reproducible. Have students select four words from the text or word wall that contain different spelling patterns and record them on the left side of the form. Suggested teacher talk might be, "How are these words alike?"

2. Ask students to search for three other words that have each of the spelling patterns chosen; have students write these to the right of each of the corresponding selected words. The spelling pattern may appear in the initial, medial, or ending parts of the new words recorded.

3. Have students share with a partner how these words connect. Suggested teacher talk could be, "How does knowing how to spell the word _____ help you spell _____?"

Motivation/Engagement: Have students use the word wall (see Word Walls technique, this chapter) to identify words that have same spelling pattern. Use magnetic letters to demonstrate changing the initial, medial, or ending part of the new words.

Note: Adapted from Taberski (2000)

Creating Words

Purpose: To manipulate letters to discover letter–sound relationships and look for patterns in words

Level: Early

ELL Technique: Yes

Multiple Intelligences: Visual/spatial, logical/mathematical, musical/rhythmic, bodily/kinesthetic, interpersonal, intrapersonal

Materials: Creating Words reproducible (see CD), words from text, paper plates or note cards, music

Procedure:

1. Select teams and decide on a specific word for each team to "create."

2. Give each team a word and have them write the individual sound unit on a plate or note card (e.g., *w-ea-th-er*) or by individual letter.

3. Copy and distribute the Creating Words reproducible.

4. Call on a team to present their word to the class but in a scrambled format. In a given time, ask the audience (i.e., class) to write on the reproducible the word they think it is.

5. Turn on some music and have the "scrambled up" team create the word by moving to the beat as they form the correct word. Stop the music and have the audience check their word and make any necessary changes below the practice box.

Look/Say/Cover/Write/Check

Purpose: To visualize and spell words

Level: Transitional (Adaptation for Early)

ELL Technique: Yes

Multiple Intelligences: Verbal/linguistic, bodily/kinesthestic, interpersonal

Materials: Look/Say/Cover/Write/Check bookmark (see CD 💿); 10 Ways to Help Know My Word reproducible (see CD 💿); text; words; notebook paper; overhead projector; note cards, folder, or chart; For Adaptation: salt, sand, flour, string, dough

Procedure:

1. Choose some spelling words and present the words to students on an overhead projector, a set of cards, a folder, or a chart.

2. **Look:** Ask students to look at the first word to visualize the overall letter patterns within the word and to see the shape of the word.

3. **Say:** Next, have students turn to a partner and say the word. Point out that this is their time to "talk" the word: They can say each of the letters, sounds, syllables, patterns they notice, and so forth. Students can close their eyes and imagine the word in their mind, stretch the word to hear the sounds, and look for patterns.

4. **Cover:** When all the students have looked at the word and pronounced it to a partner, cover the word.

5. **Write** and **Check:** Have students write the word on notebook paper, naming each letter as they write it. Show the word again to allow students to check their written word. Suggested teacher talk could be, "Look at the word you wrote; does it look right?"

6. Repeat steps 1 to 5 as needed, focusing on one word at a time. Students can use the Look/Say/Cover/Write/Check bookmark to help them remember the process.

Adaptation for Early Readers: Place salt, sand, or flour on a tray and have students trace the words. Have students use string, play dough, or bread dough to form the words. Use the 10

Ways to Help Know My Word reproducible to spell new words. Suggested teacher talk might be, "Visualize the word in your mind, and paint the word on the inside of your eyelids."

Note: Adapted from Pinnell & Fountas (1998)

Phonics Strategy: Recognizing

Students who apply the recognizing strategy are able to identify words quickly and automatically. The cognitive process allows for instant recognition of words in written form. Using text that is predictable and easy to memorize supports beginning readers in gaining word recognition abilities (Bear et al., 2008). The speed and accuracy with which a student is able to use this strategy determines the student's fluency and comprehension. "When students recognize words immediately, they find it easier to focus on the meaning of what is being read" (Bishop & Bishop, 1996, p. 53). The techniques in this section focus on supporting students in recognizing letters, sight words (words recognized and pronounced immediately), and high-frequency words (some of the most commonly used words in printed language, which are often irregular).

Appropriate text that best supports the application of the recognizing strategy has a variety of words suitable for word identification.

Recognizing Text Examples:

Cosgrove, B. (2007). *Weather*. New York: DK Children.

Pallotta, J. (1990). *The Frog Alphabet Book*. Watertown, MA: Charlesbridge.

Young, E. (1992). *Seven Blind Mice*. New York: Philomel.

Teacher Talk: Statements, Questions, and Prompts for Recognizing

Following is a list of suggested teacher talk that encourages readers to think strategically as they recognize words and letters. Try using some of these statements, questions, and prompts with your students as you work through the techniques in the following section.

- How many times have you used the high-frequency words in your writing this week?
- How does recognizing the words by sight help you when you are reading?
- Explain how you would sort these letters.
- What pictures would you select to represent this letter? Why?
- How does using your five senses help you to recognize words?
- Why do we want to be able to recognize words?

- Examine this word to see if it has a smaller word inside it to help you remember the word.

- Try to find this letter, word, or phrase around the room.

- How fast can you read this word?

As you implement the various techniques that support this strategy, use the following behaviors as a guide as you assess students' ability to recognize. Do students exhibit these behaviors never, rarely, often, always?

☐ Recognizing words instantly

☐ Identifying high-frequency words

☐ Examining words using the multiple senses

Techniques for Recognizing

Letter Recognition

Purpose: To recognize letters by matching, sorting, and creating them

Level: Emergent

ELL Technique: Yes

Multiple Intelligences: Visual/spatial, bodily/kinesthetic

Materials: Uppercase and lowercase letters, pictures relating to letters, poster paper, art supplies

Procedure:

1. Letter Matching—Have students match uppercase letters with corresponding lowercase letters, or letter-to-letter match-up.

2. Letter Sorting—Ask students to classify letters according to various attributes. Suggested teacher talk could be, "How would you sort these letters?"

3. Letter Posters—Instruct students to make posters with pictures pertaining to a specific letter. Suggested teacher talk might be, "What pictures would you use to represent this letter? Why?"

4. Letter Art—Have students make a design with a specific letter, using a variety of materials.

High-Frequency Words

Purpose: To recognize high-frequency words in text

Level: Emergent

ELL Technique: Yes

Multiple Intelligences: Visual/spatial, interpersonal

Materials: Text, word walls, highlighters, highlighting tape, pipe cleaners, magnetic letters, chalkboard or dry-erase board and markers

Procedure:

1. Word Walls—See under spelling strategy, this chapter.

2. Highlighting—Have students use highlighters, highlighting tape, pipe cleaners, or any other medium to set the high-frequency word apart from other words in the text they are reading.

3. Make and Break—Have students use magnetic letters to make a word, scramble it up, and remake it.

4. Word Games—Have students use the words to play bingo and hangman.

5. Writing and Reading—Give students as many opportunities as possible to use these words in their writing and to recognize them in their reading. This will be valuable in students' learning instant recognition of the words. Suggested teacher talk could be, "How many times have you used your high-frequency words in your writing this week? How does recognizing the words by sight help you when you are reading?"

Irregular and Sight Words

Purpose: To recognize words instantly using the five senses

Level: Emergent (Adaptation for Early–Fluent)

ELL Technique: Yes

Multiple Intelligences: Visual/spatial, logical/mathematical, bodily/kinesthetic, interpersonal

Materials: Text, board or overhead projector, fly swatter, scissors, note cards, word journal or bank, dough, oven; Optional: Audio recorder; For Adaptation: Graph paper

Procedure:

1. Select appropriate irregular or sight words (i.e., words that are not easily decoded) from text currently being read in class.

2. Introduce the words by displaying them in sentences.

3. Create a word mask by cutting a section out of the middle of a fly swatter. Place the word mask over the word to make it stand out from the other words in the sentence.

4. Have students use their sense of hearing to process the word into memory by turning to a partner and pronouncing the word aloud. Students may also record the new word to replay it in the future. Suggested teacher talk could be, "How does your sense of sight help you to recognize words?"

5. Have students visualize each word by pretending to "take a picture" of the word. The students then "develop" this picture by writing it into their word journal or word bank. (If desired, you can show students an actual object or a picture that corresponds to the word.)

6. Write the word on a note card and cut the letters apart to allow the students to remake the word.

7. To use the sense of touch to process the word, have students work in teams to roll out dough and use it to form the letters for the word.

8. Bake the words (this uses the students' sense of smell) and then have the teams eat the letters as they spell out each word (this uses the students' sense of taste).

9. Have the students read books and other texts that contain the focus words. Suggested teacher talk might be, "Why do we want to be able to recognize words?"

Adaptation for Early–Fluent Readers: Have students gradually add words to a word wall (see Word Walls technique, this chapter). Students can practice and study the displayed words. Place students in teams and have them go on word searches to find words and arrange in a grid. In addition, students can create their own word search using graph paper.

Note: Adapted from Cunningham (2000)

Phonics Wrap-Up

Phonics instruction helps students to apply their knowledge of the alphabetic system. The findings of the NRP report indicate, "it is important to emphasize that systematic phonics instruction should be integrated with other reading instruction to create a balanced reading program" (NICHD, 2000, p. 2-136). The strategies, techniques, and teacher talk presented in this chapter support teachers in maximizing their students' potential in becoming strategic readers and creating a comprehensive literacy classroom. In the craft of teaching reading, teachers use these strategies, techniques, and teacher talk as artistic tools to add dimension to the strategic readers they are helping to create.

Chapter 4

Fluency

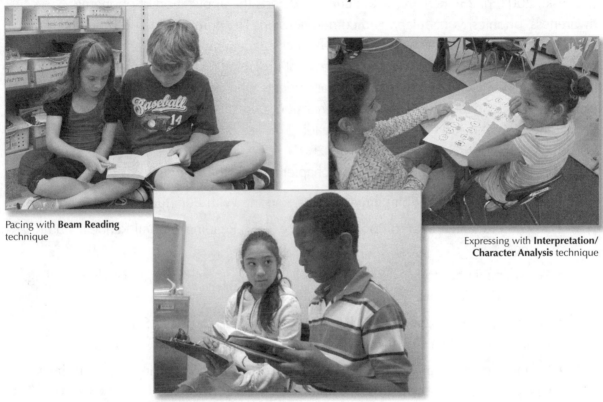

Pacing with **Beam Reading** technique

Expressing with **Interpretation/Character Analysis** technique

Phrasing with **Eye 2 Eye** technique

luency represents a level of expertise in combining appropriate phrasing and intonation while reading words automatically. The NRP report defines fluency as "the ability to read a text quickly, accurately, and with proper expression" (NICHD, 2000, p. 3-1). However, fluency is far more complex than attending to word recognition skills. Readers also demonstrate proficiency through fluency skills such as reading accuracy, reading at an appropriate rate, and using prosodic features of language to bring meaning to the text. These fluency expectations can serve as outcome measures for reading proficiency as well as for acquisition of reading skills (Klauda & Guthrie, 2008; Samuels & Farstrup, 2006; Torgesen, Rashotte, & Alexander, 2001). The ability to read efficiently brings self-assurance to a reader. Fluent readers are confident readers that apply the fluency strategies on their own, as it becomes a habit of mind (Gaskins, 2005). When readers are using all their efforts to decode unknown words within the text, they begin to lose the meaning of what they are reading.

Their confidence as readers diminishes with every moment that passes as they try to understand the intricate process that their brain is seeking to navigate. "Becoming a fluent reader has as much to do with constructing meaning as it has to do with attending to words on a page" (Forbes & Briggs, 2003, p. 3).

This chapter features strategies students need to develop independence as readers. Having a repertoire of fluency tools readily available allows "the maximum amount of cognitive energy [to] be directed to the all-important task of making sense of the text" (Rasinski, 2003, p. 26). Reading with fluency supports the application of phonemic awareness, phonics, vocabulary, and comprehension. The combination of these other four reading components, fused with fluency, enhances a reader's ability to bring meaning to reading. The National Assessment of Educational Progress (NAEP) addressed fluency in a study (Pinnell et al., 1995) that reported that students who performed poorly on fluency measures also tended to have low comprehension scores. Fluency strategies are essential to comprehension and serve as a proxy for reading proficiency (Fuchs, Fuchs, Hosp, & Jenkins, 2001; Rasinski, 2006; Samuels & Farstrup, 2006).

The strategies and techniques in this chapter include the following:

- Phrasing: Eye–Voice Span, Phrase Strips, Pausing With Punctuation, and Eye 2 Eye

- Assisted Reading: Shared Book Experience, Echo Reading, Choral Readers, and Read-Alongs

- Rereading: Listen to Me, Repeated Reading/One-Minute Reads, Recorded Reading: Record/Check/Chart, and Multimedia Reading

- Expressing: ABC Punctuation Style, Express Yourself, Dramatic Sentences, Punctuation Police, Totally Tonality, and Interpretation/Character Analysis

- Pacing: Commercial Programs, Beam Reading, Tempo Time, Time/Record/Check/Chart, and Digital Portfolio for Oral Reading

- Wide Reading: Book Baskets/Browsing Boxes, Selecting "Just Right" Books, and Book Clubs

- Accuracy: Use the techniques from Chapters 2 and 3, especially the recognizing and analyzing techniques from Chapter 3, to promote accuracy.

Table 17 aligns the instructional techniques in this chapter with the appropriate developmental levels from Chapter 1. To be effective, when using the strategies and techniques presented in this chapter, teachers should allow ample time for teacher modeling and student application, long before independent application is expected. Teachers should select and model reading aloud of appropriate text to apply the techniques in a meaningful manner, which supports authentic learning for strategic reading. By using this process, students are able to see first the whole text (i.e., appropriate literature), then see the parts systematically (i.e., strategies and techniques), and finally, apply the parts back to the whole (i.e., become metacognitively aware of strategies while reading appropriate literature). Using

TABLE 17. Fluency Techniques

	Emergent	Early	Transitional	Fluent
Before Reading	ABC Punctuation Style (E) Book Baskets/ Browsing Boxes (WR)	May include all Emergent techniques Eye–Voice Span† (Ph) Express Yourself† (E) Selecting "Just Right" Books† (WR)	May include all Emergent and Early techniques Phrase Strips (Ph) Totally Tonality† (E) Book Clubs (WR)	May include all Emergent, Early, and Transitional techniques
During Reading	Shared Book Experience (AR) Echo Reading (AR) Choral Readers (AR) Express Yourself* (E) Commercial Programs (P)	Choral Readers (AR) Read-Alongs (AR) Listen to Me (R) Punctuation Police (E) Commercial Programs (P) Beam Reading† (P) Tempo Time† (P)	Pausing With Punctuation (Ph) Choral Readers (AR) Repeated Reading/One-Minute Reads (R) Recorded Reading: Record/ Check/Chart (R) Multimedia Reading (R) Commercial Programs (P) Time/Record/Check/Chart (P)	Eye 2 Eye† (Ph) Choral Readers (AR) Interpretation/ Character Analysis (E) Commercial Programs (P) Digital Portfolio for Oral Reading (P)
After Reading		Phrase Strips (Ph) Listen to Me (R) Dramatic Sentences (E)	Eye–Voice Span*† (Ph) Recorded Reading: Record/ Check/Chart (R) Time/Record/Check/Chart (P)	

*Adaptation portion of the technique.
†Technique is illustrated on Creating Strategic Readers DVD series.
Note. The developmental levels are shown across the top of the table horizontally. Down the left side of the matrix are the suggested times when these techniques are most effective—before, during, and after reading. This matrix is a guide and is by no means an exhaustive list.
(Ph) Phrasing; (AR) Assisted reading; (R) Rereading; (E) Expressing; (P) Pacing; (WR) Wide reading

quality text and promoting language development throughout the techniques will help to enhance students' development of the strategies. In addition, teachers can use the motivation and engagement feature within many techniques as an additional means (i.e., multiple intelligence, standard) of motivating the whole child and creating 21st-century learners (refer to Chapter 1 for a description of the whole child and Figure 1, page 8, for an illustration). This allows for differentiation within the technique as needed to educate the whole child.

Fluency Strategy: Phrasing

Phrasing is the ability to read several words together before pausing, as opposed to word-by-word reading. Good strategic readers phrase words together to derive meaning rather than trying to use the meaning of each word independently. Reading word by word sounds choppy and it can stifle the overall meaning of the passage the student is reading.

When a reader "chunks" the text into syntactically meaningful phrases (e.g., by grammar), the reading rate and comprehension improve. "Studying grammar fosters fluency because grammar alerts the reader to natural phrases in a sentence" (Blevins, 2001, p. 18). The reader needs to have an understanding of noun phrases, verb phrases, and prepositional phrases. This understanding of grammar will support readers as they appropriately chunk text (Blevins, 2001; LeVasseur, Macaruso, & Shankweiler, 2008; Miller & Schwanenflugel, 2006).

The ability to connect important phrases into cohesive chunks is enhanced when the reader "learns that punctuation marks such as commas, semicolons, parentheses, and dashes signal the end of a phrase and requires a pause in reading" (Stricklan, Ganske, & Monroe, 2002, p. 135). Good strategic readers use this strategy of phrasing to make a conversational connection in their reading. The goal is to read phrases seamlessly, sounding as if the reader is holding a conversation. This permits the reading to flow, allowing the reader to concentrate on making sense of the reading.

Readers' perceptual spans dictate how much information they can take in about words in a single fixation of their eye movement (Drieghe, Pollatsek, Staub, & Rayner, 2008; NICHD, 2000; Paulson, 2005). "There are well-known individual differences in eye movement measures as a function of reading skill: Fast readers make shorter fixations, longer saccades, the jump of the eye from one fixation to another, and fewer regressions than slow readers" (Rayner, 1998, p. 392). Readers need many opportunities to practice techniques that support their ability to make shorter fixations to strategically phrase appropriately.

Appropriate text that best supports the application of the phrasing strategy has a variety of meaningful phrases throughout the text.

Phrasing Text Examples:

Lionni, L. (1970). *Fish Is Fish*. New York: Knopf.

Silverstein, S. (1996). Furniture bash. In *Falling Up* (p. 32). New York: HarperCollins.

Winstead, A., Dacey, B., & Banelin, D. (2003). *The Star-Spangled Banner*. Nashville, TN: Ideals.

Teacher Talk: Statements, Questions, and Prompts for Phrasing

Following is a list of suggested teacher talk that encourages readers to think strategically as they employ phrasing skills. Try using some of these statements, questions, and prompts with your students as you work through the techniques in the following section.

- Where are your eyes looking next?
- Try to "push" your eyes forward ahead of your voice.
- Try to "capture" several words at a time with your eyes.
- How many words do you see at a time when you are reading?
- What do you do with your eyes when you read?
- Listen to me read these sentences...which sounded better to you and why?

- How does the punctuation help you when reading?

- How did grouping the words together sound?

- Why does grouping the words together help make sense out of what you are reading?

- What would happen if you paused after each word?

- What were some of the "chunks" you found?

As you implement the various techniques that support this strategy, use the following behaviors as a guide as you assess students' ability to phrase. Do students exhibit these behaviors never, rarely, often, always?

☐ Demonstrating the value of forward eye movements and fixations

☐ Using punctuation to support inflections

☐ Reading seamlessly with a flow

Techniques for Phrasing

Eye–Voice Span

This technique is highlighted on the Creating Strategic Readers DVD/VHS series.

Purpose: To recognize and demonstrate the value of forward eye movements when reading

Level: Early (Adaptation for Transitional)

ELL Technique: No

Multiple Intelligences: Visual/spatial, verbal/linguistic, body/kinesthetic, interpersonal

Materials: Texts, overhead projector, passage of text on transparency; For Adaptation: Teacher Talk Phrase Cards (see CD 🔘)

Fluency: Phrasing

Procedure:

1. With the class, begin to read aloud a story or passage placed on an overhead transparency or visual presenter where all the students can see the text.

2. Just before finishing reading a sentence or paragraph, turn off the overhead projector or remove text from under the visual presenter. Suggested teacher talk could be, "Where are your eyes looking to next?"

3. Have students demonstrate how they can still say the next few words from the passage right after the text is removed.

4. Discuss why this happens (i.e., because of the distance, students' eyes were ahead of their voices). Suggested teacher talk might be, "Try to 'push' your eyes forward ahead of your voice."

Adaptation for Transitional Readers: Have students work in A/B pairs (A = teacher role and B = student role). The A partner listens to the B partner begin to read from text. Using the Teacher Talk Phrase Cards, partner A randomly places the strip over partner B's text and then flips the strip to model phrasing teacher talk. Partner B responds to the teacher talk presented. Have partners discuss process and then reverse roles.

Note: Adapted from Blevins (2001)

Phrase Strips

Purpose: To read more words together seamlessly before pausing

Level: Early (2–3 word phrases), Transitional (3–4 word phrases)

ELL Technique: Yes

Multiple Intelligences: Visual/spatial, verbal/linguistic, bodily/kinesthetic, interpersonal

Materials: Phrase Strips Choices (see CD 💿), texts, sentence strips, pocket chart, pencil or highlighter, pipe cleaner, transparency pens, or clay

Procedure:

1. On sentence strips, list common phrases, and place them in a pocket chart. Use the Phrase Strips Choices to get started.

2. Have students take turns selecting a strip and reading the phrase (e.g., we like to). Students may need to read the strip aloud several times before it can be read seamlessly. Suggested teacher talk could be, "What would happen if I paused after each word? Does the text make sense when I read just a word by itself? Why or why not?"

3. Then have students orally put the phrase into a complete sentence to bring meaning to the phrase (e.g., On Saturday morning we like to sleep late).

4. Record the student's sentence on a new sentence strip. If desired, laminate and place the sentence strips in a center to be used in independent practice.

5. Ask students to reread their sentences and to use phrase boundaries to indicate appropriate places for pausing between phrases (e.g., On Saturday morning/we like to sleep late).

6. Have students share their sentence strips with a partner.

Motivation/Engagement: Mark phrase boundaries at each natural break in a text with highlighters, pencil slashes, clay, or pipe cleaners. You may choose to have the students place a transparency over the text and mark with the appropriate pen. Have individual students practice reading with the marked text, trying to read fluently to the end of each marked place before pausing. Suggested teacher talk could be, "How did grouping the words together sound?"

Pausing With Punctuation

Purpose: To use punctuation to support appropriate pausing for meaning

Level: Transitional

ELL Technique: Yes

Multiple Intelligences: Visual/spatial, verbal/linguistic, logical/mathematical, interpersonal

Materials: Texts; sentences on chart paper, overhead projector, or sentence strips

Procedure:

1. Select several sentences from a passage to model how to read using punctuation. First show a sentence on chart paper, an overhead projector, or a sentence strip without punctuation to demonstrate not pausing. Suggested teacher talk could be, "Listen to someone read these sentences.... Which sounded better to you and why?"

2. Ask a volunteer to read aloud these sentences without pausing.

3. Have partners try to determine and mark where punctuation should go to encourage pausing.

4. Have pairs share with the class where they think the punctuation should go based on their interpretation of the correct meaning of the text.

5. Have students return to the text and compare their versions with where the punctuation marks actually are. Have them practice reading the text accordingly. Suggested teacher talk might be, "How does the punctuation help you when reading?"

Motivation/Engagement: Have students create sentences or use the following sentences to demonstrate through oral reading how punctuation may cause pausing in different parts of the text, which in turn can alter the meaning of the text.

The man saw the boy with the binoculars.

I know a girl with a dog who has fleas.

The girl fed Jay the big fat cat.

Note: Adapted from Strickland et al. (2002)

Eye 2 Eye

This technique is highlighted on the Creating Strategic Readers DVD/VHS series.

Purpose: To identify eye movements when reading

Level: Fluent

ELL Technique: No

Multiple Intelligences: Visual/spatial, verbal/linguistic, musical/rhythmic, interpersonal

Materials: Texts, clipboards with sheets for tally marks, pencil, copy of the passage, colored markers, CD player, music with a verse and refrain such as "The Star-Spangled Banner"

Procedure:

1. Ask students to each sit knee to knee with a partner. Have the first student read aloud 100 words from a passage while the partner observes the reader's eye movements. Suggested teacher talk could be, "Try to capture several words at a time with your eyes."

2. On a clipboard, the observer should record a tally mark for each time the reader's eye "jumps." Or he or she may record a slash mark on the copied passage.

3. Have the readers reread the passage two more times, trying to phrase more words together each time (do fewer jumps with the eye). The observers should record eye movements all three times. If working from the copied text, have the observer use a different color marking pen for noting changes that may occur.

4. Have observers discuss their observations with their readers. Suggested teacher talk might be, "What do you do with your eyes when you read?"

5. Have the partners switch roles and repeat the activity.

Motivation/Engagement: Play some short musical excerpts and have students listen to and indicate by word or gesture when they hear the end of a phrase. They can also count the number of phrases they hear or write down the last word of each phrase. Have the students sing "The Star-Spangled Banner" or listen to songs chosen that have a verse and refrain. Discuss how the text changes, but the musical phrases are the same for each verse. Suggested teacher talk, "Are the phrases about the same number in length (the same number of beats), or are they longer or shorter?" Discuss how in the musical phrases some have a more final feel in the phrase, where others seem to feel like they are asking a question waiting for the next phrase to answer them.

Fluency Strategy: Assisted Reading

Assisted reading is a strategy used to provide the reader with support while building fluency. By listening to good models of fluent reading, students learn how a reader's voice can help text make sense (Kuhn & Stahl, 2003). Many of the techniques used for assisted reading allow the teacher or modeler the opportunity to scaffold students' learning while they are gaining confidence as readers. Peers, parents, and teachers all can provide guidance and feedback on how fluent readers read and how they become aware of and correct their mistakes (Foorman & Mehta, 2002; Shanahan, 2002; Samuels & Farstrup, 2006). Scaffolding while the student is performing is critical to the development of fluency (Rasinski, 1989, 2006). This "social reading" benefits the reader because he or she knows there is support when needed and the ability to engage in conversations about the text he or she is reading.

"Classroom practices that encourage repeated oral reading with feedback and guidance lead to meaningful improvements in reading expertise for students—for good readers, as well as those who are experiencing difficulties" (NICHD, 2000, p. 3-3).

Appropriate text that best supports the application of the assisted reading strategy has repetitive patterns, interesting characters, and dialogues.

Assisted Reading Text Examples:

Bennett, R. (1988). The Gingerbread Man. In B. Schenk de Regniers, E. Moore, M. White, & J. Carr (Eds.), *Sing a Song of Popcorn: Every Child's Book of Poems* (p. 50). New York: Scholastic.

Keats, E.J. (1992). *Over in the Meadow*. New York: Scholastic.

Teacher Talk: Statements, Questions, and Prompts for Assisted Reading

Following is a list of suggested teacher talk that encourages readers to think strategically as they work on assisted reading. Try using some of these statements, questions, and prompts with your students as you work through the techniques in the following section.

- How does imitating what I read help you?

- How does hearing my voice reading help you to read better?

- Listen to _____ read. Try to use the same expression and pace to carry on the story or section.

- How does reading along with the music help you?

- Try to find one-to-one correspondences between oral words and written words.

- Tell your partner something you notice about yourself when you read.

- When you were pausing on a word, what were you thinking?

- Tell me what you think of my reading.

- How does rereading in your choral reader notebook help you?

- In what way is it easier for you to read a dictated story?

- Try to remember what you said in your story, and match your words to the print.

As you implement the various techniques that support assisted reading, use the following behaviors as a guide as you assess students. Do students exhibit these behaviors never, rarely, often, always?

☐ Listening and observing modeled reading

☐ Engaging in reflective conversations about their reading and receive feedback

☐ Imitating modeled reading and self-monitoring

Shared Book Experience

Fluency: Assisted Reading

Purpose: To listen and observe modeled reading and build fluency confidence in a shared experience

Level: Emergent

ELL Technique: Yes

Multiple Intelligences: Visual/spatial, verbal/linguistic, interpersonal

Materials: Text, Big Books or overhead projector and text on transparencies, visual document presenter; Optional: Pointer, journal

Procedure:

1. Display the text so all students can easily view it, perhaps using a Big Book or overhead transparencies. Discuss with students how to preview and make predictions about the text.

2. Read aloud the text, modeling the characteristics of a fluent strategic reader (i.e., pacing, expressing). Suggested teacher talk could be, "Reread this part using the pointer to guide your way."

3. Have the students share the reading experience orally, as they follow along with the rereading of the text.

4. After the reading, engage students in a discussion of the text, allowing them to respond to, and at times retell, what they are reading. Suggested teacher talk could be, "Respond in your journal to the book we just read."

Motivation/Engagement: Ask students to gather around a chart, board, computer, or overhead set up for dictation. Discuss the topic and read a section from the text. Record or have a volunteer "Recorder" write or type stories the students dictate. Pause to clarify and reread the recorded transcription with students. Suggested teacher talk could be, "Try to remember what you said in the story and match your words to the print." Continue to dictate from students until the story, experience, or responses are complete. Students reread their words with partners, maintaining ownership of the text and reflecting on what they are reading. Place these simple scripts at centers for further readings to increase fluency. Suggested teacher talk might be, "In what way is it easier for you to read a dictated story?

Note: Adapted from Allington (2001); Eldredge, Reutzel, & Hollingsworth (1996); Holdaway (1979)

Echo Reading

Purpose: To gain confidence by listening and imitating a strategic reader

Level: Emergent

ELL Technique: Yes

Multiple Intelligences: Visual/spatial, verbal/linguistic, interpersonal, intrapersonal

Materials: Texts, audio recorder

Procedure:

1. Ask a fluent reader to model a sentence or paragraph using all the strategies of a strategic reader. The student rereads the modeled segment, striving to repeat exactly how the fluent reader modeled the reading. This technique may be one on one, small group, or whole group. Suggested teacher talk could be, "How does imitating what I read help you?"

2. Continue this echoing effect throughout the text.

Motivation/Engagement: If a student is struggling to echo while following the print, they may need to echo the modeled reader without the print. Use the print when the echo pattern is established. Suggested teacher talk might be, "How does hearing my voice reading aloud help you to read better?" Use this technique at a center, or for a "take home" activity. Record on an audio recorder "modeled reading" leaving a pause after sentences or short paragraphs. This pause allows the student to "echo" the voice on the recording. Using the recordings gives the student privacy, while they continue to gain the confidence and fluency needed to sound more like strategic readers.

Choral Readers

Purpose: To monitor and practice oral reading in a risk-free setting

Level: Emergent–Fluent

ELL Technique: Yes

Multiple Intelligences: Visual/spatial, verbal/linguistic, musical/rhythmic, bodily/kinesthetic, interpersonal

Materials: Text; three-ring binders; songs, poems, charts, or excerpts from text

Procedure:

1. Give students a three-ring binder to use as their choral reader notebooks. At the beginning of each week, insert a text selection into the choral reader notebooks. These selections may be songs, poems, chants, or excerpts from texts that correspond with the topic or theme you are studying. You also can use these entries in the choral readers as the springboard for minilessons from all five areas of reading described in this book.

2. Have students listen as you, using all the strategies of a strategic reader, model the selection.

3. After modeling the reading, echo read the selection with students. Have students reread the modeled segment, attempting to repeat the reading exactly as it was modeled. Choral reading should follow as the students gain confidence with the selection. Suggested teacher talk could be, "How was it helpful to have me beside you when you were reading?"

4. Guide the students in reading the selection together. Students should read aloud at the pace of the modeler, using all the appropriate expressions to bring the selection to life.

5. Have students reread daily the previous selections together before beginning their assisted reading with the new selection. Suggested teacher talk could be, "How does rereading in your choral reader notebook help you?" These choral reader notebooks may periodically be sent home for the students to show their fluent reading skills to family members.

Motivation/Engagement: Have groups of students perform a choral reading of one of their favorite selections to an audience. Students can use a variety of ways to bring the text to life (i.e., clapping words while reading, whispering the rhyme, dramatic role play).

Read-Alongs

Fluency: Assisted Reading

Purpose: To gain confidence by listening to modeled reading and by reading along

Level: Early

ELL Technique: Yes

Multiple Intelligences: Visual/spatial, verbal/linguistic, interpersonal

Materials: Texts, audio books, tape/CD player

Procedure:

1. Make your own prerecorded book tapes or purchase audio books according to the readers' level.

2. Have students listen to, and follow along with, the tapes or CDs. Suggested teacher talk could be, "How does reading along with the tape/CD help you?"

3. Encourage students to note one-to-one correspondences between spoken words on the tape and the printed text. Students can practice this technique at a learning center or at home. Suggested teacher talk could be, "Try to find one-to-one correspondences with oral words and written words."

Motivation/Engagement: Ask a student to sit slightly in front of you so that your mouth is close to the student's ear. Read aloud a passage of text with the student. You should read a little louder and slightly ahead of the student. Suggested teacher talk could be, "How does hearing my voice help you read better?" Track the words by smoothly running your forefinger under the words while reading. Reread the passage several times together before going on to new sections of the text. As the student gains confidence, lower your voice and have the student take the lead as the reader. Gradually release the responsibility of tracking and reading to the student. Continue to speed up, challenging the student to keep the pace. Suggested teacher talk might be, "Listen to me read. Try to use the same expression and pace to carry on the story or section."

Note: Adapted from Heckelman (1969)

Fluency Strategy: Rereading

Rereading is a strategy used to develop rapid, fluent oral reading. This strategy is one of the most frequently recognized approaches to improving fluency (NICHD, 2000; Rashotte & Torgesen, 1985). When students repeat their reading, their amount of word recognition errors decreases, their reading speed increases, and their oral reading expression improves (O'Connor, White, & Swanson, 2007; Samuels, 2002; Vadasy & Sanders, 2008).

An extensive opportunity for practice in pattern recognition is readily available through rereading text passages. When students acquire the rhythm within a predictable pattern book, they benefit from their desire to reread the text.

> Just as a traveler going down a winding road for the second or third time begins to notice specific houses along the way, children on their second and third trip through a text will begin to focus on specific words—committing them to memory. (Morris, 1992, p. 123)

Musicians, athletes, and actors also use this practice strategy to gain fluency; they rehearse the same aspect of their performance repeatedly until they gain independence and confidence. This type of commitment by students to improving the quality of their reading is vital.

Appropriate text that best supports the application of the rereading strategy is meaningful, is relatively short, possibly contains rhythm, and is enjoyable for readers.

Rereading Text Examples:

Carle, E. (1983). *The Very Hungry Caterpillar*. New York: Philomel.

Stevenson, J. (1998). *Popcorn: Poems*. New York: Greenwillow.

KIDiddles website (Song lyrics and printable lyric sheets): www.kididdles.com/lyrics

Teacher Talk: Statements, Questions, and Prompts for Rereading

Following is a list of suggested teacher talk that encourages readers to think strategically as they employ rereading skills. Try using some of these statements, questions, and prompts with your students as you work through the techniques in the following section.

- How does knowing the pattern of a text help you?

- What text features are similar?

- What happens each time you read the text?

- Compare your first reading with your second or third reading.

- Try to reread to the point in the text where it stopped making sense to you.

- How does rereading help you make sense of the text?

- Why do readers sometimes need to reread?

- How did reading the text make you feel?

- Let's determine what caused you to need to reread the sentence or passage.

- When you reread the text, try to add expression and pick up your pace just a little.

As you implement the various techniques that support this strategy, use the following behaviors as a guide as you assess students' rereading. Do students exhibit these behaviors never, rarely, often, always?

☐ Analyzing repetitive features

☐ Interacting as a listener and a reader

☐ Self-assessing and evaluating one's own reading

Techniques for Rereading

Listen to Me

Purpose: To interact as a listener and a reader, and to give and receive feedback

Level: Early

ELL Technique: Yes

Multiple Intelligences: Visual/spatial, verbal/linguistic, interpersonal, intrapersonal

Materials: Reading Bookmark (see CD 🖸), Listen to Me form (see CD 🖸), texts, learning logs

Procedure:

1. Have students select books at their independent level to read aloud to others. They also may use books made in class.

2. Have students practice reading aloud to several listening buddies in the classroom. These listening buddies can practice their active listening strategies by leaning in toward the reader, keeping their eyes on the reader, and waiting until the reader is finished before speaking. Students can use the Reading Bookmark as a reminder of the steps students can follow before, during, and after reading.

3. Have students use the Listen to Me form to score and give feedback on the reader's oral reading. Suggested teacher talk could be, "How was your reading according to the Listen to Me form?"

4. After a student has had several practice reads with a book, send the book home with the student to read to three others. Attach a Listen to Me form to the book. The other listeners should sign the form and provide positive feedback on the student's reading.

5. Place the books being used in the student's independent reading basket for him or her to return to during independent reading time. Suggested teacher talk might be, "What happens each time you read the text again?"

Motivation/Engagement: Have students reflect and record in their learning logs reasons why rereading is important (e.g., helps readers make sense out of what is being read, helps readers understand better, helps readers notice words that were skipped before, helps readers understand difficult words in context, helps readers read faster). Suggested teacher talk might be, "Why do readers sometimes need to go back and reread?" Add rereading to a class chart of strategies readers use.

Repeated Reading/One-Minute Reads

Purpose: To increase time of words per minute read with accuracy

Level: Transitional

ELL Technique: No

Multiple Intelligences: Visual/spatial, verbal/linguistic

Materials: Texts, stopwatch

Procedure:

1. Select a short, meaningful, and appropriate leveled passages for rereading.

2. Discuss with students a baseline for the number of words they should try to read per minute.

3. Have students read aloud a text that is slightly above their independent reading level.

4. Using a stopwatch, time students reading for one minute and keep data on errors (see pacing strategy, this chapter, for formula and graphs).

5. After reading, discuss reading strategies for problem solving the incorrect words.

6. Have the student then reread the same passage while you time the reading with a stopwatch and record any errors again.

7. Continue this process for at least three times. Suggested teacher talk might be, "How did reading it again make you feel?"

8. Record results each time, followed by a discussion of results. Suggested teacher talk could be, "Compare your first reading with your second or third rereading."

Note: Adapted from Blevins (2001), Rasinski (2003), Samuels (1979), Samuels & Farstrup (2006)

Recorded Reading: Record/Check/Chart

Purpose: To self-assess using a visible marking process, and to chart progress

Level: Transitional

ELL Technique: No

Multiple Intelligences: Visual/spatial, verbal/linguistic, interpersonal, intrapersonal

Materials: Texts, photocopy of text, three different-colored pens, audio recorder, stopwatch, reflective journals

Procedure:

1. **Record**: Have students record their own readings and replay the recording to check for mispronunciations.

2. **Check**: As students listen to their first readings, ask them to mark any misreads they hear on a photocopy of the text.

3. **Chart**: Ask students to read the text aloud for a second time into the recorder. Have them listen to the second recording, and, with a different-colored pen, have them mark the same photocopy of the text to show any mispronunciations of words read the second time. Suggested teacher talk could be, "What happens each time you read the text again?"

4. Have students record a third reading into the audio recorder and mark a third round of misreads on the same photocopy of the text, with a third color.

5. Have students tally the different-colored pens' markings. Generally, with each reading, the errors will decrease. Suggested teacher talk might be, "Compare your first reading with your second or third reading. What do you notice?"

Motivation/Engagement: Use a stopwatch to time students as they read for one minute and then record the results. Time repeated readings, and discuss the results with students (see Repeated Reading/One-Minute Reads in this chapter). Have the students reflect in their journals how this technique made them feel about their reading and record goals for the next recorded reading. Students may also partner with one student as the timekeeper and the other the reader.

Note: Adapted from Allington (2001)

Multimedia Reading

Purpose: To utilize technology to evaluate one's own reading

Level: Transitional

ELL Technique: No

Multiple Intelligences: Visual/spatial, verbal/linguistic, intrapersonal

Materials: Texts, variety of multimedia resources (e.g., video, podcast, slideshow), video camera, TV, VCR/DVD player, computers

Procedure:

1. Work with students individually or in small groups to record a video or podcast or create a slideshow of a student reading aloud a selection from the text.

2. Have the student listen to and watch the recording and reflect on the reading.

3. Ask the student to reread the text, without being recorded, to practice correcting any errors that occurred on the recorded reading. Suggested teacher talk could be, "Try to reread to the point in the text where it stopped making sense to you." When the student is comfortable with the text, have the student record a second reading of the same passage using the same medium or perhaps switching to another if they so choose.

4. Ask the student to share his or her recorded readings with family members or caregivers at home. After the student watches the recording with family members, have the student read the same passage to them again to show their ability to self-evaluate their reading.

Motivation/Engagement: Have students reflect on and make observation notes about their oral reading in their learning logs.

Fluency Strategy: Expressing

Teachers need to incorporate reading with expression into the beginning stages of reading instruction. Thus, students will learn that through expressive reading the text comes to life and has meaning and purpose. Without expression, students' readings will be monotone, laborious, and incomprehensible. "Many times concepts appear in ambiguous, confusing language that students can read but do not understand" (Kinniburgh & Shaw, 2007, p.16). Applying the expressing strategy through techniques like Readers Theatre enhances students' understanding that reading is a meaning-making process even in content area reading. Speeches, poetry, journal entries, song lyrics, scripts are all examples of text that support the student to apply prosodic functions (Rasinski & Lenhart, 2007/2008).

When students concentrate on prosodic functions and forms when reading, they can indicate syntax and attitudes and can add appropriate stresses, pitch, and tone where needed to give a conversational sound to their reading. This allows the reader to convey the text's mood and meaning. It is also important that students know the difference between just reading loudly when expressing themselves and actually reading with warm but firm voices (Dowhower, 1994).

Appropriate text that best supports the application of the expressing strategy has a variety of words and phrases that allow for students to use their voices to bring the text to life.

Expressing text examples:

Braun, W., & Braun, C. (2000). *A Readers Theatre Treasury of Stories*. Winnipeg, Canada: Portage and Main.

Hoose, P., & Hoose, A. (1998). *Hey Little Ant*. Berkeley, CA: Tricycle.

Layne, S., & Hoyt, A. (2007). *Love the Baby*. Gretna, LA: Pelican.

Teacher Talk: Statements, Questions, and Prompts for Expressing

Following is a list of suggested teacher talk that encourages readers to think strategically as they employ expressing skills. Try using some of these statements, questions, and prompts with your students as you work through the techniques in the following section.

- What expression do you think the reader was trying to share in his or her dramatic expression statement?

- How can you make your reading sound more exciting?

- What does a period (or other mark of punctuation) mean?

- What does your voice do when you read a sentence that ends with a question mark?

- Change your voice to sound like the character you are portraying.

- In your mind, do you hear different voices for the different characters?

- Did you use the proper tone to convey the meaning? Why or why not?

- How did the tone of your voice set the mood for your statement?

- What feeling do you think the author wanted the character to have in this part? How do you know what the author wanted?

- What message can the volume of your voice send to the audience?

- What are some expressions you could use when reading?

- How would the character say that line?

- Try to make your reading sound as real as it can be.

- Does your reading sound like you are holding a conversation?

As you implement the various techniques that support expressing, use the following behaviors as a guide as you assess students. Do students exhibit these behaviors never, rarely, often, always?

- ☐ Identifying prosodic functions

- ☐ Demonstrating how text "comes to life" with voice and body language

- ☐ Conveying the text's mood and meaning

ABC Punctuation Style

Purpose: To use voice to apply the meaning of punctuation marks and demonstrate the ability to move left to right as a reader

Level: Emergent

ELL Technique: No

Multiple Intelligences: Visual/spatial, verbal/linguistic, logical/mathematical

Materials: Sentence strips

Procedure:

1. Create ABC punctuation sentences by grouping letters from the alphabet on sentence strips or other means to display for all to see.

2. Have students read them with expression with the proper punctuation (e.g., *abc. de! fgh? ijk? lmn. op! qrs. tuv? wx! yz.*).

Motivation/Engagement: At the writing station have students create ABC punctuation sentences to summit for the class to practice reading with expression.

Note: Adapted from Blevins (2001)

Fluency: Expressing

Express Yourself

This technique is highlighted on the Creating Strategic Readers DVD/VHS series.

Purpose: To demonstrate voice and body language as a form of expression to bring "life to reading"

Level: Early (Adaptation for Emergent)

ELL Technique: No

Multiple Intelligences: Visual/spatial, verbal/linguistic, logical/mathematical, bodily/kinesthetic, interpersonal, intrapersonal

Materials: Express Yourself reproducible (see CD), texts, note cards, platform or stool; Optional: Microphone

Procedure:

1. Use note cards to create your own expression cards and statement cards or cut out the cards from the Express Yourself reproducible. Expression cards should each include an emotion that students will be asked to use as they read (e.g., surprise, sadness, wistful,

Fluency: Expressing

anger). Statement cards should each include one simple statement, such as "Don't do that."

2. Have students take turns standing on a platform or stage (this can be a stool, sturdy wooden box, or so forth) at the front of the room. If desired, the student performing on the stage can use a standing or handheld microphone.

3. Have the performing student draw one expression card and one statement card.

4. Instruct the rest of the class—the audience—to say together, "Express yourself!"

5. Have the student think about the card and then read the statement with the specified dramatic expression. For example, if the student draws an expression card that says "surprise" and a statement card that says "Don't do that," the student would say to the audience, "Don't do that!" in a very surprised voice. Suggested teacher talk could be, "What expression do you think the reader was trying to share in his or her dramatic expression statement?"

6. Have the audience respond with what kind of expression they think the student performed. Suggested teacher talk might be, "How can you make your reading sound more exciting?"

Motivation/Engagement: Ask students to share with partners how they might use the expression sentence in the proper order and in context that would make sense to them (e.g., Oh, no! Don't do that! You might get hurt.).

Adaptation for Emergent Readers: Model sentences from a read-aloud and have the students show with their face what the character is feeling.

Dramatic Sentences

Purpose: To dramatize a sentence through body movement

Level: Early

ELL Technique: No

Multiple Intelligences: Visual/spatial, verbal/linguistic, body/kinesthetic, interpersonal

Materials: Text, sentences, scripts; Optional: Supplies to make props

Procedure:

1. Select sentences from a text you are reading.

2. Read and display sentences for all students to see, omitting punctuation.

3. Have the students think of which punctuation would best make the sentence complete and then dramatize the sentences using bodily representation of the punctuation. Select a volunteer to "be" the sentence (e.g., walking left to right, taking a hop between each word to represent space, bending and pausing for commas, jumping up and down holding body straight like a pencil for an exclamation point).

4. Have the audience (i.e., observing students) read the sentences on display as the volunteer actively moves and dramatizes the sentence.

Motivation/Engagement: Provide a dialogue-rich script for students to use to perform Readers Theatre. (There are numerous websites that offer free scripts such as www.readers-theatre.com.) Have students read the original text and then the scripted version to help them compare and contrast the two and determine the appropriate means of dramatizing the script. Have each student select a character and practice reading that character's lines, bringing the character to life with prosodic features. After several practice redundant readings, have students perform the script in teams with a dramatic presentation in front of a live audience. Teams may also design their own props. Students can even create their own scripts based on their interests.

Note: Adapted from Hoyt (1992), Shepard (1994), Sloyer (1982), Strickland et al. (2002), Young & Vardell (1993)

Punctuation Police

Purpose: To recognize the value of punctuation in oral reading

Level: Early

ELL Technique: Yes

Multiple Intelligences: Visual/spatial, verbal/linguistic, bodily/kinesthetic, interpersonal

Materials: Punctuation Police tickets (see CD 🔘), texts, sheriff or police badge, dry-erase board

Procedure:

1. Choose one student to wear a badge and act as the "punctuation police." Have other students read from a text, while the police student follows along with another copy of the same text, listening carefully to the student reading aloud.

2. The student acting as the punctuation police should record on a dry-erase board if or when the reader runs through "punctuation signs" (e.g., fails to pause properly at punctuation marks). The police student should issue a Punctuation Police ticket if the reader makes a punctuation infraction. Suggested teacher talk could be, "What does a period (or other mark of punctuation) mean?"

3. Continue this technique with partners, encouraging students to try to keep a "clean record" for reading. Suggested teacher talk might be, "What does your voice do when you read a sentence that ends with a question mark?"

Motivation/Engagement: Give each student in a small-group setting a set of the punctuation color-coded cards. They receive six in total (inadequate verbal expression, skipped comma, skipped end mark, word addition, word omission, and pace too fast). Instead of having the other students write their names down and select the infraction as on the original punctuation tickets, students are quickly able to just push forward on the table the specific "infraction" card. (The small-group idea was contributed by third-grade teacher Christina Leach.)

Totally Tonality

Fluency: Expressing

This technique is highlighted on the Creating Strategic Readers DVD/VHS series.

Purpose: To adjust tone of voice appropriately to convey the text's mood and meaning

Level: Transitional

ELL Technique: No

Multiple Intelligences: Visual/spatial, verbal/linguistic, bodily/kinesthetic, interpersonal

Materials: Texts, chart, note cards

Procedure:

1. On a chart, write some words describing a variety of tones that readers can use to express an author's purpose (e.g., ironic, serious, sarcastic, humorous). Point out that the tone of voice a reader uses reflects the emotion the character is feeling and the mood of the text.

2. Discuss how tones of voice can completely change the meaning of a text. For example, if a character says, "You are so funny" in a sarcastic tone, then he or she means someone is not funny.

3. On note cards, write some phrases students can read and different tones of voice they can use. Separate the two types of cards and have students take turns selecting a tone card and a phrase card to practice reading with the selected tone. Suggested teacher talk could be, "Did you use the proper tone to convey the meaning? Why or why not?"

4. After practicing reading with phrases, have students read sections from texts while using a chosen tone.

5. Discuss the reason students used a certain tone when reading aloud. Suggested teacher talk might be, "How did the tone of your voice set the mood for your statement?"

Motivation/Engagement: Select 8–10 quoted sentences from the text and either write the sentences on note cards or locate sentences in text and mark with highlighting tape. Pass out the text selections or the note cards to volunteers and have them form a circle facing outward. Next pass out tone cards with a variety of expressions and have these volunteers find one person in the circle to stand opposite, so there are two circles of people facing each other. Ask the outside (tone) group to demonstrate their card with facial or body expressions only. The inside partner then decides the tone being demonstrated and begins to read the quoted sentence in the tone given. After the sentence is read with the outside partners tone, the partners then reread the sentence in the context in the text and decide if they used the proper tone to convey the meaning or did they change the meaning completely with the tone presented. The partners exchange roles (i.e., inside partner hands over the sentence card or text to the outside partner, and the outside partner gives the tone card to the inside partner). Instruct inside and outside circles to make a quarter right turn and tell them how many to rotate to face a new partner and share tones and sentences. Continue the process for several rotations.

Interpretation/Character Analysis

Fluency: Expressing

Purpose: To interpret and portray the traits of character(s) in text

Level: Fluent

ELL Technique: No

Multiple Intelligences: Visual/spatial, verbal/linguistic, logical/mathematical, interpersonal

Materials: Emotion Mat (see CD 🔘), texts, numbered chips; Optional: Microphone

Procedure:

1. Ask students to read and reread a section of dialogue from a text, forming their own interpretations of how they should portray the characters' voices. Students should discuss their interpretations of the characters to ensure a correct analysis of the characters in context. This helps to keep meaning from being misconstrued.

2. Have each student perform the part of one of the characters, reading aloud with expression.

3. Discuss with students any new insights they gain from analyzing the characters' voices after the performance. Suggested teacher talk could be, "What feeling do you think the author wanted the character to have in this part? How do you know what the author wanted?"

4. Copy and distribute the Emotion Mat and numbered chips and then read aloud a selected text. Have students listen and interpret the emotions of a chosen character

5. After the read-aloud, have partners share their retell or interpretation as they pick up the numbered chips in order.

Motivation/Engagement: Have students select a text with a specific character they would like to interpret then practice to perform on a "live" syndicated radio talk show called Radio Reader based on the work of Allington (2001), Opitz and Rasinski (1998), and Stayter and Allington (1991). Have each student who will be the "radio reader on the air" prepare open-ended questions or provocative statements about their particular character. When the radio show is ready to "air," hold up a red sign to signal the beginning of the show. The student, "radio reader," reads the selection into a karaoke microphone expressively and meaningfully to capture the listening audience. After the performance, have the radio reader invite the listening audience into a discussion about the character using the questions and statements generated previously to demonstrate if they derived meaning from the reading. Suggested teacher talk might be, "What message can the volume of your voice send to the audience?"

Fluency Strategy: Pacing

Pacing is a strategy that develops through extensive exposure to reading. This strategy encompasses reading rate, which is the speed at which one reads, as well as reading flow. Table 18 demonstrates the reading rate formula and correlates the rate to grade levels. The simple fact that slow reading requires readers to invest considerably greater amounts of time in reading tasks than classmates who are reading at a rate appropriate for their grade level should be a major cause for concern for all teachers (O'Connor et al., 2007; Rasinski, 2000; Vadasy & Sanders, 2008). However, reading too fast does not always constitute proficient strategic reading.

In trying to increase fluency, educators need to be cautious not to create word callers, who have increased in speed but fail in developing meaning. Pacing permits a reader to be flexible when interacting with the text; the proficient reader is capable of slowing down and speeding up when necessary to construct meaning. Depending on the tasks, readers may need to alter their reading rate and focus on the flow of their reading.

TABLE 18. Oral Reading Fluency Target Norms for Words Read Correctly Per Minute (WCPM)

Grade	Percentile	Fall WCPM	Winter WCPM	Spring WCPM
1	90	0	60	103
	50	0	21	52
	10	0	7	20
2	90	95	125	140
	50	49	76	94
	10	15	30	49
3	90	125	151	168
	50	73	96	110
	10	30	50	57
4	90	142	167	180
	50	94	114	124
	10	48	66	75
5	90	169	184	189
	50	117	131	137
	10	65	78	88

Adapted from an electronic aggregation using AIMSweb Norms 2003–2009.

Note. To figure rate formula: Words per minute = number of words in passage divided by reading time (in seconds) x 60

TABLE 19. Reading Levels and Accuracy Formula

Level	Error Rate	
Independent	95–100%	(able to read without assistance)
Instructional	90–94%	(able to read with some assistance)
Frustration	89% and below	(unable to read even with assistance)

Note. To figure accuracy rate: $\dfrac{\text{\# words read} - \text{\# errors}}{\text{\# words read}}$ = word accuracy rate

Appropriate text that best supports the application of the pacing strategy needs to be at the student's independent or instructional reading level. A student's independent reading level is the level at which he or she has an accuracy rate of 95% or better at word recognition; it is considered the "level at which a student can read a text without the teacher's assistance" (Blevins, 2001, p. 23). The instructional level is the level at which a student should be able to read the text with some assistance. (See Table 19 for a formula to figure out students' accuracy rates.)

Pacing Text Examples and Resources (provided that these resources happen to be at your students' independent or instructional reading level):

Adams, P. (1990). *This Is the House That Jack Built*. New York: Child's Play.

Mazzoni, D., & Dannenberg, R. (1999). Audacity (voice-recording program): audacity. sourceforge.net

Noble, T. (1980). *The Day Jimmy's Boa Ate the Wash*. New York: Dial.

Teacher Talk: Statements, Questions, and Prompts for Pacing

Following is a list of suggested teacher talk that encourages readers to think strategically as they employ pacing skills. Try using some of these statements, questions, and prompts with your students as you work through the techniques in the following section.

- Try to keep up with the light to increase your rate. (For use with Beam Reading)
- Is it easy or difficult for you to keep up with the pace being modeled, that is, with the tempo? (For use with Tempo Time)
- What is happening as you hear the tempo in the background? (For use with Tempo Time)
- Tell how increasing your rate will help you read.
- How does hearing yourself read and tracking how long it takes you to read help you to pace better?
- Listen to me read these paragraphs. (Read very fast and then at a normal pace.) Which pace is more appropriate?

- How does the speed at which you are reading make a difference for you?

- Do you often have to reread a sentence? Why?

- Does the computer program help you pace yourself as a reader? Why or why not?

As you implement the various techniques that support pacing, use the following behaviors as a guide as you assess students. Do students exhibit these behaviors never, rarely, often, always?

☐ Distinguishing appropriate rhythm in reading

☐ Adjusting reading rate accordingly

☐ Tracking and observing the flow of their reading

Techniques for Pacing

Commercial Programs

Fluency: Pacing

Purpose: To develop pacing skills and improve reading rate using a computer program as a supplemental resource

Level: Emergent–Fluent

ELL Techniques: No

Multiple Intelligences: Visual/spatial, verbal/linguistic

Materials: Texts, computer, computer-based program

Procedure:

1. Select an appropriate computer program (see list below). The programs listed are supplemental and may be used for immediate, intense intervention in several of the areas of reading noted in Chapters 2–6.

2. Incorporate one of the following computer-based fluency programs into your comprehensive literacy-based classroom. Suggested teacher talk could be, "Does the computer program help you pace yourself as a reader? Why or why not? How does the speed to which you are reading make a difference for you?"

- Great Leaps (K–12 updated; Campbell, 1995) is a tutorial program divided into three major areas: (1) phonics, which concentrates on developing and mastering essential sight–sound relationships or sound awareness skills, (2) sight phrasing, which supports students in mastering sight words while developing and improving focusing skills, and (3) reading fluency, which provides age-appropriate stories specifically designed to build reading fluency, reading motivation, and proper intonation.

- QuickReads (Hiebert, 2005) is composed of high-interest nonfiction texts at the second- through sixth-grade levels. QuickReads develops automaticity by using text that is composed of 98% high-frequency and decodable words. The program combines leveled texts with speech recognition technology. The program provides instant feedback and corrects errors by prompting repeated pronunciation of unknown words.

- REWARDS (Reading Excellence Attack and Rate Developing Strategies; Archer, Gleason, & Vachon, 2000) is intended for intermediate to secondary students. It supports students in decoding and reading multisyllabic words in context, increasing reading accuracy and fluency, and improving comprehension. The first 12 lessons support the skills necessary to learn multisyllabic words (blending syllables and pronunciations of affixes and vowel combinations). The last seven lessons focus on helping readers utilize fast and accurate decoding to increase reading rate.

Beam Reading

This technique is highlighted on the Creating Strategic Readers DVD/VHS series.

Fluency: Pacing

Purpose: To track and observe reading rate using a light

Level: Early

ELL Technique: Yes

Multiple Intelligences: Visual/spatial, verbal/linguistic, bodily/kinesthetic, interpersonal

Materials: Texts, chart or overhead projector, laser pen or flashlight, teacher anecdotal notes

Procedure:

1. Display the text on a chart or overhead projector for all students to see. Use a laser pen or flashlight to shine a light on the words as the students read aloud.

2. Move the light along the words at a steady pace. Suggested teacher talk could be, "Try to keep up with the light to increase your reading rate."

3. Encourage students to follow along with the light as they read aloud. The rate at which you shine the light on the words should increase with each rereading of the text selected.

4. Have students practice this technique with partners, taking turns using the light and practicing keeping the pace of the light. Suggested teacher talk might be, "Is it easy or difficult for you to keep up with the pace being modeled?"

Motivation/Engagement: Place small handheld flashlights at small group area to use when the students read independently or give one for all students to keep in their browsing boxes for independent reading. This allows the teacher to observe students reading rate without the students knowing they are being observed. This creates a risk-free environment.

Tempo Time

This technique is highlighted on the Creating Strategic Readers DVD/VHS series.

Purpose: To distinguish rhythm in reading and maintain the reading pace with a predetermined rhythm while reading orally

Level: Early

ELL Technique: No

Multiple Intelligences: Visual/spatial, verbal/linguistic, musical/rhythmic, bodily/kinesthetic

Materials: Texts (preferably poetry or pattern books), musical instruments, nursery rhymes

Procedure:

1. Use maracas or other musical instruments to beat out a tempo. The reader's ability should determine the tempo, and the tempo can increase as the reader improves. Suggested teacher talk could be, "What is happening as you hear the tempo in the background?"

2. Ask students to listen to the tempo that you provide and begin to read, trying to keep up with the tempo time. Suggested teacher talk might be, "Is it easy or difficult for you to keep up with the tempo?"

Motivation/Engagement: Use predictable nursery rhymes while tapping out a predetermined rhythm as students follow along with their maracas. For example, display the words to "Twinkle, Twinkle Little Star" and shake the maraca to match one to one with the word as it is read together orally. Change the tempo periodically for students to practice a variety of reading paces.

Time/Record/Check/Chart

Purpose: To increase reading rate and evaluate progress

Level: Transitional

ELL Technique: No

Multiple Intelligences: Visual/spatial, verbal/linguistic, intrapersonal

Materials: Texts, photocopies of text, stopwatch, audio recorder, graph paper

Procedure:

1. **Time:** Have a student read aloud a text while you or a volunteer times the student with a stopwatch, measuring how long it takes the student to read the chosen text. Chart the time on graph paper. Suggested teacher talk could be, "Tell how increasing your rate will help your reading."

2. **Record:** Have the student record the same reading on an audio recorder and time his or her reading.

3. **Check**: The student should replay the recording while following along using a photocopied version of the text.

4. **Chart**: Chart the time for the second reading on graph paper. Suggested teacher talk might be, "How does hearing yourself read and tracking how long it takes you to read help you to pace better?"

5. Have the student mark miscues on the photocopy.

6. The student should compare reading times and continue the previous steps as needed.

Motivation/Engagement: Have students reflect on and self-assess the reading and the graphed results. Repeat the process two more times. Have students create self goals as they note their progressions.

Note: Adapted from Allington (2001)

Digital Portfolio for Oral Reading

Purpose: To increase reading rate and evaluate progress digitally

Level: Fluent

ELL Technique: No

Multiple Intelligences: Visual/spatial, verbal/linguistic, logical/mathematical, intrapersonal

Materials: Texts, photocopies of text, audio recorder, any voice recording program like *Audacity* free software program (audacity.sourceforge.net)

Procedure:

1. Prepare an area for students to read aloud and record their reading to create a digital portfolio.

2. Download a voice-recording program like *Audacity* (runs on both MAC OS and PC).

3. Have the students save their sample readings to create a digital portfolio, efolio.

4. Set up one-to-one conferences for the students to access their recordings and discuss and evaluate their progress. Their readings can be incorporated into class iMovies, iPods, slideshows, and so forth. (This part of the technique was contributed by classroom teachers Shannon McCoy and Sherry Perny.)

Fluency Strategy: Wide Reading

Students need to understand that wide reading is imperative to build fluency. It is a powerful realization when students discover that the more they read and want to read, the more fluent they become as readers. Research by Nathan and Stanovich (1991) indicates that [if students are] to become fluent readers, they need to read a lot. Our job as educators is to see to it that children want to read, that they seek new knowledge via written word and derive satisfaction and joy from the reading process. (p. 79)

Providing the opportunities for students to read and to find enjoyment in their reading is the challenge for today's educators. The wide reading techniques will support students on their journey to becoming fluent readers.

Appropriate text that best supports the application of the wide reading strategy is high interest, is in a variety of genres, and is at the independent or instructional levels of the students (refer to Table 19, page 119).

Wide Reading Text Examples:

Brown, M. (1998). *Buster's Dino Dilemma* (Arthur Chapter Book #7). New York: Little, Brown.

Cleary, B. (1981). *Ramona Quimby, Age 8*. New York: Morrow.

Comic books (e.g., Owly, Archie, TinTin).

Teacher Talk: Statements, Questions, and Prompts for Wide Reading

Following is a list of suggested teacher talk that encourages readers to think strategically as they employ wide reading skills. Try using some of these statements, questions, and prompts with your students as you work through the techniques in the following section.

- How do you feel when you are reading a book that is at your level?
- Has your reading rate improved each time you read and reread books from your browsing box?
- How do you know if a book is just right for you?
- What are signs that a book is too easy or too difficult for you?
- Try to pick a book that interests you.
- How does being in a book club help your reading?
- Why is it important to independently read books at your appropriate level?
- How does your reading sound (in your head or aloud) when you are independently reading?

As you implement the various techniques that support wide reading, use the following behaviors as a guide as you assess students. Do students exhibit these behaviors never, rarely, often, always?

☐ Choosing to read independently

☐ Self-selecting books based on reading level

☐ Determining purpose for reading

Book Baskets/Browsing Boxes

Purpose: To self-select text and find enjoyment in reading

Level: Emergent

ELL Technique: Yes

Multiple Intelligences: Visual/spatial, verbal/linguistic, bodily/kinesthetic, intrapersonal

Materials: Baskets and boxes; variety of interests, genre, and leveled texts; flashlight

Procedure:

1. Place multiple levels of books (fiction and nonfiction) and magazines into baskets or boxes. These may be books that were previously read during guided reading time.

2. Have students at different stages of development browse through the book selections to choose one book that is "just right" for them. Students should select books with which they are familiar and that are at their own independent reading level from book baskets. Teachers should discuss with students what books seem to be just right for them. Suggested teacher talk could be, "How do you feel when you are reading a book that is at your level?"

3. Have students place their selections into their own browsing box (a box or plastic bin that holds each student's collection of independent-level reading books).

4. During independent reading time, have the students read and reread texts from their boxes. Reading these books ensures quality time spent on reading at the appropriate level of each reader. Suggested teacher talk might be, "Has your reading rate improved each time you've read and reread books from your browsing boxes?"

Motivation/Engagement: Place a flashlight in each student's browsing box and have the students following along with their flashlights as they read silently. This gives students a guide as they are reading and allows the teacher to view each student's pace with the flow of the beam light. (See Beam Reading in this chapter for a more detailed explanation of this technique.)

Note: Adapted from Fountas & Pinnell (1996)

Selecting "Just Right" Books

This technique is highlighted on the Creating Strategic Readers DVD/VHS series.

Purpose: To identify and select books at students' independent reading level

Level: Early

ELL Technique: Yes

Multiple Intelligences: Visual/spatial, verbal/linguistic, interpersonal

Materials: Variety of leveled texts, three chairs of different sizes, "Goldilocks and the Three Bears," chart paper or blank poster

Procedure:

1. Demonstrate how to choose a just-right book, and discuss the value of independently reading a book that fits the reader. For example, have students read a page from a text and note each time they have difficulty with a word by raising a finger. If early in the reading students have up five fingers, they should stop reading because the text is not at the independent level.

2. Read aloud the story of "Goldilocks and the Three Bears." Line up three chairs: one too small, one too big, and one just right for the students. Select three books for the demonstration: one too easy, one too hard, and one just right for the students. Suggested teacher talk could be, "How do you know if a book is just right for you?"

3. After modeling how to select a book that is just the right match, have the class generate three posters or charts. The first chart should list what makes a text too easy (e.g., your reading rate is too fast, you know all the words, you use less energy decoding). The second one should list the traits of a text that is too hard (e.g., your reading rate is too slow, you lose focus as you are reading, you have trouble understanding or decoding words). The third chart should show what type of book is just right (e.g., your reading rate is just right, you can read most of the words, you can get the meaning from the story).

4. Post the charts in the classroom library area as a reminder for students when selecting their independent reading materials. Suggested teacher talk could be, "What are the signs that the book is too easy or too difficult for you?"

Motivation/Engagement: Have a schoolwide poster contest on how to select just right books.

Note: Adapted from Fountas & Pinnell (1999)

Book Clubs

Purpose: To determine a purpose for reading, and to develop an interest in sharing books with others

Level: Transitional

ELL Technique: No

Multiple Intelligences: Visual/spatial, verbal/linguistic, interpersonal

Materials: A variety of texts (four to six copies of the same title)

Procedure:

1. Display a variety of book sets. Each book title should have at least four additional copies on display. Suggested teacher talk could be, "Try to pick a book that interests you for your book club selection."

2. Have students select a book that is at their independent reading level and is interesting to them, and sign them up to be in a book club. Each student will be in a book club with students who are reading the same selection.

3. Have the groups meet and plan how much reading they will do independently before they get together to share and discuss the book. Each week, the clubs should meet to share their ideas, feelings, questions, concerns, and general comments about what they read.

4. Continue the process with new book selections and new clubs being formed. Suggested teacher talk might be, "How does being in a book club help your reading?"

Fluency Strategy: Accuracy

Students who read fluently read with accuracy. The accuracy strategy focuses on being able to identify and apply the graphophonic cueing system (i.e., the relationship between letters and sounds) with ease and precision. In order for students to accurately read, they need to use the phonemic awareness and phonics strategies described previously (see Chapters 2 and 3). Gaining independence at their developmental reading level in these two areas of reading will ensure a higher level of automaticity and accuracy as students read.

Research indicates that the brain devotes only a limited amount of attention to any given cognitive task (LaBerge & Samuels, 1974). The more attention a reader devotes to trying to decode an unknown word, the less time and energy he or she has to cognitively gather meaning from the text. Teachers need to assess students' accuracy by using oral reading inventories (e.g., running records, analytical reading inventories, informal reading inventories). (See Table 19, page 119, for a formula to help calculate a student's accuracy rate.) This type of assessment can be used to analyze what the student's specific needs are within the cueing system. It is important to note that this is only one strategy for helping students to read fluently.

McEwan (2002) explains that "students who make no errors but read very slowly have as little likelihood of comprehending what they read as students who read very quickly but guess at and misidentify many words" (p. 54). There must be a balance for the student to read with both fluency and comprehension. Accuracy is a vital link to reading with ease. However, teachers must keep in mind that reading is an art, with many facets that fuse together for a proficient reader to evolve.

The techniques found in Chapters 2 and 3 are appropriate for building accuracy, especially the techniques for teaching sight word recognition (i.e., recognizing) and decoding (i.e., analyzing). The techniques for teaching the rereading strategy, found in this chapter, also are appropriate for promoting accuracy.

Fluency Wrap-Up

Fluency instruction extends beyond word recognition. The fluent reader recognizes words automatically and can now attend to comprehension. The strategies, techniques, and teacher talk presented in this chapter support teachers in maximizing their students' potential in becoming strategic readers. Fluency is yet another medium by which teachers can create their masterpieces—strategic readers.

Vocabulary

Word Awareness with **Word Jars** technique

Associating with **Reflection Connection** technique

Categorizing with **Alphaboxes** technique

The NRP report states, "reading vocabulary is crucial to the comprehension process of a skilled reader" (NICHD, 2000, p. 4-3). Research shows that the size of a reader's vocabulary influences both comprehension and fluency (Beck, McKeown, & Kucan, 2002, 2008; Blachowicz & Fisher, 2000, 2006; Flood, Jensen, Lapp, & Squire, 1991; Robb, 1997). Students need many opportunities for developing a rich vocabulary through listening, speaking, reading, and writing in an integrated manner. Vocabulary instruction should be an integral component in a daily literacy block. Integrating vocabulary instruction provides students with numerous opportunities to manipulate and learn new vocabulary words. Incorporating vocabulary instruction throughout the content areas will encourage students to make connections to new and already known information, discuss meanings of new words, and demonstrate and appropriately apply the new words, providing multiple re-exposures to the words. Encouraging students to think strategically when learning new words is essential.

Vocabulary knowledge is cumulative and takes multiple exposures in a variety of meaningful contexts for words to be applicable and committed to long-term memory (Akhavan, 2007; Marzano et al., 2001; Misulis, 1999; Stahl & Nagy, 2006).

This chapter offers vocabulary strategies and techniques that enhance students' understanding of new words and concepts. These strategies include giving both definitional and contextual information about new words, performing cognitive operations when introducing words, and talking about new words constantly (McEwan, 2002). If students do not understand the meaning of the words they read, the reading process merely becomes meaningless decoding (Pinnell & Fountas, 1998). These strategies will help provide students with powerful, in-depth learning as they strive to become successful readers.

The strategies and techniques detailed in this chapter are as follows:

- Associating: Move to the Meaning, Compare 'n Share, Reflection Connection, and Semantic Feature Analysis

- Contextualizing: Cloze Passages With Semantic Gradients, Contextual Redefinition, What Do You Mean?, Collaborate and Elaborate, and Context Complex Clues

- Categorizing: Interactive Word Walls, Picture and Word Sorts, Alphaboxes, and List/Group/Label

- Visual Imaging: Charades, Museum Walk, Four Corners, and Eye Spy With My Eye

- Analyzing: Playing With Plurals, Vocabulary Tree Notebook, Flip-a-Chip, and Root Words

- Word Awareness: Word Jars, Journal Circles, Knowledge Rating, and Quick Writes

- Wide Reading: Read-Alouds, Author Study, Book Talks, and Genre Study

- Referencing: Resource Buddies, Glossary Use, and Thesaurus Use

Table 20 matches the instructional techniques discussed in this chapter to the appropriate developmental levels from Chapter 1 (emergent, early, transitional, and fluent). To be effective, the strategies and techniques presented in this chapter should allow ample time for teacher modeling and student application, long before independent application is expected. Teachers should select and model reading aloud of appropriate literature to apply the techniques in a meaningful manner, which supports authentic learning for strategic reading. By using this process, students are able to see first the whole text (i.e., appropriate literature), then see the parts systematically (i.e., strategies and techniques), and finally, apply the parts back to the whole (i.e., become metacognitively aware of strategies while reading appropriate literature). Using quality text and promoting language development throughout the techniques will help to enhance students' development of the strategies. In addition, teachers can use the motivation and engagement feature within many techniques as an additional means (i.e., multiple intelligence, standard) of motivating the whole child and creating 21st-century learners (refer to Chapter 1 for a description of the whole child and

TABLE 20. Vocabulary Techniques

	Emergent	Early	Transitional	Fluent
Before Reading	Move to the Meaning (A) Interactive Word Walls (Ca) Picture and Word Sorts† (Ca) Alphaboxes*† (Ca) Charades (V) Read-Alouds (WR)	May include all Emergent techniques Semantic Feature Analysis* (A) Interactive Word Walls (Ca) Picture and Word Sorts† (Ca) List/Group/Label (Ca) Read-Alouds* (WR)	May include all Emergent and Early techniques Compare 'n Share (A) Contextual Redefinition† (Co) What Do You Mean? (Co) Interactive Word Walls (Ca) Picture and Word Sorts† (Ca) List/Group/Label* (Ca) Four Corners* (V) Eye Spy With My Eye (V) Knowledge Rating (WA) Read-Alouds* (WR) Author Study (WR)	May include all Emergent, Early, and Transitional techniques Compare 'n Share* (A) Reflection Connection*† (A) Context Complex Clues† (Co) Interactive Word Walls (Ca) Picture and Word Sorts† (Ca) Read-Alouds* (WR) Genre Study (WR)
During Reading	Playing With Plurals (An) Read-Alouds (WR)	Cloze Passages With Semantic Gradients (Co)	Author Study (WR)	Genre Study (WR)
After Reading	Collaborate and Elaborate* (Co) Museum Walk (V) Word Jars (WA) Journal Circles* (WA) Read-Alouds (WR) Resource Buddies (R)	Collaborate and Elaborate* (Co) Alphaboxes† (Ca) Museum Walk* (V) Four Corners (V) Vocabulary Tree Notebook (A) Word Jars (WA) Journal Circles (WA) Glossary Use (R)	Reflection Connection (A) Semantic Feature Analysis (A) Collaborate and Elaborate* (Co) Contextual Redefinition† (Co) Flip-a-Chip (An) Word Jars (WA) Quick Writes (WA) Author Study (WR) Book Talks (WR) Thesaurus Use (R)	Move to the Meaning* (A) Collaborate and Elaborate (Co) Flip-a-Chip* (An) Root Words (An) Word Jars (WA)

*Adaptation portion of the technique.
†Technique is illustrated on Creating Strategic Readers DVD series.
Note. The developmental levels are shown across the top of the table horizontally. Down the left side of the matrix are the suggested times when these techniques are most effective—before, during, and after reading. This matrix is a guide and is by no means an exhaustive list.
(A) Associating; (Co) Contextualizing; (Ca) Categorizing; (V) Visual imaging; (An) Analyzing; (WA) Word awareness, (WR) Wide reading; (R) Referencing

Figure 1, page 8, for an illustration). This allows for differentiation within the technique as needed to educate the whole child.

Vocabulary Strategy: Associating

The ability to associate words is an important strategy. Proficient readers develop flexibility in using and manipulating words as they apply various techniques to acquire word associations. Understanding how words connect enables the proficient reader to analyze and synthesize information, determining the ways in which words relate to one another. To associate words, a reader processes in "linguistic form that includes print and meaning and nonlinguistic form that includes visual and sensory images" (Bromley, 2007 p. 531).

Word associating allows readers to use alternative words to construct meaning from the text. To link prior experiences with new information, one may construct many kinds of word relationships. When readers use analogies, they draw inferences, and an opportunity for critical thinking occurs. This process of attaching a new concept to an existing one allows the reader to connect and bring meaning to the text.

Appropriate texts that best support the application of the word associating strategy have keywords that provide reinforcement of meaning.

Associating Text and Resource Examples:

Flocabulary (featuring Hip-Hop in the Classroom): www.Flocabualry.com

Harrison, B., & Rappaport, A. (2006). *Flocabulary: The Hip-Hop Approach to SAT-Level Vocabulary Building*. Kennebunkport, ME: Cider Mill Press.

Henkes, K. (1993). *Owen*. New York: Greenwillow.

Tocci, S. (2006). *Mercury*. New York: Scholastic.

Teacher Talk: Statements, Questions, and Prompts for Associating

Following is a list of suggested teacher talk that encourages readers to think strategically as they employ word-associating skills. Try using some of these statements, questions, and prompts with your students as you work through the techniques in the following section.

- What made you think of that association?

- What features do these words have in common?

- What connects all these examples together?

- Explain how you would connect these two words together.

- Why did you connect these two words?

- What does the similarity tell you about these features?

- How are these words similar and different?

- What connections do these words have?

- What are examples/nonexamples of the word (i.e., synonyms and antonyms)?

As you implement the various techniques that support associating, use the following behaviors as a guide as you assess students. Do students exhibit these behaviors never, rarely, often, always?

☐ Making connections among words

☐ Determining how words relate

☐ Generating analogies to extend content knowledge

Techniques for Associating

Move to the Meaning

Purpose: To use music to connect words with their meaning

Level: Emergent (Adaptation for Fluent)

ELL Technique: No

Multiple Intelligences: verbal/linguistic, musical/rhythmic

Materials: Text, items related to content, music instruments, hip-hop music (see, for example, www.flocabulary.com)

Procedure:

1. Pass out musical instruments and have the students create movement and music to associate to selected words (i.e., emotion words such as *excited* and *scared* or weather words such as *thunder* and *rain*).

2. Ask students to share their musical creation of their word and to describe why they chose the instrument, tune, and rhythm for their word.

Adaptation for Fluent Readers: Use a hip-hop song such as "The Chipmunk Rap" below found on the Flocabulary website (www.flocabulary.com) and other hip-hop songs to help students make connections to words from well-known children's literature (as indicated by the words in caps and boldface below). Create your own hip-hop or rap songs using selected vocabulary words.

First I saw this **ENORMOUS** tree.

Incredible! The biggest tree I ever did see,

And what did I see, in this huge oak tree?

A chipmunk on a branch, winking at me.

The wind was blowing and his tale **QUIVERED**.

It shook back and forth while he ate his dinner.

The chipmunk uncurled his tale, **UNFURLED** it.

I wanted to get closer, but I was nervous,

So I stayed at a **DISTANCE**, not too close.

I didn't move toward him, I didn't **APPROACH**.

Compare 'n Share

Purpose: To make connections among words

Level: Transitional (Adaptation for Fluent)

ELL Technique: No

Multiple Intelligences: Visual/spatial, interpersonal

Materials: Text, plain note cards, colored note cards; For Adaptation: Apples to Apples Jr. game

Procedure:

1. Distribute a note card to each student with a vocabulary word written on it (e.g., *affordable*). Encourage students to record on their note cards several synonyms under the word (e.g., cheap, low price, economical). These cards are then referred to as the word cards. Collect these cards from the students.

2. Give each student a blank, colored note card and read the words on the word cards. Have students record one example of something that fits the description given by each word card. Repeat this process for all of the word cards. Collect all these example cards.

3. Divide the students into groups to play the game. Pass out a stack of the word cards and example cards to each group. Each student selects 5 example cards and then takes a turn revealing the word card. The students who did not reveal the word card try to find an example card in their hand that best fits the revealed word card.

Adaptation for Fluent Readers: Have games such as Apples to Apples Jr. available at a vocabulary station so students can play in teams. Students can expand their vocabulary and thinking skills with board games such as this one; the second edition contains over 576 cards, so students may make thousands of new vocabulary comparisons.

Reflection Connection

This technique is highlighted on the Creating Strategic Readers DVD/VHS series.

Purpose: To connect words that relate to one another and determine relationships among the words

Level: Transitional (Adaptation for Fluent)

ELL Technique: No

Multiple Intelligences: Visual/spatial, bodily/kinesthetic, interpersonal

Materials: Text, note cards; For Adaptation: Reflection Connection reproducible (see CD), Puzzle Pieces reproducible

Procedure:

1. Prior to reading a selection, choose and record 10 words or phrases from the selection. The first 5 words or phrases should be from the selected text; the other 5 should be from the text also, but they should relate in some way to the first 5 words (e.g., sleep/night, dirty/torn).

2. Create two sets of word or phrase cards, one set for the first 5 words or phrases, and one set for the second

3. Divide students into two groups and give each student a word or phrase card from the set (if you have more than 10 students, let the students work in pairs or small groups).

4. Have students read their word cards and work together to determine which words or phrases connect and, if so, how the words connect. Suggested teacher talk could be, "What connects all these examples together?"

5. Ask the two main teams to record their predictions to share with the class later. Figure 7 shows an example of the process using the book *Owen* by Kevin Henkes.

6. After reading the text, have teams return to their notes to confirm or modify their connections according to how each word was used in the context of the text. Suggested teacher talk might be, "How would you connect these two words together?"

Adaptation for Fluent Readers: Students use 4 chosen words to complete the following sentence and then an additional phrase to complete the explanation: _____ is to

FIGURE 7. Sample Reflection Connection

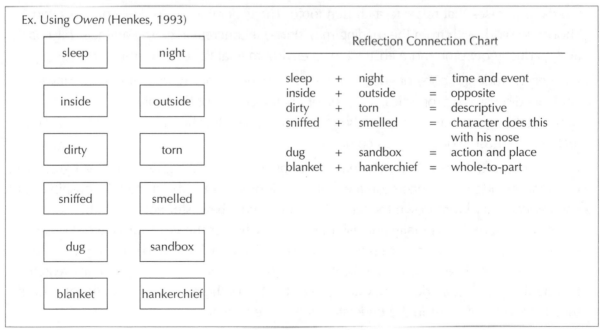

Ex. Using *Owen* (Henkes, 1993)

sleep	night
inside	outside
dirty	torn
sniffed	smelled
dug	sandbox
blanket	hankerchief

Reflection Connection Chart

sleep	+	night	=	time and event
inside	+	outside	=	opposite
dirty	+	torn	=	descriptive
sniffed	+	smelled	=	character does this with his nose
dug	+	sandbox	=	action and place
blanket	+	hankerchief	=	whole-to-part

_____ as _____ is to _____ because _____. Students determine how the words connect and record their results on the Reflection Connection reproducible. Laminate the Puzzle Pieces reproducible and have students record the words used to fill in the blanks above on their pieces and share in small groups. The dialogue within the group should focus on how the words connect and relate to one another. After a brief discussion, the students should revisit the text to examine the connected words in context.

Note: Adapted from Blachowicz & Fisher (2000), Vacca & Vacca (1996)

Semantic Feature Analysis

Vocabulary: Associating

This technique is highlighted on the Creating Strategic Readers DVD/VHS series.

Purpose: To explore how sets of key vocabulary words relate to one another and extend content knowledge

Level: Transitional

ELL Technique: Yes

Multiple Intelligences: Visual/spatial, verbal/linguistic, logical/mathematical, interpersonal

Materials: Semantic Feature Analysis matrix (see CD 💿), text; Optional: Journals or chart; For Adaptation: Computer and online lessons such as Word Storms from www. readwritethink.org

Procedure:

1. On the left column of the Semantic Feature Analysis matrix, write 5 to 10 key vocabulary words or phrases that relate to a chosen topic. The general topics or key concepts you choose to work with from the reading may start out concrete (e.g., sea animals, baseball) and gradually become more abstract (e.g., environmental issues, government).

2. Give each student a copy of your matrix with the vocabulary words written in. Have students discuss the properties, features, or characteristics of the topic and list them horizontally across the top row of the matrix. Suggested teacher talk could be, "What features do these words have in common?"

3. Before you read the text, have students collaborate with partners, work in small groups, or work independently to record on the matrix their predictions about the relationships. For each vocabulary word down the left side of the matrix, have students work their way across the matrix horizontally and ask themselves whether the vocabulary word possesses each of the features or properties written across the top. Ask them to write a plus (+) or minus (-) symbol in each box to indicate the presence or absence of a particular feature. During this process, students may add across the top of the matrix any additional features they discover that assist in the understanding of the concept.

4. Encourage students to explain their findings and to identify terms or features that they still are questioning.

5. After reading the text selection, have students modify any portion of their matrix as needed to reflect what they have learned from the reading. Students may also record a summary of their findings in vocabulary journals, use them to create a "group findings" chart, or discuss them with partners. Suggested teacher talk might be, "How are these words alike or different?"

Note: Adapted from Baldwin, Ford, & Readence (1981); Johnson & Pearson (1984); Pittelmann, Heimlich, Berglund, & French (1991)

Vocabulary Strategy: Contextualizing

One of the most effective strategies to increase vocabulary comprehension is to use the context that surrounds an unknown word to discover its meaning. This discovery process transpires through clues contained in the context. The reader can use context in several ways to help convey meaning. For example, sometimes the meaning of a word is explained within the same sentence. At times, synonyms of the unknown word can clarify words within the sentence. A contrast clue may identify meaning. Sometimes, the reader may need to make an inference or continue reading to figure out the relationship between the unknown word and the clues around the unknown word. Strategy instruction is necessary to support the reader in explicitly using context within the text to comprehend meaning.

Students need to "realize that it is okay to take a stab at unfamiliar words and figure out an approximate meaning from the context" (Calkins, 2001, p. 168). After students identify the unknown word, they may predict its possible meaning from the context. The context enables students to make an inquisitive stance toward word meaning and to monitor and verify predictions (Greenwood & Flanigan, 2007; Nelson, 2008; Tierney & Readence, 2005). Using a variety of contextual analysis techniques allows the student to be active, rather than passive, in the discovery of new words.

Appropriate text that best supports the application of the contextualizing strategy has strong word choice within the text to support the derived meaning.

Contextualizing Text Examples:

Bunting, E. (1991). *Fly Away Home*. New York: Clarion.

Polacco, P. (1988). *The Keeping Quilt*. New York: Simon & Schuster.

Westerskov, K. (2004). *Penguins*. Carlsbad, CA: Dominie Press.

Teacher Talk: Statements, Questions, and Prompts for Contextualizing

Following is a list of suggested teacher talk that encourages readers to think strategically as they employ contextualizing skills. Try using some of these statements, questions, and prompts with your students as you work through the techniques in the following section.

- Try the new meaning in place of the word in the sentence. Does it make sense?

- What do you know about the word _____ from this sentence?

- Describe how you used the word in context (definition, cause and effect, opposite).

- Explain how the context helps you understand the meaning of the word?

- What clues are in the sentence that helped you figure out the word?

- What word do you think best completes the sentence? Why?

- What words within the sentence help support the meaning of _____?

- What is the word being used to signal that an opposite, contrasting thought is occurring?

- What do these two words have in common?

- When you come to a word you don't know, how do you use context clues to determine the meaning of the unknown word?

As you implement the various techniques that support this strategy, use the following behaviors as a guide as you assess students' ability to contextualize. Do students exhibit these behaviors never, rarely, often, always?

☐ Predicting and verifying omitted words using surrounding context

☐ Cross checking using cueing systems

☐ Using background knowledge to examine and verify word meaning

Techniques for Contextualizing

Cloze Passages With Semantic Gradients

Vocabulary: Contextualizing

Purpose: To predict an omitted word using surrounding context and to cross-check with several cueing systems

Level: Early

ELL Technique: No

Multiple Intelligences: Visual/spatial, verbal/linguistic, logical/mathematical, interpersonal, intrapersonal

Materials: Text; overhead projector and transparency, board, or chart; correction tape or a large sticky note; learning logs

Procedure:

1. Select a short passage from a text, and display it on an overhead projector, the board, or a chart. Choose several words to omit and place correction tape or a large sticky note over the words.

FIGURE 8. Sample Semantic Gradient

Exhausted -------------------------| -------------------------|-------------------------|-------------------------Energetic

Word bank: tired, lively, worn out, active

2. Guide students in figuring out the missing words by using the "sense" of the surrounding words or other sentences. Suggested teacher talk could be, "What word do you think best completes the sentence? Why?"

3. Have students generate ideas for words that would best complete each of the sentences.

4. Record these ideas either on the sticky note covering each missing word or on chart paper.

5. When students are finished generating their replacement words, slowly peel back the sticky note from the first word to show the word's onset. Allow students to change their predictions if the words they predicted had a different beginning sound. Then, peel back the sticky note completely, exposing the correct word. This technique provides an opportunity for students to cross-check with several cueing systems: semantic (Does the word chosen to complete the sentence make sense with the rest of the sentence?), syntactic (Does the word chosen sound right for the English language?), and visual (Does the word chosen look right once the sticky note has been removed?).

6. Using the list of words students generated to complete the passage, have students determine where the words could be placed on a continuum.

Motivation/Engagement: Place the sticky note over the word but leave the onset visible. Students record in their learning logs their process in figuring out the unknown word. Have students discuss with a partner what strategies they used to try to figure out the meaning of the unknown word. Students may also create their own semantic gradient either by using a partially completed gradient with the words to choose from and place on the gradient or by generating words from the two extreme ends of the continuum (see Figure 8).

Note: Adapted from Blachowitz & Fisher (2006), Greenwood & Flanigan (2007), Strickland et al. (2002)

Contextual Redefinition

This technique is highlighted on the Creating Strategic Readers DVD/VHS series.

Vocabulary: Contextualizing

Purpose: To use background knowledge to examine the meanings of words and to verify the correct meaning of a word through the context or a dictionary

Level: Transitional

ELL Technique: No

Multiple Intelligences: Visual/spatial, verbal/linguistic

Materials: Text; overhead projector and transparency, board, or chart; dictionary

Procedure:

1. Select unfamiliar words from a text and present the words in isolation on an overhead transparency, the board, or a chart. Choose words that are unfamiliar to students but are necessary for their understanding of the text.

2. With partners, have students predict what they think is the meaning of each of the new words. This step allows students to tap into any background knowledge they have, bringing what they know to the meaning of the words.

3. Read aloud from the text or write and present each word in its appropriate context and develop new sentences that provide contexts for each word. Suggested teacher talk could be, "How does the context help you understand the meaning of the words?"

4. Allow students a chance to change or confirm their predictions, and discuss how hearing or seeing the context helped them understand the meanings of the words.

5. Have students verify the word meanings by using resources such as a dictionary.

6. Have students discuss how the two steps of contextual redefinition (i.e., seeing the words in isolation and seeing them placed in context) were different. Suggested teacher talk might be, "What words within the sentence help support the meaning of (word)?"

Note: Adapted from Readence et al. (2007), Tierney & Readence (2005)

What Do You Mean?

Vocabulary: Contextualizing

Purpose: To demonstrate how students use words in different contexts that change the meaning of the word

Level: Transitional

ELL Technique: Yes

Multiple Intelligences: Visual/spatial, verbal/linguistic, interpersonal, intrapersonal

Materials: What Do You Mean? reproducible (see CD 💿), text, chart, notebooks

Procedure:

1. Select words with multiple meanings or use the What Do You Mean? reproducible to demonstrate how words can be used in different contexts that change the meaning of the word.

2. Show students a word and ask them to tell a partner what they think the word means.

3. Read the word in a sentence from the selected text and have students discuss with their partners whether their predicted meaning for the word was correct. Suggested teacher talk

could be, "Show the context that surrounded the unknown word that helped to reveal its meaning."

4. Give each pair of students one word to use in two different sentences. Have one partner create a sentence using the word as one part of speech (e.g., a noun) while the other partner uses the word as a different part of speech (e.g., a verb) in a different sentence.

5. Have the partners explain their thinking (i.e., sentences) to the class, demonstrating the multiple meanings of the word.

6. List the demonstrated words on a chart and have students write these words in their notebooks to start a word collection journal. Suggested teacher talk might be, "Try to think of how you can use this word as a noun or as a verb (or other parts of speech, as applicable)."

Motivation/Engagement: Have the students create a cartoon character to share their interpretation of the word. Invite them to use a speech balloon to write the two different ways they used the multiple meaning word. The students can illustrate the scene around the character to correspond with the appropriate meaning of the word.

Collaborate and Elaborate

Purpose: To explore, discuss, and formulate a definition that the students perceive from clues within the sentence or related sentences and integrate newly formed words into a working vocabulary

Level: Fluent (Adaptation for Emergent–Transitional)

ELL Technique: Yes

Multiple Intelligences: Visual/spatial, verbal/linguistic, interpersonal,

Materials: Texts, vocabulary notebook; For Adaptation: Bingo file folders for groups, bingo word cards, bingo colored cards

Procedure:

1. Invite students to write unknown words or phrases they encounter in a vocabulary notebook.

2. Arrange students in groups to explore, discuss, and formulate a definition of the words or phrases that they perceive from clues within the sentence or related sentences.

3. Teams select a recorder to capture their examples and non-examples of the word from personal experiences and background knowledge, which helps to illustrate what the word is or is not, depending on the related words in context. Suggested teacher talk could be, "What clues are within the sentence that helped you figure out the word?"

4. The group agrees upon a definition that best describes the meaning of the word or phrases according to the related words and compares it with resources (i.e., dictionary, teacher, glossary).

5. Students continue to add new vocabulary words as they encounter them in their reading. Suggested teacher talk could be, "How have you used your new word in your written or oral presentation?"

Adaptation for Emergent–Transitional Readers: Have students create a visual representation of the word. Play the word game bingo. Students select words from their team list and create group bingo boards and their bingo color word cards. Draw a word card and use the cloze procedure by reading a sentence omitting the selected word. Students listen and match the word from their bingo cards that they think best completes the sentence. Draw a bingo color card and have the student that represents that color from each group determine if they have a place on their team bingo board. Return each color card word to be drawn again until a group completes their board. (This cooperative bingo idea was adapted from second-grade teacher Stephanie Dix.)

Context Complex Clues

Vocabulary: Contextualizing

This technique is highlighted on the Creating Strategic Readers DVD/VHS series.

Purpose: To use context clues to figure out the meaning of an unfamiliar word

Level: Fluent

ELL Technique: No

Multiple Intelligences: Visual/spatial, verbal/linguistic, interpersonal

Materials: Context Complex Clues reproducible (see CD), text, notebooks

Procedure:

1. Select a word from a text that may cause the students difficulty in understanding the meaning of the sentence or text passage.

2. Demonstrate a variety of ways students may use the context to figure out the meaning of the unfamiliar word. Copy and distribute the Context Complex Clues reproducible to show students some methods for using context.

3. Read a sentence that uses the word in a different context but that keeps the same meaning for the word (e.g., definition or description clues, linked synonym clues, compare and contrast clues, inferring clues). Chart these words as "clue glue" words for each category of contextual clues. See Figure 9 for a sample of clue glue words. Suggested teacher talk could be, "What clue glue words within the sentence help support the meaning of _____?"

FIGURE 9. Sample Clue Glue Words for Context Complex Clues

Definition	Synonym/compare	Antonym/contrast	Cause and effect
means	like	differ	because
is	as if	not	due to
describes	same as	different	if...then
states	and	unlike	consequently

4. Have students write their predictions in their notebooks (you can ask them to start vocabulary logs for this activity) and discuss what clues in the sentence helped to convey the meaning of the word. Suggested teacher talk might be, "Describe how you used the word in context."

Motivation/Engagement: In small groups, have students select words that challenged them in their independent reading time. Use the chart with the group to try to figure out the meaning of the unknown words.

Vocabulary Strategy: Categorizing

Categorizing is a strategy that actively engages students and encourages them to organize new concepts and experiences in relation to prior knowledge about the concept. This strategy enlists the use of graphic organizers as visual representations of relationships. Graphic organizers such as concept maps, webs, and Venn diagrams make thinking visible to students (Fogarty, 1997). As Stull and Mayer (2007) note, "The limits of the learner's cognitive capacity should be addressed in the design of graphic organizers" (p. 818). Students can also gain cognitive knowledge by properly designing their own graphic organizers as they process the text. Categorizing features of vocabulary words enables students to use higher order thinking and promotes cognitive word awareness in a visible manner. To categorize successfully, students need to be able to internalize the patterns under study and begin to make connections (Miller & Eilam, 2008; Strickland et al., 2002). Categorizing vocabulary words gives students an opportunity to develop an understanding of the essential attributes, qualities, and characteristics of a word's meaning.

Appropriate text that best supports the application of the categorizing strategy has a variety of words in the text suitable for sorting according to features and noticeable patterns.

Categorizing Text Examples:

Cherry, L. (1990). *The Great Kapot Tree: A Tale of the Amazon Rain Forest*. San Diego, CA: Gulliver Green/Harcourt.

Henkes, K. (1988). *Chester's Way*. New York: Greenwillow.

Suen, A. (2005). *Finding a Way: Six Historic U.S. Routes*. Parsippany, NJ: Celebration Press, Pearson Learning Group.

Teacher Talk: Statements, Questions, and Prompts for Categorizing

Following is a list of suggested teacher talk that encourages readers to think strategically as they categorize. Try using some of these statements, questions, and prompts with your students as you work through the techniques in the following section.

- How do you know that word belongs with this group?
- Tell some things that come to your mind when you think of the word _____?
- Describe what you know about this word?
- What features do these words have in common?
- What connects all these examples together?
- Check to make sure all the examples given have a commonality.
- What does the similarity tell you about these features?
- Check with a partner to see if you both agree with the categories.
- Explain how using a word map helps you.
- Describe how you categorized your words.
- How do the words you are studying relate to the story?

As you implement the various techniques that support this strategy, use the following behaviors as a guide as you assess students' ability to categorize. Do students exhibit these behaviors never, rarely, often, always?

- ☐ Describing the attributes, qualities, and characteristics of a word's meaning
- ☐ Choosing and sorting words by specific features
- ☐ Connecting ideas to form the meaning of words

Techniques for Categorizing

Interactive Word Walls

Vocabulary: Categorizing

Purpose: To actively find, write, chant, and discuss features of words posted on a word wall

Level: Emergent–Fluent

ELL Technique: Yes

Multiple Intelligences: Visual/spatial, verbal/linguistic, logical/mathematical, bodily/kinesthetic, interpersonal

Materials: Texts, collection of words, colored tag board, trifold display board, vocabulary notebooks, word jars

Procedure:

1. Select and add approximately five words to a systematically organized collection of words displayed for all to view and use as a resource and tool for studying words.

2. Integrate daily how to actively find, write, discuss, and chant these words. Use the word wall as an active process throughout the daily schedule. Suggested teacher talk could be, "How do you know that word belongs with this group?"

3. Write words on a strip of colored tag board and place them on the wall according to the categories (e.g., alphabet, by first and last names, theme words, rime wall, homophone word wall). Work the words with a variety of activities (i.e., clapping words, rhyming words, reviewing endings, making sentences, playing bingo, word sorting, and doing a cheer).

4. Engage the students in conversations noticing the features of how the words sound, look, what they mean, and how the words chosen connect to other words they know. Suggested teacher talk might be, "How can you use the word wall to help you daily?"

Motivation/Engagement: Create a portable wall by using tri-fold display boards for ease in moving around the room. These walls are great for content related words (e.g., math center with math concepts and symbols; science exploration area with words related to theme). The students can also record these words in a vocabulary notebook. It can have a section for their individual sorted words or a file folder sectioned according to how the student categorized the words for future referencing. Students can place words in their word jars (see Word Jars technique in this chapter).

Picture and Word Sorts

This technique is highlighted on the Creating Strategic Readers DVD/VHS series.

Purpose: To determine and sort words by specific features

Level: Emergent–Fluent

ELL Technique: Yes

Multiple Intelligences: Visual/spatial, verbal/linguistic, logical/mathematical, bodily/kinesthetic, interpersonal, intrapersonal, naturalist/environmentalist

Materials: Pictures or words from texts, note cards, highlighter, plants, camera

Procedure:

1. Choose 15 to 20 words from a selected text; they should be words that students can identify or read, but not necessarily spell. (For truly emergent readers or poorer readers, you can have students do this activity with pictures.) Write the words on note cards.

Vocabulary: Categorizing

2. Have students work in pairs or small groups to discuss the features of each word. Have students put the words into different categories by their similarities or differences. Categories may include colors, action words, or simple nouns. You may determine the categories in advance (a closed sort) or the students may discuss the common features of the words and then determine for themselves how to categorize them (an open sort). Suggested teacher talk might be, "Check with a partner to see if you both agree with the categories."

3. After students place the words within appropriate categories, have a class discussion to allow students to justify their sorting criteria. Suggested teacher talk could be, "What features do these words have in common?"

4. Provide an opportunity for students to edit their sorts if they so desire after the discussion.

5. Review the text and highlight the words the students used in the sorting activity.

Motivation/Engagement: Bring in a variety of plants and have students sort them by features and discuss their placements. Create a "human" class graph by passing out the picture or word cards and having the students walk around finding their like partners. Take a picture of the class graph and place the picture at the "Vocab Lab" (a vocabulary station where students study words). Have the students examine the words and the categories in the class photo and discuss their overall findings.

Note: Adapted from Henderson (1990); Henderson, Bear, & Templeton (1992); Zutell (1998)

Alphaboxes

This technique is highlighted on the Creating Strategic Readers DVD/VHS series.

Purpose: To notice beginning sounds of words in context and to sort words by beginning letter

Level: Early (Adaptation for Emergent)

ELL Technique: Yes

Multiple Intelligences: Visual/spatial, verbal/linguistic, bodily/kinesthetic, interpersonal

Materials: Alphaboxes reproducible (see CD 💿), text, highlighter; For Adpatation: Picture cards or objects

Procedure:

1. After reading a text selection, have students work in pairs or small groups to discuss and think of words that reflect important points from the text. Suggested teacher talk could be, "How do the words you selected relate to the story?"

2. Ask students to explain how their chosen words relate to the text. Copy and distribute the Alphaboxes reproducible. With the whole group or in pairs, have students decide which words to write in which boxes, according to the words' beginning letters. Suggested teacher talk could be, "Why did you place this word in this box?"

3. Return to the text and highlight the words the students selected for their alphaboxes.

Motivation/Engagement: Have students create sentences using the words in the boxes.

Adaptation for Emergent Readers: Pass out picture cards or objects that relate to a text you are reading (picture cards can be generated by using free images from websites such as clipart.com if needed). As you read the text, pause on selected words and have students listen to the word and then decide if the picture card or object they have begins with the sound or letter. The selected student places the picture on a large Alphabox class chart or places the object on an alphabet rug. Place the chart with pictures and the text at the literacy center for students to utilize as they reread and write about the text.

Note: Adapted from Hoyt (2008)

List/Group/Label

Purpose: To organize and connect word attributes, images, and descriptions of words

Level: Early (Adaptation for Transitional)

ELL Technique: Yes

Multiple Intelligences: Visual/spatial, verbal/linguistic, logical/mathematical, interpersonal, intrapersonal

Materials: Text; chart paper, overhead, or board; highlighter; For Adaptation: List/Group/Label reproducible (see CD 💿)

Procedure:

1. Determine a content-related topic or concept based on what the class is studying and reading.

2. As a class, in small groups, with partners, or individually, have students brainstorm words that relate to the chosen topic or concept.

3. Record these words on chart paper, an overhead projector, or the board in a list form or around an oval containing the central concept.

4. Have students decide how these brainstormed lists can be classified according to their shared relationships and share their reasoning with the whole group. Suggested teacher talk could be, "Describe how you categorized your words." Encourage students to group categories within three types of associations: class (i.e., What is it?—the broad category of things the concept fits into), properties (i.e., What is it like?—the attributes that define the concept), and examples (e.g., What is like it?—illustrations of the concept).

5. Return to the text and highlight the words students are categorizing.

6. Have students create a label or title that best describes each newly formed category.

Adaptation for Transitional Readers: Have students use the List/Group/Label reproducible or other graphic organizers as a visual representation of and a way to form a definition of the studied word. Suggested teacher talk could be, "How does the format help you to connect and generate meaning of the focused words?"

Note: Adapted from Johnson & Pearson (1984), Olson & Gee (1991), Schwartz (1988), Schwartz & Raphael (1985), Stahl & Nagy (2006)

Vocabulary Strategy: Visual Imaging

Visualizing vocabulary words enables students who are stronger in spatial rather than in verbal intelligence to find or draw pictures that illustrate the definitions of words (Silver, Strong, & Perini, 2001). Visual imaging is also referred to as mind, mental, or concept imagery. A student creates an image that represents the definition of the word and calls up this image whenever encountering the word. "The strategy of visualization provides opportunities for students to use their imaginations to facilitate both vocabulary development and comprehension across the curriculum" (Tate, 2003, p. 101). This strategy assists readers in assessing understanding of vocabulary knowledge, learning word meaning, making predictions and inferences, and concept acquisition.

When students use visual imaging, they think of a word that looks like, or even sounds like, the word they are learning. The more vivid the imagery, the more likely students will be able to connect and mentally recall the vocabulary word to its meaning. Different types of art activate different parts of the brain (Jensen, 2000, 2005), and this sensory connection is the bond for visual learners. Linking verbal and visual images increases students' ability to store and retrieve information (Ogle, 2000). "Transforming ideas from reading into artwork, poetry, etc., is an evaluative, interpretive act that reveals the students' level of understanding" (Collins, 1993, p. 3).

Appropriate text that best supports the application of the visualizing strategy has a variety of words in the text suitable for creating vivid mental images. Also, note that graphic genre is a cross between a novel and comics and is a valid reading tool in a world dominated by DVD games and high tech movies.

Visual Imaging Text Examples:

Kesselman, W. (1993). *Emma*. New York: Bantam Doubleday Dell.

Sava, S.C. (2006). *Dreamland Chronicles: Book One*. Blue Dream Studios. Available: www .thedreamlandchronicles.com

White, E.B. (1974). *Charlotte's Web*. New York: HarperTrophy.

Teacher Talk: Statements, Questions, and Prompts for Visual Imaging

Following is a list of suggested teacher talk that encourages readers to think strategically as they employ visual imaging skills. Try using some of these statements, questions, and prompts with your students as you work through the techniques in the following section.

- How does your illustration help you remember the new word?
- What do you see when you think of the word _____?
- Do the illustrations match what you imagined in your mind when you heard the story?
- What is the word _____ like? How does the example remind you of the word?
- What part of the pantomime helped you to know the word?
- Try to look at all the clay forms and create a definition of the word _____.
- Why did you choose that movement to represent the word _____?
- Which word goes with _____? Why does that word go with _____?
- Try to visualize the meaning of the word. Describe what you see.
- Try to visualize what the word looks like by using the picture.

As you implement the various techniques that support visual imaging, use the following behaviors as a guide as you assess students. Do students exhibit these behaviors never, rarely, often, always?

- ☐ Imprinting visual meanings by creating a mental image of a word
- ☐ Illustrating a word's meaning
- ☐ Giving examples and nonexamples of what the word is like or not like
- ☐ Questioning and hypothesizing for meaning of the image (purpose and context)

Techniques for Visual Imaging

Charades

Purpose: To make a mental image of a word to aid in recalling the word

Level: Emergent

ELL Technique: Yes

Multiple Intelligences: Visual/spatial, verbal/linguistic, bodily/kinesthetic, interpersonal, intrapersonal

Materials: Text, note cards, symbolic objects

Procedure:

1. Write some chosen vocabulary words or phrases from the text on note cards and have students take turns selecting a word card and acting out (i.e., role-playing or pantomiming) the meaning of the word on the card while holding or moving related or symbolic objects. Suggested teacher talk could be, "What part of the pantomime helped you to know the word?"

Vocabulary: Visual Imaging

2. Have students give suggestions for what the word might be until the correct word is identified.

3. Return to the text, and highlight the words students acted out within the text.

Motivation/Engagement: Have teams of students use several of the vocabulary words to create a skit to perform for the entire class. Teams can use pantomime and some verbal interaction while dramatizing the text. Teams also can select a few word cards and take a few minutes to improvise a situation demonstrating each word. This interaction with drama and words helps to develop vocabulary words through dialogue. Suggested teacher talk might be, "Why did you choose that movement to represent the word _____?"

Museum Walk

Purpose: To imprint visual meaning by creating a representation of a word

Level: Emergent (Adaptation for Early)

ELL Technique: Yes

Multiple Intelligences: Visual/spatial, verbal/linguistic, logical/mathematical, bodily/kinesthetic, interpersonal, intrapersonal

Materials: Text, ball of clay, highlighter, drawing notebook; For Adaption: Note card

Procedure:

1. Give each student a ball of clay and introduce a new vocabulary word.

2. Have students form a visual image of what the word means to them out of the clay.

3. Display the images around the room, and have the students do a word "museum walk" to view the visual forms of the word. Suggested teacher talk could be, "Try to look at all the clay forms and create a definition of the word _____."

4. Ask students to explain how their forms relate to the meaning of the word. Suggested teacher talk might be, "Why did you choose the way you did to represent the word _____?"

5. Revisit the text and have students highlight the words they formed.

Adaptation for Early Readers: Assign different words to students working in groups. Have each team create and share a visual image of their word from a large ball of clay. Display the creations around the room, and have the students go on the word "museum walk" as suggested above. Have students carry a drawing notebook with them and draw pictures of the images connected to each word. Students can also provide explanations of their clay by folding a note card to make a table tent. On one side have the students write the name of their creation. On the other side, the students write how they would categorize the image. Students also can use a computer graphics program to create picture cards for their words.

The cards would have the word printed at the top and a graphic, chosen by the students, under the word. The graphic should be a pictorial representation of the meaning of the word and the object that matches their clay form.

Four Corners

Purpose: To visualize the meaning of a word in multiple ways

Level: Early (Adaptation for Transitional)

ELL Technique: No

Multiple Intelligences: Visual/spatial, verbal/linguistic, bodily/kinesthetic, interpersonal

Materials: Text, unlined paper, pencils or markers, highlighter; Optional: Pictures from magazines, glue, scissors; For Adaptation: Four Corners reproducible (see CD)

Procedure:

1. Have students draw lines on a blank sheet of paper to divide the paper into fourths.

2. Have students write a key vocabulary word in the center of their paper.

3. Have students draw or paste a magazine picture that represents the opposite meaning of the word in the top left corner. Have students mark a big black X over the visual image.

4. Have students draw or paste a picture from a magazine that demonstrates an example of the word in the top right corner. Suggested teacher talk could be, "What is the word _____ like? How does it remind you of that word?"

5. Have students illustrate a personal connection they can make to the word in the bottom left corner of the paper. Suggested teacher talk could be, "Which word goes with _____? Why does that word go with _____?"

6. Have students draw—using the letters in the word—a picture that illustrates the meaning of the word in the bottom right corner.

7. Return to the text and highlight the words the students studied.

Adaptation for Transitional Readers: Place groups in teams and give each team a corner to complete. Have the teams decide on a leader to share their findings while all the students are using their vocabulary notebook or the Four Corners graphic organizer to record the presentations.

Eye Spy With My Eye

Purpose: To enter imaginatively into the picture, to question and hypothesize for meaning of the image, its purpose and its context

Level: Transitional

ELL Technique: No

Multiple Intelligences: Visual/spatial, verbal/linguistic, logical/mathematical, interpersonal, intrapersonal

Materials: Texts, magazine pictures, illustrations, photographs, story boards

Procedure:

1. Select a text with graphics and copy or show only the picture. Ask the students to look at the picture and describe what they see. Suggested teacher talk might be, "Spy with your eye who is in the picture? "What do you think they are thinking or saying?"

2. Read a part of the text that correlates with the picture and have the students try to make predictions as to what they think happened before the scene depicted in the picture.

3. Ask students to try to solve the scene by inferring what they think will be the rest of the story based on the graphic they spied.

Motivation/Engagement: Have students create several images about a personal experience. The students select one of the images from the story line to share with a partner to practice looking at the image to create meaning. Partners ask each other questions and make predictions and inferences about the images. Next, have the partners orally share their personal experience using the images. Finally, each student converts the images into a storyboard for a comic to share.

Note: Adapted from Williams (2008)

Vocabulary Strategy: Analyzing

Students use the analyzing strategy to examine the structure of words they are studying. Analyzing the structure, or word parts, is a way to determine the meaning of a word. There are three main word parts: prefixes, suffixes, and roots. Studying the morphemes of words (i.e., the smallest meaningful unit in language) allows students to acquire information about the meaning, phonological representation, and parts of speech of new words from their prefixes, roots, and suffixes (Nagy, Diakidoy, & Anderson, 1991). These word parts help to contribute to the meaning of the word. "Morphological awareness should play a more prominent role in decoding morphologically complex words because it helps beginning readers parse strings of letters at the right syllable boundary (e.g., mis-handle vs. mi-shandle)" (Kuo & Anderson, 2006, p. 172).

According to Nilsen and Nilsen (2003), spending class time on frequently used morphemes is a good teaching practice because it helps students establish structural connections among words. "Students need to learn to use word parts strategically, cautiously, and thoughtfully" (Stahl & Nagy, 2006, p. 159). Implementing techniques that support the connections between the structural analysis concepts and the basic definition will help students in understanding the word. Appropriate text that best supports the application of the analyzing strategy has a variety of words suitable for a specific structural concept.

Analyzing Text Examples:

Arnold, T. (1997). *Parts*. New York: Penguin.

Banks, K. (2006). *Max's Words*. New York: Farrar, Straus, & Giroux.

Numeroff, L. (2002). *If You Take a Mouse to School*. New York: Laura Geringer.

Teacher Talk: Statements, Questions, and Prompts for Analyzing

Following is a list of suggested teacher talk that encourages readers to think strategically as they employ analyzing skills. Try using some of these statements, questions, and prompts with your students as you work through the techniques in the following section.

- Look for any parts of a word that help you make sense of it.
- Try to cover up part of the word (e.g., the prefix). What word do you have left?
- Try to take the word apart.
- What words around it tell you something about the word?
- What does the prefix _____ do when added to the start of the word _____?
- What words go together with this word?
- What is the root word of _____?
- Which word has a prefix? Suffix?
- What is the meaning of the prefix or suffix?
- If you know what the root word for _____ means, what do you think _____ means?
- How does knowing the prefix, suffix, or root word of a word help you?
- How are all these words alike?

As you implement the various techniques that support this strategy, use the following behaviors as a guide as you assess students' ability to analyze. Do students exhibit these behaviors never, rarely, often, always?

☐ Locating morphemes in a word and examining their meaning

☐ Demonstrating how prefixes affect words and their meaning

☐ Deciphering how words derive meaning from root words

Techniques for Analyzing

Playing With Plurals

**Vocabulary:
Analyzing**

Purpose: To analyze the structure of a word to determine if it is singular or plural

Level: Emergent

ELL Technique: No

Multiple Intelligences: Visual/spatial, verbal/linguistic, naturalist/environmentalist

Materials: Text, cookies or chips, cookie tray, various items for demonstrating the (more than) plural concept; Optional: Small shoebox or paper and glue

Procedure:

1. Display a tray of cookies and have the students describe what you have in your hand. Their response may be, "cookies."

2. Go around the room and ask the students if they would like a cookie or cookies. You can also use chips and ask if they want a chip or chips. Suggested teacher talk might be, "I will listen to the end of your word to determine what to give you." Discuss with students how listening to the ending of their word would help me determine the amount to give.

3. Hold up items and have the students decide if the corresponding word is singular or plural (e.g., a ball or balls). Write and display the words of the items and highlight the letter *s* at the end of each of the words to denote when there are more than one. You can have two trays, one with singular items and one with plural. Have students compare and contrast the trays.

4. During a read-aloud have the students listen for plural words. Have them share their discoveries with a partner.

Motivation/Engagement: Go on a "plural walk" outside. Have the students collect items (e.g., leaves, rocks, flowers) and also notice items (e.g., birds, clouds) that are plural. Place collected items on display and create a label with the letter *s* highlighted. Students may put their collections in a small shoebox or glue on paper as their plural collection.

Vocabulary Tree Notebook

**Vocabulary:
Analyzing**

Purpose: To identify morphemes within a word

Level: Early

ELL Technique: No

Multiple Intelligences: Visual/spatial

Materials: Vocabulary Tree reproducible (see CD 🔘), text, three-ring binders or clasp folders

Procedure:

1. Using the Vocabulary Tree reproducible, create a notebook with several vocabulary tree pages for each student. Distribute the notebooks to the students.

2. Have students designate one page in their notebooks for each morpheme (root, stem, or affix) they study. Whenever students encounter a word with that part (e.g., *-ing*), have them write it on the appropriate tree and note where the word was encountered. Suggested teacher talk could be, "Try to take the word apart."

3. Have students share their vocabulary trees with a partner and discuss why the words on a particular tree are related. Suggested teacher talk could be, "How are all these words alike?"

4. Return to the text, and have students locate the words they studied.

Note: Adapted from Hill (1998)

Flip-a-Chip

Purpose: To mix and match four meaningful word parts to make four words

Level: Transitional (Adaptation for Fluent)

ELL Technique: No

Multiple Intelligences: Visual/spatial, verbal/linguistic, interpersonal

Materials: Texts, white chips, word journals

Procedure:

1. Record chosen words on four white round chips. Each set of chips has two prefixes and two meaningful chunks of chosen words.

2. Give each student a prefix chip and chunk of chosen word chip. Suggested teacher talk could be, "What does the prefix ____ do when added to the start of the word _____?"

3. Students flip the chips to form a word. Continue this process forming all four words.

4. Have the partners record their results in word journals. Rotate giving all the partners time to work with each set of chips. Suggested teacher talk might be, "How are all these words alike?"

5. Have the students demonstrate where their flip-a-chip word is in the text.

Adaptation for Fluent Readers: Have partners write a paragraph with blanks. These blanks represent where the newly formed words on the chips would best complete the sentences. The students place the newly formed paragraph in the bag with the chips. Other students can then have a try at completing the paragraph using the chips. Have students use word sorting techniques (see the categorizing strategy, this chapter, for more ideas) to examine the concepts of prefixes and suffixes. Students also can use word walls, journals, and word matching activities to reinforce the analysis of prefixes and suffixes. (See Tables 21 and 22 for lists of commonly used prefixes and suffixes.)

Note: Adapted from Bear et al. (2008), Mountain (2002)

TABLE 21. Commonly Used Prefixes

Prefix	Meaning	Examples
auto-	self	automatic, autograph, automobile
bi-	two	biweekly, bicycle, bilingual
de-	reverse action, remove, away	deflate, detach, deodorize
dis-	apart, negative, away	dislike, disagree, disappear
in-	not, free from, out	inactive, invisible
mis-	wrong	misspell, miscount, misfortune
pre-	before	preview, prepay, prepare
re-	back, again	redo, recall, repaint
tri-	three	triangle, tricycle, trilogy
un-	not	undo, untold, unhappy

TABLE 22. Commonly Used Suffixes

Suffix	Meaning	Examples
-tion	being, act, process (forms noun)	mention, vacation, location
-er	person connected with (forms noun)	runner, teacher, speaker
-less	without (forms adjective)	speechless, breathless, thoughtless
-ing	verb form (forms present participle)	running, singing, swimming
-ness	state of, condition of (forms noun)	likeness, forgiveness, happiness
-s, -es	plural	boys, girls, boxes
-ly	characteristic of (forms adverb)	lovely, happily
-est	comparative (forms adjective)	happiest, funniest, craziest
-ful	full of (forms adjective)	playful, helpful, grateful
-ed	verb form (forms past tense)	played, relaxed, rehearsed

Root Words

Vocabulary: Analyzing

Purpose: To understand that a word derives meaning from the root word, also known as the base or stem

Level: Fluent

ELL Technique: No

Multiple Intelligences: Visual/spatial, verbal/linguistic

Materials: Text, dictionaries, journals, highlighter

Procedure:

1. Have students research the meanings of root words found in the vocabulary for the text or topic they are studying. Tell students that analyzing this foundational part of a word helps

them to determine a word's origin and history, which will make the word more memorable. Suggested teacher talk could be, "How does knowing the root word help you?"

2. Have students generate a set of new words by adding affixes (prefixes and suffixes) to the root words. Have them write these new words in a journal. Suggested teacher talk might be, "What is the root word of _____?"

3. Ask the students to use a dictionary to look up the definition for each of the root words from the set of words they generated.

4. Lead students in a discussion on how these words all relate and can be categorized.

5. Have students return to the text and highlight the words they studied.

Vocabulary Strategy: Word Awareness

Students gain a sense of ownership of a word when they can transfer a new vocabulary word to their writing and speaking in a meaningful way (Routman, 2000). Word awareness, also known as word consciousness, is a strategy that brings one's thinking about the usage of a word to an application level and personalizes word learning. Effective readers acquire up to seven new vocabulary words each day. To enhance vocabulary, students need to have a desire to know words and gain "enjoyment and satisfaction from using them well and from hearing them used well by others" (Graves, 2000, p. 127).

When students know a word, they are able to use that word in speech and writing and to understand the word in text when it appears. Word-conscious students know and use many words, and they are aware of the subtleties of word meaning and the power words can have (Graves, Juel, & Graves, 1998; Graves & Watts-Taffe, 2008). Applying word awareness strategies is a natural, motivating way to support students while they are building their vocabulary and increasing their comprehension.

Appropriate text that best supports the application of the word awareness strategy has a variety of words for students to use in their everyday conversations.

Word Awareness Text Examples:

Degross, M. (1994). *Donavan's Word Jar*. New York: HarperCollins.

O'Connor, J. (2009). *Fancy Nancy: The Dazzling Book Report*. New York: HarperCollins.

Parish, H. (1995). *Good Driving, Amelia Bedelia*. New York: Greenwillow.

Teacher Talk: Statements, Questions, and Prompts for Word Awareness

Following is a list of suggested teacher talk that encourages readers to think strategically as they employ word awareness skills. Try using some of these statements, questions, and prompts with your students as you work through the techniques in the following section.

- What do you know about the word _____?

- How can you find out more about a chosen word?

- How often did you use your chosen word in your journal writing?

- Try to use a new word when you are sharing today.

- Try to rate the word according to how much you know about the word.

- How did being aware of one word today help you to learn about that word?

- Do you feel confident to use the word _____ in a conversation or in your writing? Why? Why not?

- How did your word choice affect the other students' understanding of your journal entry?

As you implement the various techniques that support word awareness, use the following behaviors as a guide as you assess students. Do students exhibit these behaviors never, rarely, often, always?

☐ Gaining ownership of words by applying new words in everyday conversations

☐ Transferring a new vocabulary word to their writings

☐ Indicating levels of knowledge of words

Techniques for Word Awareness

Word Jars

Purpose: To examine words in their environment and use new words in everyday language

Level: Emergent–Fluent

ELL Technique: Yes

Multiple Intelligences: Visual/spatial, verbal/linguistic, logical/mathematic, bodily/kinesthetic, interpersonal, intrapersonal

Materials: Word Jar template (see CD 🔘), *Donavan's Word Jar* (Degross, 1994); Optional: paper strips, plastic jars, sticky labels, vocabulary log

Procedure:

1. Prepare word jars using the Word Jar template or give each student a plastic jar.

2. Read *Donavan's Word Jar* to the students and discuss how Donavan shares his encounters with a variety of people and their reactions to his word jar.

3. Invite the students to create their own word jar and have them search for words to add to the jar each day.

Motivation/Engagement: Have students select a word from their word jar that they would like to use throughout the week in their conversations. Have students keep a daily vocabulary log and during independent writing time write how they used their vocabulary word in context for that day. Encourage students to have at least five entries per word before adding a new vocabulary word. Students can write their word on a sticky label and wear it on their clothes. Each time that a student uses his or her chosen word in conversation, the listener should add a tally mark to the sticky label. Read a text, and have students highlight the words they chose to study. Students can periodically use their word jar to categorize their words and add them to their vocabulary notebooks or a word wall. Have students share their words from their jars with teams and have a word-card trading day.

Note: Adapted from Barger (2006)

Journal Circles

Purpose: To express an awareness of words in writing

Level: Early (Adaptation for Emergent)

ELL Technique: Yes

Multiple Intelligences: Visual/spatial, verbal/linguistic, interpersonal

Materials: Text, journals

Procedure:

1. Establish a daily journal writing time and have students make an effort to use vocabulary words they are currently studying when they write in their journals.

2. When writing time is complete, ask students to join journal circles in which small groups of mixed or similar ability take turns sharing their daily entries and noting the word choices they used in their writing. Journal circle time gives students a chance to "try out" sharing how they used words in context. Suggested teacher talk could be, "Try to use a new word when you are sharing today."

3. After hearing each student orally read his or her journal entry, have the other team members make comments, ask questions, or compliment the reader regarding his or her word choices and overall journal entry. Suggested teacher talk might be, "How did your word choice affect the other students' understanding of your journal entry?"

4. Read a text, and have students point out what words they heard in the text that they have used in their journal entries.

Adaptation for Emergent Readers: Read aloud stories and record on a vocabulary chart words from the text that are important or interesting for students to know. Have students sign their names on the vocabulary chart next to the vocabulary word identified for them to use. Place a tally mark beside the student's name each time he or she uses the assigned word in a meaningful way orally or in their journals.

Knowledge Rating

Purpose: To identify the level of knowledge of a word

Level: Transitional

ELL Technique: No

Multiple Intelligences: Visual/spatial, verbal/linguistic, interpersonal, intrapersonal

Materials: Knowledge Rating reproducible (see CD 🔘), text, notebooks

Procedure:

1. Present students with a list of vocabulary words related to the topic you are studying.

2. Have students analyze their familiarity with the chosen words, and ask them to place a check mark beside their level of word knowledge on a matrix. Suggested teacher talk might be, "Try to rate the word according to how much you know about it."

3. Ask students to discuss with partners what they know about the list of words and select words to focus on during the upcoming reading of the text.

4. Copy the Knowledge Rating reproducible and distribute to each student. Before reading, have the students use the rating matrix to record the selected words and to rate them according to their level of knowledge of each word. Suggested teacher talk could be, "What do you know about the word _____?"

5. After reading, have students reflect on their rating matrix and determine whether their knowledge of certain words changed.

6. Have students place an *X* in the appropriate column of the matrix to represent any changes. Ask students to keep their rating charts in a personal vocabulary log and review them periodically, making adjustments on words that are becoming more familiar to them.

7. Reread the text, and have students listen for the new words they are studying and think about how they are used in context.

Note: Adapted from Blachowicz (1986)

Quick Writes

Purpose: To utilize background knowledge to formulate meanings of words

Level: Transitional

ELL Technique: Yes

Multiple Intelligences: Visual/spatial, verbal/linguistic, interpersonal, intrapersonal

Materials: Text, vocabulary journals

Procedure:

1. Present one new vocabulary word to students prior to reading a text selection.

2. After presenting the vocabulary word, have students write about the word for a few minutes in a vocabulary journal. This writing may include a definition of the word, a synonym or antonym for the word, or a response to a question you present using the word or about the word. Suggested teacher talk might be, "What do you know about the word _____?"

3. Have students share in groups their Quick Write responses and discuss similarities and differences among the responses.

4. Read the text and emphasize the vocabulary word within the context of the selection.

5. Ask students to revisit their written responses and make any adjustments necessary to correspond with the way the word is used in the context of the text.

6. Have groups discuss their ideas about the word, helping students to put new concepts in their own words. Suggested teacher talk might be, "How did being aware of the word today help you learn about that word?"

Note: Adapted from Tate (2003)

Vocabulary Strategy: Wide Reading

Wide reading is a strategy that fosters vocabulary development through a variety of opportunities for students to read. Students need at least 20 minutes of daily reading to help increase their vocabulary list by 1,000 words per year (Nagy, Anderson, & Herman, 1987). This daily exposure is a natural way to increase vocabulary. "Children learn new words by reading extensively on their own. The more children read on their own, the more words they encounter and the more word meaning they learn" (Armbruster, Lehr, & Osborn, 2001, p. 35).

Encountering words in reading passages or speaking them in context multiple times is one of the best ways to commit words to long-term memory. Students will benefit from techniques geared toward rehearsing and talking about some of the words and concepts in a book (Calkins, 2001). "Encountering words repeatedly in text builds a fabric of meaning that makes it easier to learn new words" (Fountas & Pinnell, 1996, p. 166).

Appropriate literature that best supports the application of the wide reading strategy appeals to the students' reading levels and interests and fits into a range of genres.

Wide Reading Text Examples:

Biel, T. (2003). *Zoobooks: Tigers*. Poway, CA: Wildlife Education.

DiCamillo, K. (2000). *Because of Winn-Dixie*. Cambridge, MA: Candlewick.

Layne, S. (2006). *Mergers*. Gretna, LA: Pelican.

Teacher Talk: Statements, Questions, and Prompts for Wide Reading

Following is a list of suggested teacher talk that encourages readers to think strategically as they employ wide reading skills. Try using some of these statements, questions, and prompts with your students as you work through the techniques in the following section.

- What are some of the interesting vocabulary words the author uses?

- Why are these words interesting to you?

- How have you used some words from your vocabulary club in your everyday conversation?

- What pattern do you notice the author using for his or her word choice?

- Tell me about some interesting words you are encountering while you are reading.

- How did you select your words for your book talk?

- What kind of words did you notice are common in this specific genre?

- In what genre would you most likely find these words?

- Tell me about some interesting words you heard while listening to the read-aloud.

As you implement the various techniques that support wide reading, use the following behaviors as a guide as you assess students: As you implement the various techniques that support wide reading, use the following behaviors as a guide as you assess students. Do students exhibit these behaviors never, rarely, often, always?

- ☐ Listening and absorbing vocabulary from hearing and reading text

- ☐ Imitating author's words in conversation

- ☐ Identifying characteristics of words among genres

Techniques for Wide Reading

Read-Alouds

Vocabulary: Wide Reading

Purpose: To listen to and absorb the vocabulary from a chosen text

Level: Emergent (Adaptation for Early–Fluent)

ELL Technique: Yes

Multiple Intelligences: Visual/spatial, verbal/linguistic, interpersonal

Materials: Text, chart; For Adaptation: Note cards

Procedure:

1. Read aloud a story to the class. Have students listen during the read-aloud and try to absorb the vocabulary from the chosen text. Suggested teacher talk might be, "Tell me about some interesting words you heard while listening to the read-aloud."

2. Instruct students to discuss with a partner interesting words they heard during the read-aloud. Suggested teacher talk could be, "Why are these words interesting to you?"

3. Set the text that you read in an area in the classroom where students can reread it or otherwise revisit the text on their own.

4. Keep a class chart of all the titles read aloud each month. Have students discuss and record their reflections on the texts on this chart and periodically compare previously noted connections with new connections (e.g., text-to-text connections, text-to-self connections).

Adaptation for Early–Fluent Readers: Write selected words from the story on note cards, and pass them out to the students before the read-aloud. As the students are listening to the story, have them hold up their word cards when they hear the words in the story. After the read-aloud, have the students share how each word was used in the story.

Author Study

Purpose: To imitate authors' words in conversation

Level: Transitional

ELL Technique: No

Multiple Intelligences: Visual/spatial, verbal/linguistic, intrapersonal

Materials: Multiple texts by the same author, sticky tabs, chart paper, materials for students to create their own written versions

Vocabulary: Wide Reading

Procedure:

1. Have students read several books by a particular author. During this author study, have students look for keywords the author uses frequently in his or her writing.

2. List the author's name at the top of a sheet of chart paper and have students list the words from step 1 in addition to other interesting words the author uses. Suggested teacher talk might be, "What pattern do you notice the author using for his or her word choice?"

3. Encourage students to imitate the author by using the author's words in their everyday conversations. Suggested teacher talk could be, "What are some of the vocabulary words the author uses that are interesting to you?"

4. Create an area in the classroom to display the books and other information about the author you are studying (e.g., an Awesome Author center). Display the author's books with sticky tabs on the pages with the studied words. Encourage students to revisit the author's books.

Motivation/Engagement: Have students imitate the featured author by creating their own versions of the stories at the writing center.

Book Talks

Purpose: To identify vocabulary words that support the meaning of a book

Level: Transitional

ELL Technique: Yes

Multiple Intelligences: Visual/spatial, verbal/linguistic, interpersonal

Materials: Text, student vocabulary logs, materials for students to create a poster display

Procedure:

1. Encourage students to read a variety of books. Tell students that they will be giving book talks using the vocabulary from each story to introduce classmates to a particular book. Suggested teacher talk could be, "Tell me about some interesting words you are encountering while you are reading."

2. As they are reading, have students keep vocabulary logs in which they write interesting vocabulary words that help them relate to the meaning of the book.

3. Ask students to share these words when giving their classmates an orientation of the book. Suggested teacher talk might be, "How did you select your words for your book talk?"

Motivation/Engagement: Have students create a poster that illustrates their book talk and display these at the classroom library area with the books to entice others to read it.

Genre Study

Purpose: To identify similarities and differences among vocabulary words within genres

Level: Fluent

ELL Technique: No

Multiple Intelligences: Visual/spatial, verbal/linguistic, interpersonal

Materials: Texts in a variety of genres, chart, materials for creative writing, highlighters

Procedure:

1. Expose students to several different genres of reading material.

2. During this genre study, keep a chart of specific vocabulary words that correlate with each particular genre (see Table 23 for examples). Suggested teacher talk might be, "What kinds of words did you notice that are common in the specific genre?"

TABLE 23. Vocabulary Words for Genre Study

Genre	Description	Vocabulary Words and Phrases
Fantasy	Fiction that contains elements that are not real such as magical powers and animals that talk	Wizard, magical, hero, powers, imagine
Mystery	Story that contains suspense; mysterious	Secret, classified, investigation, discover, clue, evidence, witness, suspense
Folk tale	Story passed on from one generation to another by word of mouth	Once upon a time, This is the story of, Long ago, There once was
Fable	A fictitious story meant to teach a lesson; characters are usually animals	Responsibility, moral, courage, freedom, noble, kindness
Science fiction	Content not pattern, what if, infinite possibilities, imagination	Aliens, encounter, outer space, scientific, time travel, consequences

3. Have students frequently discuss the similarities and differences among the vocabulary words within the various genres. Suggested teacher talk could be, "In what genre would you most likely find these words?"

Motivation/Engagement: Using the genre chart, have students select a genre and create a writing piece using at least 10 words that indicate strongly their genre choice. Have partners read the writings and decide the chosen genre and highlight the words that correlate with the genre.

Vocabulary Strategy: Referencing

Referencing is a strategy that allows readers to use resources to bring meaning to an unknown word. Students simply select a resource to search for the meaning of the word. However, teachers and students can overrely on this traditional strategy. "Definitions alone can lead to only a relatively superficial level of word knowledge. By itself, looking up words in a dictionary or memorizing definitions does not reliably improve reading comprehension" (Nagy, 2003, p. 5). Instruction for students should focus on how these resources can aid in learning meanings of words in the appropriate context. The quality of the definition also is an important factor in being able to use the dictionary as an aid to understanding text (McKeown, 1993; Nist & Olejnik, 1995). Teachers need to work with students in selecting the definition that best supports the meaning of the chosen word. "To make deriving the meaning from the dictionary definitions most effective, it needs to be modeled for students and practiced in a scaffold way" (Beck et al., 2008, p. 47). Several techniques are possible, including using a book's glossary, a dictionary, a thesaurus, or a resource buddy.

Appropriate text that best supports the application of the referencing strategy has a variety of words in the text suitable for sorting according to features and definitions.

Referencing Text and Resource Examples:

Freeman, M. (2002). *Go Facts: Insects*. Littleton, MA: Newbridge/Sundance.

Priddy, R. (2001). *My Big Book of Everything*. New York: Dorling Kindersley.

Wikipedia (online dictionary): www.wikipedia.com

Wordsmith.org (provides opportunities to work with words, word play, language, and literature): www.wordsmith.org

Teacher Talk: Statements, Questions, and Prompts for Referencing

Following is a list of suggested teacher talk that encourages readers to think strategically as they employ referencing skills. Try using some of these statements, questions, and prompts with your students as you work through the techniques in the following section.

- How did the dictionary help you to figure out the word?
- Try to select words to examine and record that are interesting to you.
- What feature helps you to know if a word will be in the glossary?
- Which word means _____? How did you find the meaning for the word?
- How do you use the glossary to help you understand the meaning of a word?
- How do you use a thesaurus, glossary, or dictionary?
- Try to tell your buddy what you think the word means. Discuss it together.
- How did your buddy help you understand the unknown word?

As you implement the various techniques that support referencing, use the following behaviors as a guide as you assess students. Do students exhibit these behaviors never, rarely, often, always?

☐ Analyzing unknown words for meaning

☐ Using glossaries, dictionaries, and thesauruses to determine meaning of words

☐ Selecting meaning of a word that best supports the use of the word in context

Techniques for Referencing

Resource Buddies

**Vocabulary:
Referencing**

Purpose: To work with a partner to analyze unknown words for meaning

Level: Emergent

ELL Technique: Yes

Multiple Intelligences: Visual/spatial, verbal/linguistic, interpersonal

Materials: Text, journals, note cards, writing supplies for creating class dictionary

Procedure:

1. Assign each of your students an older student from a different classroom to be their resource buddy.

2. Throughout the week, have students keep track of words from their reading for which they need assistance to understand the meaning. Have students write these unknown words in their word journals. Suggested teacher talk might be, "Try to tell your buddy what you think the word means. Discuss it together."

3. Once each week, have students get together with their resource buddies to analyze the unknown words.

4. Have students write in their journals any information the buddy shares about the words. Suggested teacher talk might be, "How did your buddy help you understand the unknown word?"

Motivation/Engagement: Create vocabulary word cards (using a large font) and definition cards (on a word processor in landscape mode). Laminate, cut apart, and pass out one card, either the word or a definition, to each student. On a predetermined signal, have students walk around the room trying to find the match between students. When a match is found, students line up and share their word's meaning with the group. Partners can create a definition page for a class dictionary for a content area study. (This idea was contributed by third-grade teacher Sherry Perny.)

Glossary Use

Purpose: To utilize a glossary to help identify the definitions of keywords

Level: Early

ELL Technique: No

Multiple Intelligences: Visual/spatial, verbal/linguistic, interpersonal

Materials: Texts with glossaries, supplies such as markers and crayons for creating illustrated glossary

Vocabulary: Referencing

Procedure:

1. Work with students to select several words from an informational text and look up their definitions in the book's glossary. Make students aware that nonfiction books often have glossaries of the terms used throughout the text, and that words that appear in the glossary are often boldfaced or italicized in the running text.

2. Have students look for a word in the glossary. Suggested teacher talk could be, "How do you use the glossary to help you understand the meaning of a word?"

3. After reading the definition from the glossary, ask students to retell the definition to a partner and point out where that chosen word is in the text. Suggested teacher talk might be, "What feature helps you to know if a word will be in the glossary?"

Motivation/Engagement: Have students create an illustrated glossary.

Thesaurus Use

Purpose: To use the thesaurus to help determine the meaning of a word

Level: Transitional

ELL Technique: Yes

Multiple Intelligences: Visual/spatial, verbal/linguistic, interpersonal

Materials: Text, thesaurus, dictionary, sticky notes

Procedure:

1. Select several words to examine with the students using a thesaurus. Show the students how to use a thesaurus to look up multiple words to represent the word chosen and how, from these choices, one is able to get a better understanding of what the word could mean.

2. With partners, have the students choose a known or unknown word from a text and put a sticky note over the word.

3. Have the students predict other words they could substitute for that word that would still make sense in the passage.

4. Ask students to look up the word in a thesaurus and compare the word they chose to the ones that are under that entry in the thesaurus. Suggested teacher talk might be, "How do you use a thesaurus?" Students can put a check mark by the words that are both on their sticky note and in the thesaurus. They also can add words to their sticky note if desired.

5. As a class, discuss how students can see several words listed together in the thesaurus that all have similar usages in a sentence and can use that list to infer what they think the meaning of a particular word is.

6. Have students compare and contrast the thesaurus to a dictionary. Students can work with partners to examine and identify the various parts of a dictionary (e.g., guide words, parts of speech, definitions, etymologies).

Motivation/Engagement: Have students use an online thesaurus (www.merriam-webster.com) to highlight a chosen word and then search for some word choices that correspond with the original word. Suggested teacher talk could be, "What feature of the online program helps you understand the word better? How does it help you?"

Vocabulary Wrap-Up

Vocabulary is a key component of effective reading instruction. Both fluency and comprehension are affected by vocabulary knowledge (Flood et al., 1991; Robb, 1997). Vocabulary "is the glue that holds stories, ideas, and content together and that facilitates making comprehension accessible for children" (Rupley, Logan, & Nichols, 1999, p. 5). The NRP report findings indicate that vocabulary seems to occupy an important middle ground in learning to read. Oral vocabulary is a key to learning to make the transition from oral to written forms, whereas reading vocabulary is crucial to the comprehension processes of a skilled reader (NICHD, 2000, p. 4-15).

The strategies, techniques, and teacher talk presented in this chapter support teachers in maximizing their readers' potential in becoming strategic readers. When teachers brush this stroke (techniques and teacher talk in vocabulary) across their canvases, they are adding another dimension to their masterpieces—strategic readers.

Chapter 6

Comprehension

Determining Importance with
Main Idea Wheel technique

Visualizing and Sensory Imaging
with **Sensory Impressions**
technique

Summarizing with **Summary Ball** technique

Comprehension is the essence of reading; therefore, teachers should weave comprehension strategies into their everyday teaching across the curriculum. According to the NRP report, "Comprehension strategies are specific procedures that guide students to become aware of how well they are comprehending as they attempt to read and write" (NICHD, 2000, p. 4-5). In fact, teachers need to begin teaching these strategies in kindergarten. "To delay this sort of powerful instruction until children have reached the intermediate grades is to deny them the very experiences that help them develop the most important of reading dispositions" (Pearson & Duke, 2002, p. 248). These emerging readers are able to begin using higher thinking skills to bring meaning to the text. The ability to comprehend is far from being passive. "Comprehension occurs when a reader is able to act on, respond to, or transform the information that is presented in written text in ways that it demonstrates understanding" (Brassell & Rasinski, 2008, p. 18).

Comprehension as a strategic process enables readers to make connections and move beyond literal recall. Teachers need to remember that good comprehension instruction needs to be taught explicitly and strategically. With every technique, it is vital that teachers explain and model directly, guiding students on how the technique builds the corresponding comprehension strategy (Boulware-Gooden, Carreker, Thornhill, & Joshi, 2007; Fisher, Frey, & Lapp, 2009; Hilden & Pressley, 2007; Israel & Duffy, 2009; Pressley, 2002). Comprehension instruction requires making "the strategy a part of our unconscious reading process, so that students are able to combine any number of strategies to problem solve before, during, and after they read" (Routman, 2003, p. 129). This transactional approach has been proven to support readers to becoming active, independent readers who bring meaning to reading (Brown, 2008).

The strategies and their corresponding techniques detailed in this chapter are as follows:

- Previewing: What I Know…What I Wonder…, Book Introduction, Text Traits: Getting to Know the Text, and Skim and Scan

- Activating and Building Background Knowledge: Connect and Reflect, Tapping 'N To (TNT) Reading, Anticipation/Reaction Guides, and Think Sheet

- Predicting: Picture Walk, Story Impression, Journaling, and Two-Column Note Prediction

- Questioning: Ripple Effect, Question–Answer Relationships (QARs), Question Logs: 3Rs, and Survey, Question, Read, Recite, Review (SQ3R)

- Visualizing and Sensory Imaging: Sketch to Stretch, Wordless Picture Books, Frame This, Drama, and Sensory Impressions

- Inferring and Drawing Conclusions: Interpreting Text, Save the Last Word for Me, Talk Show, and Scenarios With T-Charts

- Summarizing: Detail/Retell, Journaling or Group Chart, Summary Ball, Narrative Pyramid, and Somebody/Wanted/But/So

- Determining Importance: Picture This, Chapter Tours, Main Idea Wheel, and Highlighting

- Synthesizing: Creating a Play, Mind Mapping, Rewriting a Story, Say Something, and Synthesizing Target

Table 24 matches the techniques in this chapter to the developmental levels from Chapter 1 (emergent, early, transitional, and fluent). To be effective, the strategies and techniques presented in this chapter should allow ample time for teacher modeling and student application, long before independent application is expected. Teachers should select and model reading aloud of appropriate text to apply the techniques in a meaningful manner, which supports authentic learning for strategic reading. By using this process,

TABLE 24. Comprehension Techniques

	Emergent	Early	Transitional	Fluent
Before Reading	What I Know… What I Wonder… (P) Book Introduction (P) Text Traits: Getting to Know the Text (P) Anticipation/Reaction Guides*† (A) Picture Walk (Pr) Story Impressions (Pr)	May include all Emergent techniques Book Introduction (P) Text Traits: Getting to Know the Text (P) Skim and Scan (P) Tapping 'N To Reading (A) Journaling (Pr) Wordless Picture Books* (V) Chapter Tours (D)	May include all Emergent and Early techniques Book Introduction (P) Text Traits: Getting to Know the Text (P) Skim and Scan (P) Anticipation/Reaction Guides† (A) Think Sheet (A) Question–Answer Relationships (Q)	May include all Emergent, Early, and Transitional techniques Book Introduction (P) Text Traits: Getting to Know the Text (P) Skim and Scan (P) Story Impressions* (Pr) Two-Column Note Prediction (Pr) Survey, Question, Read, Recite, Review (Q)
During Reading	Connect and Reflect (A) Ripple Effect (Q) Wordless Picture Books (V) Sensory Impression*† (V)	Skim and Scan (P) Connect and Reflect (A) Interpreting Text (I) Journaling or Group Chart (S) Somebody/Wanted/But/So* (S)	Connect and Reflect (A) Question Logs: 3Rs† (Q) Somebody/Wanted/But/So (S) Highlighting (D)	Connect and Reflect (A) Survey, Question, Read, Recite, Review (Q) Scenarios With T-Charts (I) Highlighting* (D)
After Reading	Sketch to Stretch (V) Frame This (V) Detail/Retell (S) Picture This (D)	(V) Drama† (V) Sensory Impressions† (V) Interpreting Text (I) Detail/Retell (S) Summary Ball (S) Main Idea Wheel* (D) Creating a Play (Sy)	Save the Last Word for Me (I) Talk Show (I) Detail/Retell (S) Narrative Pyramid (S) Somebody/Wanted/But/So (S) Main Idea Wheel (D) Mind Mapping (Sy) Rewriting a Story (Sy) Say Something (Sy)	Survey, Question, Read, Recite, Review (Q) Detail/Retell (S) Synthesizing Target (Sy)

*Adaptation portion of the technique.
†Technique is illustrated on Creating Strategic Readers DVD series.
Note. The developmental levels are shown across the top of the table horizontally. Down the left side of the matrix are the suggested times when these techniques are most effective—before, during, and after reading. This matrix is a guide and is by no means an exhaustive list.
(P) Previewing; (A) Activating and building background knowledge; (Pr) Predicting; (Q) Questioning; (V) Visualizing and sensory imaging; (I) Inferring and drawing conclusions; (S) Summarizing; (D) Determining importance; (Sy) Synthesizing

students are able to see first the whole text (i.e., appropriate literature), then see the parts systematically (i.e., strategies and techniques), and finally, apply the parts back to the whole (i.e., become metacognitively aware of strategies while reading appropriate literature). Using quality literature and promoting language development throughout the techniques will help to enhance students' development of the strategies. In addition, teachers can use the motivation and engagement feature within many techniques as an additional means (i.e., multiple intelligence, standard) of motivating the whole child and creating 21st-century learners (refer to Chapter 1 for a description of the whole child and Figure 1, page 8, for an illustration). This allows for differentiation within the technique as needed to educate the whole child.

Comprehension Strategy: Previewing

Previewing motivates students to want to read the text. It enables readers to examine text features, skim to get a sense of what the text is about, and identify the organizational structure. While previewing, readers begin relating to what they already know—their schema—and form several opinions about the text they are reading. Previewing is one of the best strategies for evoking relevant thoughts and memories relating to the text. Previewing allows readers to get their minds ready to read a particular type of text. When they use this strategy, students have a better understanding of what they know about the text, what they would like to learn from the text, and what they anticipate might happen as they read.

Appropriate text that best supports the application of the previewing strategy should have an interesting title, chapter headings, or illustrations.

Previewing Text Examples:

Brinckloe, J. (1986). *Fireflies*. New York: Aladdin.

Rylant, C. (1985). *The Relatives Came*. New York: Atheneum.

Tokuda, W., Hall, R., & Wakiyama, H. (1992). *Humphrey the Lost Whale: A True Story*. Torrance, CA: Heian.

Teacher Talk: Statements, Questions, and Prompts for Previewing

Following is a list of suggested teacher talk that encourages readers to think strategically as they employ previewing skills. Try using some of these statements, questions, and prompts with your students as you work through the techniques in the following section.

- The title makes me think the book will be about...

- I have read other books by this author. I think this book also will be good because...

- The illustrations help me to...

- Perhaps the pictures will provide clues about...

- What else do you notice from the picture?

- I noticed that the author...

- I noticed that the pictures are helping to tell the story because...

- This picture makes me think about…

- What is the significance of the title?

- I have a connection to this, it reminds me of...
- Are you familiar with the topic of the selection?
- What is your purpose for reading this selection?
- How is the text structured?
- What do you notice about the captions?
- What features help you when previewing the book?

As you implement the various techniques that support this strategy, use the following behaviors as a guide as you assess students' ability to preview. Do students exhibit these behaviors never, rarely, often, always?

☐ Activating background knowledge to preview text

☐ Initiating mental images

☐ Using text traits to preview purpose

Techniques for Previewing

What I Know...What I Wonder...

Purpose: To activate background knowledge to preview a text

Level: Emergent–Fluent

ELL Technique: Yes

Multiple Intelligences: Visual/spatial, verbal/linguistic, bodily/kinesthetic, interpersonal, intrapersonal

Materials: Text, chart paper, marker, hula hoops

Procedure:

1. Through class discussions, activate students' prior personal experiences that are pertinent to the text you are about to read. Suggested teacher talk could be, "What comes to your mind as you view this text? Think about what you know."

2. Begin to build with students any necessary background knowledge they might need for studying this text (for ideas, see the activating and building background knowledge strategy and its techniques in this chapter). Suggested teacher talk might be, "Ask yourself, 'Am I familiar with the topic of the selection?'"

3. Have students reflect on what they wonder as they preview a text. Place two colored hula hoops on the floor to represent what I know and what I wonder. Have students model their thinking as they step into each hoop.

Motivation/Engagement: Create a two-column graphic organizer on chart paper (or on an overhead or a visual presenter). Label the left column "What I Know" and the right column "What I Wonder." Have students use sticky notes to record their thinking in print or with illustrations and align with the column titles. Teacher talk could be, "What are you thinking? What are you wondering about? I am wondering...." This can be done with a read aloud or during independent reading (one-to-one conferring). As a follow-up to support oral language and vocabulary have students share their thinking with a partner and decide where to place their sticky notes on the chart.

Book Introduction

Comprehension: Previewing

Purpose: To stimulate interests, implant vocabulary, and initiate mental images

Level: Emergent–Fluent

ELL Technique: Yes

Multiple Intelligences: Visual/spatial, verbal/linguistic, interpersonal, intrapersonal

Materials: Text

Procedure:

1. Before reading a chosen book, discuss briefly with the students what the book is about, key concepts in the book, and new vocabulary. Eliciting vocabulary use through discussions with students and then identifying a few of those words directly within the text helps to implant the words in students' minds.

2. Have students preview some of the pictures in the book as a source of information. Suggested teacher talk could be, "Perhaps the pictures will provide clues about...."

3. Encourage students to think aloud, describing their reactions to the illustrations and the text. Suggested teacher talk might be, "What does the text seem to be about?"

Motivation/Engagement: Have students create an introduction about themselves, highlighting key traits. Have them stand and introduce themselves to the group. Discuss what information they found to help them to get to "know" each other better through the introductions. Compare this technique to using a book introduction to preview the book.

Text Traits: Getting to Know the Text

Comprehension: Previewing

Purpose: To identify and use text features, supports, and structures to help determine the purpose of a text

Level: Emergent–Fluent

ELL Technique: No

Multiple Intelligences: Visual/spatial, verbal/linguistic, interpersonal

Materials: Text Traits reproducible (see CD 🔘), text

Procedure:

1. Before reading a chosen book, preview a specific text trait (i.e., features, supports, or structure) that will support the students' ability to determine the purpose of the text. Suggested teacher talk could be, "How is the text structured? What features help you when previewing the book?"

2. Provide a "Text Trait" minilesson on an activity in which they read the headings in a text and predict what they think the text will be about based on the headings.

3. Have students work with a partner to make predictions about a particular text. Suggested teacher talk could be, "Based on the text features noted, what do you think the story is about? Which details or clues from the selection did you use to make your prediction?"

4. Have students pause throughout the reading of the text and use text features to make further predictions as well as to confirm or change their previous predictions.

Motivation/Engagement: Give each student a Text Trait card (example of text trait or the text trait terminology). Have students match their cards in a large group activity. With their matched partner, share how their text trait can help them as a reader.

Skim and Scan

Purpose: To make first impressions about a text

Level: Early–Fluent

ELL Technique: No

Multiple Intelligences: Visual/spatial, verbal/linguistic, bodily/kinesthetic, interpersonal, intrapersonal

Materials: Text

Procedure:

1. Have students skim the text they are about to read, noting their first impressions. Suggested teacher talk could be, "I noticed that the author...."

2. Encourage student to scan the "lead-ins," subheadings, diagrams, and any other portions of the text that give them a feel for the text they will be reading. Ask students to use these first impressions to begin selecting strategies that they will need to comprehend the text. Teachers may post these strategies in the classroom so the names are more readily accessible to students. Suggested teacher talk might be, "How can skimming and scanning be helpful? When would you use it?"

3. Discuss and record a variety purposes for skimming and scanning.

Motivation/Engagement: Distribute to teams a scenario to bring to "life" (e.g., You need a job, you want to bake a cake, you want a new video game). Invite students to select a resource to skim and scan for their scenario. Have students describe how the resource supports the purpose. Have teams act out their scenario results.

Comprehension Strategy: Activating and Building Background Knowledge

Proficient strategic readers bring their prior knowledge to a text to help them discern the meaning of what they are reading. When readers are thinking about what they already know, they are using their schemas to better understand the text. According to Keene and Zimmermann (2007), students connect new information to their own experiences (text to self), to other texts they have experienced (text to text), and to real-world issues (text to world). Strategic readers add or alter their thinking as they encounter new ideas and information from the text. It is critical that teachers not only activate their students' knowledge of topics they are reading about but also are aware of situations in which students have little or no background knowledge so that they can build, through scaffolding, essential understandings before their students begin reading (Fisher et al., 2009; Jensen & Nickelsen, 2008; Strickland et al., 2002).

Appropriate text that best supports the application of the activating and building background knowledge strategy needs to have ways for students to connect with the text and use their schemas (i.e., what they already know) or to add to what they need to know about the text selected.

Activating and Building Background Knowledge Text Examples:

Henkes, K. (1991). *Chrysanthemum*. New York: Greenwillow.

Martin, B., Jr, & Archambault, J. (1987). *Knots on a Counting Rope*. New York: Henry Holt.

Local newspaper and magazines articles

Teacher Talk: Statements, Questions, and Prompts for Activating and Building Background Knowledge

Following is a list of suggested teacher talk that encourages readers to think strategically as they activate and build background knowledge. Try using some of these statements, questions, and prompts with your students as you work through the techniques in the following section.

- Read the title or opening paragraph, and name another book similar to this one.
- Make a connection to other texts written by the same author or books that may be related to the same theme.
- What do you know that will help you understand the information in this section?
- Which details from the text connected to your own experiences?

- What other stories did this story remind you of?

- What personal connection did you make with the text?

- How are the events described in this story related to your own experiences? Were they similar? Were they different?

- What do you already know about the text?

- Do you agree or disagree with the statement presented? Why or why not?

- Try to read and confirm whether your answer to the statement is true or false.

- Based on your prior knowledge of the topic, what questions come to mind?

- Identify how you supported your thinking—with the text, background knowledge or both.

- What comes to your mind when you hear the word (or phrase) _____ ?

As you implement the various techniques that support this strategy, use the following behaviors as a guide as you assess students' ability to activate and build background knowledge. Do students exhibit these behaviors never, rarely, often, always?

☐ Making connections to self, text, and world

☐ Confirming or changing predictions

☐ Enlarging background knowledge

Techniques for Activating and Building Background Knowledge

Connect and Reflect

Comprehension: Activating and Building Background Knowledge

Purpose: To associate text with self, another text, and other aspects of the world

Level: Emergent–Fluent

ELL Technique: No

Multiple Intelligences: Visual/spatial, verbal/linguistic, bodily/kinesthetic, intrapersonal

Materials: Connect and Reflect reproducible (see CD ⬤), text

Procedure:

1. Explain that a text-to-self connection is made when something in the story reminds you of something in your life.

2. Model for students text-to-self connections. For example, after reading the first page the teacher talk could be, "This reminds me of a time when…. I have made a text-to-self connection in this story."

3. Distribute the text-to-self puzzle pieces from the Connect and Reflect reproducible and have the students illustrate or write the event from the text on one piece and what their personal connection on the other puzzle piece. Suggested teacher talk might be, "What made the event so memorable?"

4. Have students share the connections and display puzzle pieces for future discussions.

Motivation/Engagement: Use the puzzle pieces for text-to-text connections (i.e., related books, characters, and so forth) and text-to-world connections (i.e., a broader connection to people and places around us through newspaper articles, magazine interviews, and so forth). Use the following questions for students to respond to literature they have read at a writing station.

Text To... Questions?

Text-to-self

How does this relate to my life?

What does this remind me of in my life?

What is this similar to in my life?

Has something like this ever happened to me?

Text-to-text

Have I read in another book about something like this?

What does this remind me of in another book I've read?

How is this text similar to other things I've read?

How is this different from other books I've read?

Text-to-world

What does this remind me of in the real world?

How did that part relate to the world around me?

How is this text similar to things that happen in the real world?

How is this different from things that happen in the real world?

Note: Adapted from Keene & Zimmermann (2007), Harvey & Goudvis (2007)

Tapping 'N To (TNT) Reading

Purpose: To develop, add, or modify new insights to text

Level: Early

ELL Technique: Yes

Multiple Intelligences: Visual/spatial, verbal/linguistic, logical/mathematical, interpersonal, intrapersonal

Materials: Text, chart paper, hammer, nail, piece of wood, paper and pencils for creating a KWLS graphic organizer, sticky notes

Procedure:

1. Demonstrate tapping into wood with a hammer and nail. Explain how with each "tap" the nail goes deeper into the wood. Relate the tapping into the wood to the steps in this technique and how each time you tap with a step, you are either activating or building background knowledge.

2. Identify the central concept in a text selection and introduce it to the students by saying, "What comes to your mind when you hear the word (or phrase) _____?" For example, you could use images like a farm or best friend.

3. Individually, have students record all of their associations with the topic and what they know about it.

4. Have students share and list their responses on a chart. Prompt students to reflect on and clarify their background knowledge by asking, "What made you think of _____?"

Motivation/Engagement: Have students create a KWLS graphic organizer by making four columns in a table format and labeling each one *K*, *W*, *L*, and *S*. Students record what they already know about the theme, topic, or concept in the *K* column (what we *K*now) to activate their prior knowledge and demonstrate the correlation between what they already know, and the information in the text. In the *W* column (what we *W*ant to know), have the students generate questions they would like to have answered as they read the text. As they are reading, have the students use sticky notes to mark sections of the text that helped them to answer their questions. After reading, have students record new knowledge in the *L* column (what we have *L*earned) reflecting on their original questions and use it to create a smooth transition into writing about their reading. Revisit the columns with students to modify or confirm statements from what they knew. Revisit the W column to assure the students' questions were addressed in the discussions. Use a final *S* (what we *S*till want to know) column to further their quest for a broader understanding based on their predictions.

Note: Adapted from Langer (1981), Ogle (1986), Sippola (1995)

Anticipation/Reaction Guides

This technique is highlighted on the Creating Strategic Readers DVD/VHS Series.

Purpose: To confirm or change predictions about text

Level: Transitional (Adaptation for Emergent)

ELL Technique: No

Multiple Intelligences: Visual/spatial, verbal/linguistic, intrapersonal

Materials: Anticipation/Reaction Guide (see CD 💿), text, notebook paper

Procedure:

1. Identify the main topic or concept of a text prior to meeting with students.

2. Create three to five statements that will challenge or support students' beliefs or that may reflect common misconceptions about the subject, topic, or concept. Record these statements on the Anticipation/Reaction Guide.

3. Have students read each statement and note whether they agree (+) or disagree (×). Suggested teacher talk could be, "Do you agree or disagree with the statement presented? Why or why not? Try to read and confirm whether your answer to the statement is true or false."

4. Have students return to the statements after they have read the text and engage in a discussion on how the textual information supported, contradicted, or modified their first opinions. Suggested teacher talk could be, "Identify how you supported your thinking, with the text, background knowledge, or both."

Adaptation for Emergent Readers: Make the statements you created about the subject, topic, or concept before the class read aloud and then have students decide what they think they know about the statements with signals (e.g., thumbs up, thumbs down). Then listen to the read aloud and share reactions to previous statements. Figure 10 provides an example of an Anticipation/Reaction guide.

Note: Adapted from Herber (1984)

Think Sheet

Purpose: To generate and record background knowledge to guide reading

Level: Transitional

ELL Technique: No

Multiple Intelligences: Visual/spatial, intrapersonal

Materials: Think Sheet reproducible (see CD ⊙), text

Comprehension: Activating and Building Background Knowledge

Procedure:

1. Copy the Think Sheet reproducible and distribute to each student. Choose a text to study and have students write the text's main topic in the rectangular box on their sheets.

2. Have students list ideas that they have about the main topic based on their prior knowledge on the side of the sheet with the light bulb.

3. Have students record any questions they have about the main topic on the side of the sheet with the light bulb. Suggested teacher talk could be, "Based on your prior knowledge of the topic, what questions come to mind?"

4. Ask students to use what they have recorded on their think sheets to guide their reading of the text.

FIGURE 10. Sample Anticipation/Reaction Guide

Name_____ Date_____

Text_____

Directions:

1. Read the anticipation statement and decide if you agree or disagree with it.

2. In the Me column, place a + symbol to represent if you agree with the statement. (You think the statement is true.) If you disagree with the statement, place an ×. (You think the statement is false/not true).

3. Read the text to confirm or change your anticipation to the statement. Place a + in the Text column if the statement in the text is true and an × if it is not true.

4. Record your reaction to the process in the Reaction column.

Anticipation statement	Me	Text	Reaction (confirmed or changed)
1. Turtles have been on earth since the time of the dinosaurs.			
2. All turtles can pull their heads, legs, and tails into their shells.			
3. Turtles' body temperature is the same as the air or water around them.			
4. Turtles hibernate.			
5.			

5. Have students read the text. As they locate information related to their original prereading ideas and questions, have students write the information beside their corresponding original statements. Suggested teacher talk could be, "What personal connection did you make from the text?"

Note: Adapted from Dole & Smith (1987)

Comprehension Strategy: Predicting

Predicting is a strategy that helps readers set expectations for reading, connect early with the text for meaning, and decide what they think will happen. Strategic readers make predictions before reading and while reading, based on a number of skills and strategies like previewing, activating background knowledge, and asking questions (Block, Rodgers, & Johnson, 2004; Fisher et al., 2009). "When readers make predictions about what they'll learn, they activate their schema about the topic and what they know about the type of text they are about to read" (Miller, 2002, p. 145). Predictions can be based on clues in the title, the illustrations, and the details within the text. These organizational structures are the blueprints that show the author's plan for presenting information to the reader (Strickland et al., 2002).

During reading, readers may predict what content will occur in succeeding portions of the text. Readers can describe what they think will be revealed next, based on what they have read so far and based on the personal background knowledge they bring to the text. After reading a portion of the text, readers can confirm whether their predictions were accurate and adjust them as needed.

Appropriate text that best supports the application of the predicting strategy needs to have interesting titles, illustrations, and other text features that allow students to think on what the text might be about and then to be able to confirm or counter the prediction.

Predicting Text Examples:

Burns, M. (2008). *The Greedy Triangle*. New York: Scholastic.

Hutchins, P. (1986). *The Doorbell Rang*. New York: Greenwillow.

Schlein, M. (1990). *The Year of the Panda*. New York: Crowell.

Teacher Talk: Statements, Questions, and Prompts for Predicting

Following is a list of suggested teacher talk that encourages readers to think strategically as they employ prediction skills. Try using some of these statements, questions, and prompts with your students as you work through the techniques in the following section.

- What makes you think _____ is going to happen? Why?
- I wonder if _____; I want to know _____.

- What will happen next? I think I know what is going to happen.
- What do you think the text is going to tell you about? What makes you think so? What evidence supports your prediction?
- Try to imagine what is going on in the story.
- What information do you expect to read in this selection based on the title?
- What do you predict the author will reveal next, based on the first paragraph or chapter?
- Which details or clues from the selection did you use to make your prediction?
- Which predictions were confirmed by the text?
- Which predictions need to be adjusted or revised?
- Looking at the picture on the cover, what do you imagine this story will be about?
- Based on the text features noted, what do you think the story is about?

As you implement the various techniques that support this strategy, use the following behaviors as a guide as you assess students' ability to predict. Do students exhibit these behaviors never, rarely, often, always?

☐ Analyzing illustrations within text and observing clues about topic or events

☐ Forecasting what a text will be about

☐ Composing, checking, or modifying predictions

 Techniques for Predicting

Picture Walk

Purpose: To use illustrations within a text to make predictions

Level: Emergent

ELL Technique: Yes

Multiple Intelligences: Visual/spatial, verbal/linguistic, bodily/kinesthetic, naturalist/environmentalist

Materials: Text

Procedure:

1. Have students peruse a book, looking at the pictures and describing what they see. Ask students to use the pictures to make predictions. Suggested teacher talk could be, "Looking at the picture on the cover, what do you imagine this story will be about?"

2. Lead students in a discussion about understanding the concepts, keywords, or key phrases from the text based on the illustrations. Suggested teacher talk might be, "How do the pictures help you to predict what the story will be about?"

3. Have students discuss the predictions they made from the picture walk while reading the text. Suggested teacher talk might be, "Can you remember a time when…? How does this help you to predict what will happen next?"

Motivation/Engagement: Have students go on a nature walk to represent a picture walk. Have students predict what will happen on their nature walk before they begin and as they are in the process.

Story Impression

Purpose: To compose, check, and modify predictions

Level: Emergent (Adaptation for Fluent)

ELL Technique: Yes

Multiple Intelligences: Visual/spatial, verbal/linguistic, logical/mathematical, interpersonal

Materials: Fiction or other story-oriented text, chart paper

Procedure:

1. Select seven keywords that relate to significant information from the text you are studying, and display the chain of words in the order in which they appeared in the text for all students to see. These words should reflect the following story elements: main characters, setting, problem, events, and solution. Suggested teacher talk could be, "Try to imagine what is going on in the story based on the seven words presented."

2. Have students work in teams to predict a story line using the words presented.

3. Have teams create a story using all seven words after they have had time to discuss their predictions. One student in the class can be the recorder and write the teams' creations on chart paper. Suggested teacher talk could be, "Present to the entire class your story creations. Which details or clues from the selection did you use to make your prediction?"

4. After all the teams have shared their versions of the story, read the story and have students compare and contrast their stories to it.

Adaptation for Fluent Readers: Have students create a Venn diagram to compare and contrast their story predictions to the original story.

Note: Adapted from McGinley & Denner (1987)

Journaling

Purpose: To predict in written form what a text will be about

Level: Early

ELL Technique: Yes

Multiple Intelligences: Visual/spatial, verbal/linguistic, interpersonal, intrapersonal

Materials: Text, journals

Procedure:

1. Have students keep reading response journals in which they draw or write what they think a story they are preparing to read will be about and justify why they think it will be that way. Suggested teacher talk could be, "What will happen? I think I know what is going to happen. What do you think the text is going to tell you about _____? What makes you think so? What evidence supports your prediction?"

2. As in Journal Circles (see Chapter 5, page 159), have students share their journal entries.

3. Read the text and have students discuss the predictions they recorded in their journals in comparison with the actual events in the text.

Motivation/Engagement: Offer sentence stems in written form (e.g., "I think…," "My prediction is…," "I am wondering…"). Have the students sit knee to knee and make predictions about the text. Suggested teacher talk could be, "What will happen next ? I think I know what is going to happen." Have students listen to their partner's prediction to help support any additional predictions. This process encourages the more reluctant reader to contribute what they think might happen.

Two-Column Note Prediction

Purpose: To record and justify predictions

Level: Fluent

ELL Technique: No

Multiple Intelligences: Visual/spatial, verbal/linguistic, interpersonal, intrapersonal

Materials: Two-Column Note Prediction Form (see CD 💿), text

Procedure:

1. Copy the Two-Column Note Prediction Form and distribute to each student. Have students record their predictions about a text on the left side of the form.

2. On the right side, have students record their thought processes behind these predictions. Suggested teacher talk might be, "What makes you think _____ is going to happen? Why?"

3. Have students share their predictions and then read the text to see whether their predictions were correct. Suggested teacher talk could be, "Which predictions were confirmed by the text?"

Note: Adapted from Miller (2002)

Comprehension Strategy: Questioning

Questioning is a strategy that helps readers to review content and to relate what they have learned to what they already know. Generating and asking questions also helps students to identify issues and ideas in all content areas, construct meaning, enhance understanding, discover new information, clarify confusion, and solve problems (Kinniburgh & Shaw, 2009; Raphael, Highfield, & Au, 2006). Asking questions before reading allows readers to set purposes for reading and helps them to determine what they want to learn while reading.

Strategic readers move from general questions to story-specific questions during their interaction with the text, and they integrate information from different segments of text. When the text becomes unclear, strategic readers formulate questions and then continue reading to find details that may later help answer those questions and make sense of the text. Asking and answering questions encourage readers to notice pieces of information within the text that support the main idea. This process of asking and answering questions allows readers to think actively as they read.

Appropriate text and resources that best support the application of the questioning strategy need to capture the mind of the reader and encourage questions before, during, and after reading.

Questioning Text Examples:

Abercrombie, B. (1990). *Charlie Anderson*. New York: M.K. McElderry.

Lasky, K. (1994). *The Librarian Who Measured the Earth*. New York: Little, Brown.

Survey forms (to collect and analyze data) and interview forms (to ask questions to obtain information about the interviewee)

Teacher Talk: Statements, Questions, and Prompts for Questioning

Following is a list of suggested teacher talk that encourages readers to think strategically as they employ questioning skills. Try using some of these statements, questions, and prompts with your students as you work through the techniques in the following section.

- What questions did you have while you were reading this text?
- What questions do you have about the story after reading it? How can you answer your questions?

- Where do you find the answers to your questions?

- What differences of opinion between (name two characters) did you notice?

- Before you start reading, ask three questions that you would like to find out about the text.

- While you are reading, try to find the answers to the questions you asked.

- What questions do you hope this story will answer?

- What information do you hope this text will include?

- How does asking questions help the reader?

- How do readers figure out the answers to their questions?

- How does forming a question about the text help you comprehend it?

- Try to think of a question that will support comprehension of the text. What do you understand now because of your questions?

As you implement the various techniques that support this strategy, use the following behaviors as a guide as you assess students' ability to question. Do students exhibit these behaviors never, rarely, often, always?

☐ Establishing a purpose for reading by asking questions

☐ Generating questions to discover new information

☐ Using questions for clarification and problem solving

Techniques for Questioning

Ripple Effect

Purpose: To activate questions and stimulate thinking based on the generated questions

Level: Emergent

ELL Technique: Yes

Multiple Intelligences: Visual/spatial, verbal/linguistic, bodily/kinesthetic, interpersonal, naturalist/environmentalist

Materials: Text, small inflatable pool or fish bowl, colored pebbles, colored construction paper, large blue butcher paper for pond

Procedure:

1. Select a text, theme, or concept to introduce to the class.

2. Bring in a small child's inflatable pool or fish bowl and place for all to see. Hold a few small colored pebbles in your hand. Demonstrate the rippling concept of when you throw

a pebble into water and there is a splash and you may even hear the pebble hit the water. You will notice concentric circles rippling out from the entry point. There may even be other effects when the pebble enters the water (i.e., scare a fish, hit another rock, frighten someone near it). By throwing the pebble into the water, you have caused change through the ripple effect.

3. Connect the concrete demonstration to what happens in your head as you think about a story or idea. The pebble can represent a question that you form and toss "out there" into the sea of unknown. A ripple of thoughts (wave of thinking) begins to spread and expand from the point of origin.

4. During a read-aloud, hold some colored pebbles in your hand and when a thought or question occurs in your mind, stop and toss the pebble in the water. Share the question and let the "wave of thinking" ripple into the conversation about the text.

Motivation/Engagement: Use the colored construction paper as a visual tool for students to record their questions and place on the class pond. The pond can be titled based on the text you are reading or the concept you are studying. You can draw ripple waves and record the students' thoughts on each wave.

Question–Answer Relationships (QARs)

Comprehension: Questioning

Purpose: To determine various questioning techniques to aid in comprehension of the text

Level: Transitional

ELL Technique: Yes

Multiple Intelligences: Visual/spatial, verbal/linguistic, interpersonal, intrapersonal

Materials: QARs reproducible (see CD 🔵), text, notebooks

Procedure:

1. Copy and distribute the QARs reproducible. Introduce the four question–answer relationships: Right There, Think and Search, Author and Me, and On My Own.

2. Explain that these four question–answer relationships can be categorized into the two ways the reader derives the answers:

   • **In the Book** (text-based)—Suggested teacher talk for these questions could be, "Can you find the exact words in the book?" This type of question requires students to remember exactly what the author said and to return to the text to find where the author said it.

   "Right There" questions ask readers to respond at the literal level; words from the question and words from the answer will usually be found exactly stated in the text very close to each other. Key Words: who, what, when, where, identify, list, name, define

"Think and Search" questions are inferential ones that require readers to derive the answer from more than one sentence, paragraph, or page. Key Words: compare and contrast, explain, tell why, find evidence, problem and solution, cause and effect

- **In My Head**—These questions are not found in the book; they require readers to utilize their background knowledge and understanding of what they are reading to answer the questions.

  "Author and You" questions are inferential; the words from the book are in the question, but these questions also require input from readers' own prior knowledge to connect with the text and derive an answer. Key Words: in what ways, how is the author using, what might happen based on, what is the author's message

  "On My Own" questions require application from readers' background knowledge and experiences. Key Words: in your opinion, this is what I think, I derived, I feel, I believe it will, I already know that

3. After discussing the four types of questions, ask groups of students to practice answering the different types of questions, which teachers should produce beforehand. Partners or teams could practice generating their own questions for each other to answer.

4. Have students determine the question–answer relationship of each question and record and justify their answers in their notebooks. Suggested teacher talk might be, "Where do you find answers to your questions?"

5. Have students share their responses and then reread the text to verify their accuracy.

Note: Adapted from Raphael (1986), Raphael et al. (2006)

Question Logs: 3Rs

This technique is highlighted in the Creating Strategic Readers DVD/VHS series.

Purpose: To bring meaning to the text by recording, reacting, and reflecting to questions

Level: Transitional

ELL Technique: No

Multiple Intelligences: Visual/spatial, verbal/linguistic, intrapersonal

Materials: Question Logs: 3Rs form (see CD 🔘), text, question logs (binders for recording)

Procedure:

1. Have students create three columns in their question logs and label them to record questions (1R), reactions (2R), and reflections (3R).

2. **Record**: Have students record questions that they think or wonder about before and during reading in the (1R) column.

3. **React**: Have students note their reactions in the (2R) column as they continue to read the text. Suggested teacher talk could be, "What did you wonder about while you were reading this text?"

4. **Reflect**: Have students use the final column to reflect, make connections, or note any other thoughts that help bring meaning to the text. Suggested teacher talk could be, "What questions do you have about the story after reading it?"

Survey, Question, Read, Recite, Review (SQ3R)

Purpose: To establish a purpose for reading by asking questions

Level: Fluent

ELL Technique: No

Multiple Intelligences: Visual/spatial, verbal/linguistic, interpersonal, intrapersonal

Materials: SQ3R reproducible (see CD), text, journals

Procedure:

1. Copy the SQ3R reproducible and distribute to each student. Have students survey the text material by looking at the title, headings, illustrations, graphics, and key terms. Use the questions in the far left column of the SQ3R sheet to guide students through this survey process.

2. **Survey**: Invite students to skim and scan the text traits before reading to survey what they are about to read.

3. **Question**: Ask students to think about how each of these items might relate to the text, and have them ask questions about the text to establish a purpose for reading. Encourage students to turn the title, heading, and pictures into questions. Have students write their questions in the middle column of the SQ3R sheet. Suggested teacher talk might be, "Think about the title. What do you know about this subject? What do you want to know? Turn the title into a question. While you are reading, try to find the answers to your questions."

4. **Read**: Have students read the text to search for answers to their questions and have them discuss the columns of the SQ3R sheet.

5. **Recite**: Have students recite or write answers to the questions, looking away from the text to recall what was read. Students may need to reread the text for any remaining unanswered questions.

6. **Review**: Have students review the information learned by applying it in another context. Examples may be creating a graphic organizer that depicts the main idea, role-playing parts of the text, drawing a flowchart, summarizing, and participating in group discussions. Suggested teacher talk could be, "How were your questions answered? Were some questions answered through making an inference or synthesizing? What examples can you share?"

Motivation/Engagement: Discuss with students some possible answers to the following questions and allow time for students to think about them before responding: What do we know about asking questions? How does asking questions help a reader? How do readers figure out the answers to their questions? Write students' answers on a chart in separate columns. Ask students to write in a reflective journal their thoughts about questioning. Have students share their journal responses during one-to-one conferencing.

Note: Adapted from Martin (1985), Miller (2002), Robinson (1961)

Comprehension Strategy:
Visualizing and Sensory Imaging

Visualizing is a strategy that enables readers to make words on the page of a text real and concrete (Keene & Zimmermann, 2007). This strategy helps readers engage with the text, strengthens their relationship to the text, and stimulates imaginative thinking, which aids in comprehension. The reader visualizes by creating a picture in his or her mind based on descriptive details within the text to assist understanding. Before and after reading, sensory language helps readers form appropriate mental images in their heads about what is happening in the text.

Visualizing provides a springboard for memory recall and retention and makes reading an active process by stimulating the mental interchange of new ideas and experiences. "Visualizing personalizes reading, keeps us engaged, and often prevents us from abandoning a book" (Harvey & Goudvis, 2000, p. 97). Creating sensory images equips readers to draw conclusions, bring to mind details, and create interpretations of the text. Forming these images during reading seems to increase the amount readers understand and recall (Fisher et al., 2009; Irwin, 1991; Johnston, Barnes, & Desrochers, 2008; Sprenger, 2005).

Using drama is another way to explore a story and its content in a visual way. A research study on drama by McMaster (1998) found that vocabularies presented in a drama content provided students with the opportunity to acquire the meanings visually. "Drama for language learning not only provides a whole learning experience but brings language learning to life" (Robbie, Ruggierello, & Warren, 2001, p. 2). Using drama appeals to all the senses and encourages the use of sensory imaging as a strategy for acquiring meaning of text.

Appropriate text that best supports the application of the visualizing strategy needs to have words and phrases that provoke thinking and are full of images for the mind.

Visualizing and Sensory Imaging Text Examples:

Yolen, J. (1991). *Greyling*. New York: Philomel.

Zolotow, C. (1994). *The Seashore Book*. New York: HarperTrophy.

Magazines such as *Weekly Reader* or *Time For Kids*

Teacher Talk: Statements, Questions, and Prompts for Visualizing and Sensory Imaging

Following is a list of suggested teacher talk that encourages readers to think strategically as they employ visualizing skills. Try using some of these statements, questions, and prompts with your students as you work through the techniques in the following section.

- Try to imagine the setting. Describe how it looked in your mind.

- What pictures came to your mind as you read this page?

- As you listen to this story, create a picture in your mind of what you think is happening.

- What sensory details did the author use to help you create a picture of the story in your mind?

- What images did you see in your mind as you read?

- What sounds did you hear as you read?

- What words or phrases did the author use to help you create an image in your mind?

- Did you create a movie in your mind? If so, describe it.

- Try to picture in your mind someone who would remind you of a character in the story.

- In my mind's eye, I imagine _____. How do you think it would look?

- In my head, I can see _____.

- How did you visualize the beginning of the text in your head?

- I imagine _____.

- I can imagine what it is like to _____.

As you implement the various techniques that support this strategy, use the following behaviors as a guide as you assess students' ability to visualize. Do students exhibit these behaviors never, rarely, often, always?

- ☐ Recording mental images of text

- ☐ Creating illustrations to support meaning of a text

- ☐ Using senses to attend to story details

Sketch to Stretch

Purpose: To sketch visual images of text to aid in memory and recall of the story

Level: Emergent

ELL Technique: Yes

Multiple Intelligences: Visual/spatial, verbal/linguistic, logical/mathematical, interpersonal, intrapersonal

Materials: Texts, drawing paper, markers or colored pencils

Procedure:

1. Have students sketch what the text means to them after they finish reading or hearing a story. Suggested teacher talk could be, "What images did you see in your mind as you were sketching?"

2. Arrange students in groups. Select one student at a time to share their sketches and have group members tell their interpretations of the sketch. When everyone in the group has given their version of the sketch, the student who drew the picture describes his or her interpretation of the illustration. Suggested teacher talk could be, "What words or phrases did the author use to help you create an image in your mind?"

3. Continue repeating this process until all members of the group have shared their sketches.

4. Reread the text and have students reflect on the words or phrases that were sketched.

Motivation/Engagement: Have teams add all the sketches together to create a sequential mural of their version of the text and share with class.

Note: Adapted from Short, Harste, & Burke (1996); Whitin (2009)

Wordless Picture Books

Purpose: To create illustrations that support the meaning of a text

Level: Emergent (Adaptation for Early)

ELL Technique: Yes

Multiple Intelligences: Visual/spatial, verbal/linguistic, logical/mathematical, interpersonal

Materials: Text, drawing paper, TV show theme songs or instrumentals, CD player

Procedure:

1. As you read a story with students, discuss how to create mental pictures of it. Suggested teacher talk could be, "What picture comes to mind as I read the text, or as you read the text?"

2. After reading a text, have students create their own pictures of the parts of the text that were not illustrated. Ask students to draw the "missing parts" that they created in their minds and to share their drawings with a small group. Suggested teacher talk could be, "Try to imagine what the setting looks like." Compile students' drawings to create a picture book.

3. Reread the original text, reflecting on the illustrations the students drew to capture the mental images.

Adaptation for Early Readers: Use similes to create mental images by attaching what is known to the unknown. For example, the icicle was as cold as a popsicle. The shape of the Earth looks like a blue and green marble. Also, have students listen to TV show theme songs or instrumentals and imagine the music as the background for a movie. Have students describe what they think the movie could be about based on the music.

Note: Adapted from Harvey & Goudvis (2000)

Frame This

Purpose: To frame images of a story by creating a life-size picture to aid in visualizing details from a story

Level: Emergent

ELL Technique: No

Multiple Intelligence: Visual/spatial, verbal/linguistic, bodily/kinesthetic, interpersonal, intrapersonal

Materials: Text, 11 × 14 picture frame

Procedure:

1. Show a picture in a frame and discuss how the frame holds the picture, but the picture tells or captures the story.

2. Use the outer section of an 11 × 14 frame to create a life-size talking picture frame. Have a volunteer hold the frame in front of his or her face so the "audience" can "see" the picture (the volunteer's face).

3. Have the student volunteer (also known as the "picture frame") begin to talk about the images that he or she recorded in his or her mind during the read-aloud. The volunteer can use facial and voice expressions to convey his or her message.

> Comprehension: Visualizing and Sensory Imaging

Drama

This technique is highlighted on the Creating Strategic Readers DVD/VHS series.

Purpose: To bring story images to life

Level: Early

> Comprehension: Visualizing and Sensory Imaging

ELL Technique: Yes

Multiple Intelligences: Visual/spatial, verbal/linguistic, logical/mathematical, bodily/kinesthetic, interpersonal

Materials: Text, props

Procedure:

1. Have students read a text with no pictures and then ask them to use appropriate props to act out images that were in their minds as they read the selection. Suggested teacher talk might be, "Did you create a movie in your mind? If so, describe it."

2. Ask several students to read the same unillustrated text. Suggested teacher talk could be, "How did you visualize the beginning of the text?"

3. Have students come to the front of the room, perform, and try to create the images in the minds of the other students (the audience) who did not read the text.

4. Ask the audience to discuss what they saw and to predict what they think the text would be about based on the dramas performed.

Motivation/Engagement: Play charades (see visual imaging strategy in Chapter 5). Without using words, students act out scenes from the story while the audience tries to guess the events.

Sensory Impressions

Comprehension: Visualizing and Sensory Imaging

This technique is highlighted on the Creating Strategic Readers DVD/VHS series.

Purpose: To utilize senses to attend to story details

Level: Early (Adaptation for Emergent)

ELL Technique: Yes

Multiple Intelligences: Visual/spatial, verbal/linguistic, bodily/kinesthetic, interpersonal, naturalist/environmentalist

Materials: Sensory Impressions reproducibles (see CD 💿), text; Optional: Sensory items

Procedure:

1. Create scenarios for students to attend to the use of their senses. For example, ask students to close their eyes and think of the school cafeteria. Ask them to describe to a partner what they see, smell, touch, taste, and hear. The class could also go on a nature walk to utilize the senses to attend to the detail of their surroundings. Students may use the hand reproducible to record one sensory item for each finger. Transfer this sensory thinking to the text.

2. Have students read a text selection that is rich in sensory details. Suggested teacher talk could be, "What sensory details did the author use to help you create a picture of the story in your mind?"

3. Copy the second reproducible and distribute to each student. Ask students to stop throughout their reading to write or draw their responses under the appropriate sense. Suggested teacher talk might be, "What sounds did you hear in your mind as you read? Record it under the picture of the ear."

4. Ask students to work in groups to compare their answers and discuss any differences in their responses.

Adaptation for Emergent Readers: Distribute a variety of sensory items (e.g., glasses, gloves, clown nose, headphones, spoon) to all students or select five. As students listen to a read-aloud, they will reflect upon their particular sense and record appropriate sensory responses that pertain to the text being read. Have students retell the story through the appropriate sense (e.g., I could smell the cookies baking.).

Comprehension Strategy: Inferring and Drawing Conclusions

Inferring is a strategy that permits readers to merge their background knowledge with text clues to come to a conclusion about an underlying theme or idea. Drawing conclusions helps readers gather more information and ideas and understand the writer's point of view. Readers gather and question details from the text and reach a decision that makes sense. They arrive at a decision or opinion by reasoning from known facts or evidence that seem to require that a specific conclusion be reached. This cognitive model builds "text-based representation through processes critical for semantic coherence such as pronominal reference and inferences that connects parts of text" (Johnston et al., 2008, p. 125). Such readers use implicit information to make a logical guess or read between the lines.

Strategic readers create unique understandings of the text, make predictions and inferences, and confirm or deny those predictions based on textual information. These readers test their developing comprehension of the text along with extending their comprehension beyond literal understandings of the printed page (Keene & Zimmermann, 2007). "Inferencing is the bedrock of comprehension...it is about reading faces, reading body language, reading expressions, and reading tone, as well as reading text" (Harvey & Goudvis, 2000, p. 105).

Appropriate text that best supports the application of the inferring and drawing conclusions strategy needs to have pictures or language that help to elicit inferences.

Inferring and Drawing Conclusion Text Examples:

Bunting, E. (1988). *How Many Days to America? A Thanksgiving Story*. New York: Clarion.

Cannon, J. (1993). *Stellaluna*. New York: Scholastic.

Poetry such as sonnets, ballads, limericks

Teacher Talk: Statements, Questions, and Prompts for Inferring and Drawing Conclusions

Following is a list of suggested teacher talk that encourages readers to think strategically as they employ inferring skills. Try using some of these statements, questions, and prompts with your students as you work through the techniques in the following section.

- I wonder...

- What evidence does the author provide to support _____?

- What does the author want you to realize?

- What facts can you derive based on the following clues?

- What clues did the author give that led to your conclusion?

- What is the main conclusion from _____?

- What details or evidence support your conclusion?

- What reasoning helped you draw your conclusion?

- What is the story beneath the story?

- What would happen if _____?

- Why do you think that would happen?

- Try to read between the lines.

- How do you think the character feels?

- This statement means _____.

- How do you combine the clues in the paragraph with what you already know to draw a conclusion?

As you implement the various techniques that support this strategy, use the following behaviors as a guide as you assess students' ability to infer and draw conclusions. Do students exhibit these behaviors never, rarely, often, always?

- ☐ Merging background knowledge with text clues

- ☐ Constructing interpretations by reading between the lines

- ☐ Making judgments after considering all information presented in text

Interpreting Text

Purpose: To read between the lines to construct meaning

Level: Early

ELL Technique: No

Multiple Intelligences: Visual/spatial, verbal/linguistic, interpersonal, intrapersonal

Materials: Texts, copies of text excerpt, overhead projector, transparency of text excerpt, newspaper pictures or illustrations from text, greeting cards, paper and art supplies

Procedure:

1. Enlarge a section of a text that supports inferring and display it with an overhead projector, or make and distribute copies so that all students can see the text and follow along.

2. Read aloud the passage, pausing at key sections to ask, "So what's really going on?"

3. Discuss with students what you and they think is really going on. If desired, you can have students read a section silently and then stop to talk in pairs about how every part of the text takes on a deeper layer when readers make their own interpretations. Suggested teacher talk could be, "Why do you think that would happen? What is the story beneath the story?"

Motivation/Engagement: Display a newspaper picture and ask the students to view it and determine what they would create as the heading for the article. Have them think of ways to write the heading to correspond with the picture, without giving the reader all the information literally. Have partners read each heading and determine what they think will be the rest of the story. Their goal is to capture a reader to infer the meaning of the picture based on the heading and entice them to read the rest of the article. They can also use greeting cards with symbolic language and discuss the real meaning of the card. Have students create their own greeting cards using metaphors and similes and various poetic structures.

Note: Adapted from Calkins (2001)

Save the Last Word for Me

Purpose: To construct interpretations and compare with others

Level: Transitional

ELL Technique: Yes

Multiple Intelligences: Visual/spatial, verbal/linguistic, interpersonal

Materials: Texts, paper or note cards

Procedure:

1. Have students read independently and select a passage, phrase, word, or sentences within the text that "stands out" or catches their attention.

2. Ask the students to write what the text said (word, phrases, or sentences) that caught their attention on the front side of a piece of paper or note card. These can be interesting points worthy of discussion. Suggested teacher talk could be, "Try to read between the lines."

3. Have the students explain why they selected the passage, phrase, sentence, or words on the back of the paper or card.

4. Place students into small groups for discussion and have them prioritize their cards in order (e.g., from most to least importance or according to interests) with regard to the student's desire to discuss what was written on the cards.

5. Each student reads aloud the front of the card to their group and gets feedback on how the other students react to what was written, what the quote means, and if they agree or disagree with it. Suggested talk could be, "I think this statement means...."

6. The student who reads the card can then turn the card over and read to the group why they chose this particular quote. This gives the student who reads the card the "last word" to either alter or stand by what was written as a reflection to the phrase.

Note: Adapted from Short et al. (1996)

Talk Show

Comprehension: Inferring and Drawing Conclusions

Purpose: To reflect on and discuss the content of a book

Level: Transitional

ELL Technique: Yes

Multiple Intelligences: Visual/spatial, verbal/linguistic, interpersonal, intrapersonal

Materials: Text, microphone, T-chart, journals

Procedure:

1. Choose a group of three students to pretend that they are on a talk show: One student should host the show, one should pretend to be the author of a book the students have read, and one should pretend to be the reader of the book. Give the students a microphone to hold when they speak.

2. Have the host open the show by giving an introduction about the book they will be discussing on the show. Have students begin with their discussion of the book. The author should make statements that imply information, and the reader should make inferences from those statements. For example, if the author states, "The main character discovered real joy," then readers might infer that the main character was unhappy or upset about

something but an event occurs that results in his or her happiness. Suggested teacher talk could be directed to the reader from the host: "What evidence does the author provide? What does the author want you to realize?"

3. Have the host begin to summarize the discussion with statements like, "So, what I hear you saying is _____."

4. Make notes during the talk show on a T-chart (i.e., a chart with a large T separating the author's statements from the readers' inferences) to discuss later with the "audience" (i.e., the other students in the classroom).

5. Reread the text and have students reflect on the show and on how it supported their comprehension of the text.

Motivation/Engagement: Have students record in reflection journals their interpretation of the interview by reflecting on and thinking about what was said and not said (i.e., body language, tone of voice).

Scenarios With T-Charts

Purpose: To make inferences about a scenario based on evidence

Level: Fluent

ELL Technique: No

Multiple Intelligences: Visual/spatial, verbal/linguistic, interpersonal, intrapersonal

Materials: Text, paper

Procedure:

1. Use scenarios from the text from which students can practice inferring. Have students listen to these scenarios or read them to each other and decide what inferences they can draw based on the evidence in the scenarios.

2. Have partners take turns stating their inferences and then noting what evidence from the scenario helped to lead them to their inferences about the section of the text. Suggested teacher talk could be, "What clues did the author give that led to your conclusion?"

3. Have the pairs create T-charts on paper. Students should write their inferences on the left side and write the evidence, or the "why" behind their thinking, on the right side of the chart. Suggested teacher talk might be, "What reasoning helped you draw your conclusion?"

4. Reread the text, having students note any changes directly on the T-chart as they listen to you read. Suggested teacher talk could be, "How did inferring support you in comprehending the text?"

Motivation/Engagement: Create a courtroom scenario. Have students listen to the evidence presented. In the deliberation room, have students use multiple strategies (i.e., what they visualized, connections made, questions answered) and then discuss their judgment from their point of view. Have them use their ability to gather the details and draw a conclusion. Ask them to record their conclusion and read their verdict.

Comprehension Strategy: Summarizing

Summarizing is a strategy that helps the reader identify and organize the essential information found within a text. Strategic readers summarize during reading by putting together information and focusing on the key elements of what they are reading. These key elements are brief and related to important ideas, events, details, structural clues, or other information that supports the reader in bringing meaning to the text. Students continually organize these key elements throughout their reading of a text while filtering out less significant details. Research by Pearson and Duke (2002) suggests instruction on summarizing to improve students' overall comprehension of text content.

To make generalizations about a story rather than simply retell the specifics, strategic readers select important information after reading and bring together these ideas in their own words. Retelling allows students to recall story structure and gives them guidance as they discuss the setting, theme, plot episodes, resolution of conflicts, and sequence of events (Hoyt, 2008). A summary is an objective retelling; it does not make obvious judgments. Summarizing is a succinct reduction of passages into a simple compilation of facts. "Text guides" are used as resources to support the ability to deconstruct, as it requires the reader to break down the main ideas that comprise the text to form a summary (Montelongo, 2008).

Appropriate text that best supports the application of the summarizing strategy needs to have identifiable story elements (characters, setting, events, problem, solution).

Summarizing Text Examples:

Brooke, L. (2000–2008). Heartland series. New York: Scholastic. (20 chapter books)

Konigsburg, E.L. (1997). *The View From Saturday*. New York: Scholastic.

Naylor, P.R. (1992). *Shiloh*. New York: Bantam Doubleday Dell.

Teacher Talk: Statements, Questions, and Prompts for Summarizing

Following is a list of suggested teacher talk that encourages readers to think strategically as they employ summarizing skills. Try using some of these statements, questions, and prompts with your students as you work through the techniques in the following section.

- How can you describe the overall understanding of the story in a few sentences? Complete the statement, The text is mainly about…

- What words from a story jump out at you to help make an artistic representation?

- What was the focus of the reading selection?

- Think of all the parts in the story and put them together as if you were going to tell another person about the story. How could you say this using only a few sentences: in brief…, in conclusion…, to sum it up…?

- What clues are within the text features?

- What does the author say?

- Which details are most and least significant?

- How can you use key ideas to condense the information in this story?

- Which words helped you describe the gist of the story?

- What do you think is the main idea of this story? Of this paragraph?

- What clues are within the text?

- What visual clues can you identify?

As you implement the various techniques that support this strategy, use the following behaviors as a guide as you assess students' ability to summarize. Do students exhibit these behaviors never, rarely, often, always?

☐ Reconstructing the text through a retell

☐ Identifying and organizing essential information

☐ Examining and filtering less significant details

Techniques for Summarizing

Detail/Retell

Purpose: To recount story details in a sequential order and develop story grammar

Level: Emergent–Fluent

ELL Technique: Yes

Multiple Intelligences: Visual/spatial, verbal/linguistic, logical/mathematical, bodily/kinesthetic, intrapersonal

Materials: Detail/Retell Rubric (see CD 🔘), text, one of the following: story props, gardening glove, baseball base mats, three hula hoops

Procedure:

1. Discuss and practice with students ways they retell daily. With partners, have the students tell what they did either over the weekend, last night, on vacation, and so forth. Discuss how they may have used words like first, next, and then while they were retelling the events to their partners.

Comprehension: Summarizing

2. Demonstrate retelling after you read a short text. Suggested teacher talk might be, " I am going to retell the story to you as if you never heard it before." Remind them just like they told their partners about their weekend or vacation, when you retell a story, you are providing the details of the story to create a mental image to the other person of all the story details.

3. To guide students with visual props use one of the following to increase their detail retells.

   • Story glove—Write on a garden glove with a permanent marker thumb the terms characters (thumb), setting (pointer finger), problem (middle finger), events (ring finger) and ending (pinky finger). Use the glove as a visual reminder of the narrative story elements for a retell. Students can trace their hand and create a retell to share by drawing or writing the story elements on the their fingers.

   • Baseball mats—Create or purchase a first base, second base, and third base and have the students stand on each base and give their detail retell what happened first in the story, then what happened next in the story, and finally share how the story ended while standing on third base. You can use the home plate for students to share the information from the detail retell to "bring the retell home" by selecting key pieces of information and creating a concise summary statement.

   • Hula hoops—Place at least three different-colored hula hoops on the floor before a read aloud. As you are reading, stand inside a hula hoop and move to the next hoop when there is a transition in the text. When you have finished the section, step out of the hula hoops and ask the students what was happening when you were in the first red hoop, next in the green hoop, etc. This allows students with a more spatial awareness to follow the sequence of the story and supports their Detail/Retell.

   • Table of contents—Have the students use the table of contents as a review and an opportunity to guide them through a retell. Students read aloud the table of contents stopping on each entry and giving the details that were within that chapter.

Motivation/Engagement: Use the Detail/Retell Retelling Rubric as a guide for students to reflect on their ability to retell and as an evaluation tool of the student's comprehension of the text.

Journaling or Group Chart

Purpose: To identify and record summaries for discussion

Level: Early

ELL Technique: Yes

Multiple Intelligences: Visual/spatial, verbal/linguistic, logical/mathematical, interpersonal

Materials: Story Mapping reproducible (see CD 💿), text, chart paper or journals

Procedure:

As a story is being read (individually or as a read-aloud), have students stop to discuss and record important issues, themes, and ideas. Have students keep journals to use for this purpose or take notes from group discussions on chart paper. Suggested teacher talk could be, "What was the focus of the reading selection? Which details are most and least significant?"

Motivation/Engagement: Copy the Story Map reproducible and distribute to each student. Ask students to complete the map while the story is being read and identify the characters (who they are and what the author tells about them), the setting (where and when the story takes place), the problems and events (what problems the characters is facing, whether those problems are changing throughout the story), and the solution (the conclusion, or how things work out).

Summary Ball

This technique is highlighted on the Creating Strategic Readers DVD/VHS series.

Purpose: To create a group summary

Level: Early

ELL Technique: Yes

Multiple Intelligences: Visual/spatial, verbal/linguistic, interpersonal

Materials: Text, beach ball, chart paper, permanent marker

Procedure:

1. After reading a narrative, write the questions Who, What, Where, When, Why, and How on an inflated beach ball using a permanent marker.

2. Have students toss around the ball in a small group. Ask each student who catches the ball to look to see which word is closest to his or her right thumb and to answer that question with regard to the text just read.

3. If more than one student gets the same question, the first student can answer the question, and subsequent students can elaborate on what the first student said about that topic. Suggested teacher talk could be, "How could you say this using only a few sentences?"

4. Record the students' responses in a list on chart paper to provide a group story summary.

5. Have students reread the text and reflect on the summary created. Suggested teacher talk might be, "How did creating a group summary support your understanding of the story we read?"

Note: Adapted from Cunningham & Allington (2007)

Narrative Pyramid

Purpose: To organize events in a story

Level: Transitional

ELL Technique: No

Multiple Intelligences: Visual/spatial, verbal/linguistic, interpersonal

Materials: Narrative Pyramid reproducible (see CD ⊙), text

Procedure:

1. Choose a story the students have read and tell the students they will be constructing an eight-line narrative pyramid of words. Suggested teacher talk could be, "Think of all the parts in the story and put them together as if you were telling another person the story."

2. Have the students construct their pyramids as follows:

    - The top line should include the character's name in a single word.

    - Have students choose two words to describe that character for the second line.

    - Have students use three words to portray the setting on the third line.

    - Ask students to explain the problem using four descriptive words or four conflicts within the story on the fourth line.

    - Lines five, six, and seven should present three different events that occurred, each line using five, six, and seven words, respectively.

    - Have students select eight words to express the solution(s) to the problem for the eighth line.

3. Have students use their pyramids as a reference to summarize the text. Suggested teacher talk might be, "Using your pyramid, what was the text about?"

Motivation/Engagement: Use the Narrative Pyramid reproducible for the students to reflect on story details and record during a class read-aloud. Have them justify their sections with a partner.

Note: Adapted from Waldo (1991)

Somebody/Wanted/But/So

This technique is highlighted on the Creating Strategic Readers DVD/VHS series.

Purpose: To organize key information in a story and construct a graphic organizer to outline the story elements

Level: Transitional (Adaptation for Early)

ELL Technique: Yes

Multiple Intelligences: Visual/spatial, verbal/linguistic, interpersonal

Materials: Text, paper; For Adaptation: Hula hoops

Procedure:

1. Have students fold a sheet of paper into fourths and write the following headings on the four sections: Somebody, Wanted, But, and So.

2. Using a story that the students have read, have students complete their individual charts by writing a statement under each section: Somebody (identify the character), Wanted (describe the character's goal or motivation), But (describe a conflict that impedes the character), and So (describe the resolution of the conflict). Suggested teacher talk could be, "How can you use key ideas to condense the information in this story?"

Adaptation for Early Readers: Place four hula hoops on the classroom floor and tell students that each hoop represents one of the four headings (Somebody, Wanted, But, So). Have students stand inside the hoops after reading a story and summarize each corresponding aspect as they walk through the hoops. Suggested teacher talk might be, "Which details are the most and least significant?"

Note: Adapted from Schmidt & Buckley (1990)

Comprehension Strategy: Determining Importance

Determining importance is a strategy that requires the reader to distinguish between what is important and what is merely interesting. "When great readers are reading this stuff that has so many ideas in it, they have to listen to that mental voice tell them which words, which sentences or paragraphs, and which ideas are important" (Keene & Zimmermann, 1997, p. 86).

Readers are required to identify the topic and supporting details and to identify or invent their own main idea or summary statement by combining ideas across sentences. Reading requires the memory to hold and process a massive amount of information. "Readers cannot store all the information presented in a text in their minds. Sifting through information to determine the most important points ensures that working memory is not overloaded and continues to process information" (Fisher et al., 2009, p. 51). Sometimes, however, the reader needs to understand and remember more information than can be summed up in a brief statement. Finding the essence of the text is the key to determining what is important. The reader needs to make decisions as to what parts of a text deserve the most attention, remembering that not all the information presented is of equal value. Determining importance is critical when reading texts that emphasize learning of information, as in nonfiction. "When kids read and understand nonfiction, they build background for the topic and acquire new knowledge. The ability to identify essential ideas and salient information is a prerequisite to developing insight" (Harvey & Goudvis, 2000, p.

119). Strategic readers are able to look for text features that signal cues and for ideas that help to distinguish the important from the unimportant within the text and between fiction and nonfiction text.

Appropriate text that best supports the application of the determining importance strategy needs to have strong essential information made evident through text features, ideas, and themes.

Determining Importance Text Examples:

Donnelly, J. (1988). *The Titantic: Lost—And Found.* New York: Random House.

Eaton, D., & Lee, J. (1996). *The Three Silly Cowboys.* Parsippany, NJ: Pearson.

Rylant, C. (1996). *Henry and Mudge.* New York: Simon & Schuster.

Teacher Talk: Statements, Questions, and Prompts for Determining Importance

Following is a list of suggested teacher talk that encourages readers to think strategically as they determine importance. Try using some of these statements, questions, and prompts with your students as you work through the techniques in the following section.

- What is essential?
- How did you know these details were more important than other details?
- What does the author offer as a theme or opinion?
- What is the author's message?
- Look carefully at the first and last line of each paragraph.
- Tell me about some of the important ideas that struck you.
- Which facts are important or essential to the text?
- Notice that the cue words are followed by important information.
- Use the margin to make notes.
- Highlight only necessary words and phrases.
- Show in the text what you read that was the most important idea.

As you implement the various techniques that support this strategy, use the following behaviors as a guide as you assess students' ability to determine importance. Do students exhibit these behaviors never, rarely, often, always?

☐ Previewing text and identifying key features

☐ Determining essential information and main ideas

☐ Identifying story elements and organizing and reflecting on supporting details

Picture This

Purpose: To examine a photograph for details and determine the main purpose of the photo

Level: Emergent

ELL Technique: Yes

Multiple Intelligences: Visual/spatial, verbal/linguistic, logical/mathematical, interpersonal, intrapersonal

Materials: Photographs, newspaper/magazine pictures, plastic sleeve or picture frame, items from family events such as photos or postcards

Procedure:

1. Gather several photographs and share with the class. Place pictures in a plastic sleeve, glass picture frame, or laminate. Circulate the photos and ask the students to describe what they think is happening in the picture(s). Suggested teacher talk could be, "Looking at the photograph, what might you state is the main reason this picture was taken? Why?"

2. Have students generate and share a headline they think would best support the picture if it were in a newspaper or magazine.

3. Record their generated words and details directly on the picture (e.g., use a dry-erase marker on the plastic film or lamination, or use permanent marker on the glass which can be cleaned with rubbing alcohol).

4. Come to a consensus on the main purpose of the picture(s) and then read and compare the headline or caption that actually supports the picture from the newspaper or magazine article with the students' ideas.

Motivation/Engagement: Place several pictures at each table group. Ask students to discuss the pictures and place pictures in a story format. Students use the pictures to capture the main concept and share what they interpret, based on the pictures, the title of the story could be and which picture they think represents the main idea of the "picture this" story line. Have students bring in pictures, postcards, or other items to document family vacations, events, and so forth. Have the students generate a single statement that summarizes their trip, activity, or experience based on the pictures.

Chapter Tours

Purpose: To preview text and identify key nonfiction features

Level: Early

Comprehension:
Determining
Importance

ELL Technique: Yes

Multiple Intelligences: Visual/spatial, verbal/linguistic, interpersonal, intrapersonal, naturalist/environmentalist

Materials: Text, a hat marked "Tour Guide"

Procedure:

1. Have students take a "tour": nature tour, school tour, or virtual tour on the web. Have them listen to the tour guide for keywords that help them connect and relate to the tour.

2. Ask students to transfer the tour concept to a nonfiction text they will be reading. Ask them to preview the text and identify features such as photographs, labels, and keywords that will help them determine what is important. Suggested teacher talk could be, "Look carefully at the first and last line of each paragraph."

2. Have students take turns putting on the tour guide hat and leading a small group through a tour of the text students will be reading. Encourage students to make comments like a real tour guide. Suggested teacher talk could be, "Tell me about some of the important ideas that struck you."

3. Read the text and have students reflect on how the tour guide activity supported their comprehension.

Motivation/Engagement: Have students create a "story/concept" travel brochure using the tour guide words. Students can become a tour guide by applying words identified in their brochure as guided imagery. The following is a sample of tour guide talk:

As we look over to the left, you will notice…

Focus your attention on…

Coming up now is one of the highlights of…

Today you will see…

Note: Adapted from Wood, Lapp, & Flood (1992)

Main Idea Wheel

This technique is highlighted on the Creating Strategic Readers DVD/VHS series.

Purpose: To identify what is essential within the text

Level: Transitional (Adaptation for Early)

ELL Technique: Yes

Multiple Intelligences: Visual/spatial, verbal/linguistic, bodily/kinesthetic, interpersonal

Materials: Main Idea Wheel: Intermediate Grades (see CD), text; For Adaptation: Main Idea Wheel: Primary Grades (see CD), items for creating spinning wheel such as pencil, brad, or paperclip

Procedure:

1. Copy the Main Idea Wheel and distribute to each student. Have students identify and record the important concept from a text in the center part of the wheel. Suggested teacher talk could be, "What is essential?"

2. Have students record important details that support the main concept on the spokes of the wheel. Suggested teacher talk might be, "How did you know it was important?"

3. Have students share their wheels with the class and lead a discussion about what various students placed on their spokes as being important.

4. Reread the text and have students reflect on the ideas and statements they wrote on their spokes and on how these ideas supported their process of making meaning from the text.

Adaptation for Early Readers: Students can complete the same activity using the Main Ideal Wheel for primary grades. Then, have students cut out their wheels and create spinners of the wheel by attaching them to an item like a pencil using a brad or paperclip. Students spin their wheels and share the section it lands on with a partner. Students' discussions should focus on why they feel it was an essential part of the story/concept.

Note: Adapted from Irwin & Baker (1989)

Highlighting

Purpose: To identify essential information

Level: Transitional (Adaptation for Fluent)

ELL Technique: Yes

Multiple Intelligences: Visual/spatial, verbal/linguistic, logical/mathematical, interpersonal

Materials: Texts, overhead transparencies, highlighters or transparency pens, plain and colored sticky notes

Comprehension:
Determining
Importance

Procedure:

1. Make a transparency of a section from the text and have the students work in groups to determine and highlight on the overhead transparency or directly on the text, essential information. Suggested teacher talk: "Highlight only necessary words and phrases."

2. Ask students to share their markings and the purposes for them.

3. Read the text and have students reflect on how highlighting important information guided them to a clearer understanding of the author's purpose for the text.

Adaptation for Fluent Readers: Have students use sticky notes to mark sections in their text that helps them to determine what information is important. On the sticky note, have them record why they selected that particular section of the text. Students may use color sticky notes to categorize their facts. Have students highlight relationships between facts on sticky notes.

Note: Adapted from Santa, Havens, & Maycumber (1996)

Comprehension Strategy: Synthesizing

Synthesizing is the merging of new information with prior background knowledge to create an original idea. Strategic readers stop periodically while reading to digest what they have read and what it means before continuing. This process personalizes reading by allowing readers to form opinions and "[combine] separate pieces of knowledge to come up with knowledge that is new, at least new to the person doing the thinking" (Irwin, 1991, p. 102). This process allows readers to make judgments that promote higher-order "elaborative" thinking. The teacher who abandons the "one right answer" approach will elicit these divergent responses (Irwin, 1991).

Synthesizing usually occurs in conjunction with analysis. Readers sift through a plethora of information, pulling out key ideas and putting these ideas together to have an overall sense of what they are reading. This process draws together the results of developing thoughts into a conclusion to interpret or evaluate, and adding information to the summary (Fisher et al., 2009). The synthesizing strategy "combines elements into a pattern not clearly there before" (Tate, 2003, p. 6). The ability to synthesize when reading requires that readers integrate all of the comprehension strategies described previously in this chapter—which itself, actually, is synthesizing.

Appropriate text (whether fiction or nonfiction) and resources that best supports the application of the synthesizing strategy needs to have strong text elements and patterns.

Synthesizing Text Examples:

Cartoons and caricatures (for example, use editorials in newspapers, magazines, and student creations)

Lionni, L. (1976). *A Color of His Own*. New York: Knopf.

Penn, A. (1993). *The Kissing Hand*. Washington, DC: Child Welfare League of America.

Teacher Talk: Statements, Questions, and Prompts for Synthesizing

Following is a list of suggested teacher talk that encourages readers to think strategically as they employ synthesizing skills. Try using some of these statements, questions, and prompts with your students as you work through the techniques in the following section.

- What new ideas or information do you have?
- What parts of this text can you use to create a new idea?
- What is the gist of the story?
- How could you test your theory?
- Try to propose an alternative to the situation.
- How has your thinking changed since reading that part of the text?
- How else could you _____?

- Try to verbalize what is happening within the text.

- What did you think about first? Now what are you thinking?

- How would you re-create _____?

- What do you understand now that you did not understand before?

- I didn't understand it when the author said _____, but now I understand _____.

- Try to write down what you are thinking and continue to think as you add new thoughts to your previous ones.

As you implement the various techniques that support this strategy, use the following behaviors as a guide as you assess students' ability to synthesize. Do students exhibit these behaviors never, rarely, often, always?

☐ Interpreting understanding of text through drama and artwork

☐ Combining information and forming new thoughts

☐ Monitoring and evaluating text for meaning

Techniques for Synthesizing

Creating a Play

Purpose: To interpret students' understandings of text through drama or music

Level: Early

ELL Technique: Yes

Multiple Intelligences: Visual/spatial, verbal/linguistic, musical/rhythmic, bodily/kinesthetic, interpersonal

Materials: Text, props that correspond with text, variety of song title selections

Procedure:

1. Read a story and tell students they will be acting it out. Suggested teacher talk could be, "Think about how would you bring the text to life."

2. Give students time to discuss, plan, and practice their interpretations of the text in small groups. Students can use whatever props they need to re-create the story that they read.

3. Have students discuss how their understanding of the text has changed after students perform their interpretations for the class, if it has changed at all. Suggested teacher talk could be, "I did not understand it when the author said _____, but now I understand that _____."

Motivation/Engagement: Have students select song titles that correspond to the story and then justify why they selected the titles.

Mind Mapping

Purpose: To make connections to words or concepts from a text with artwork

Level: Transitional

ELL Technique: No

Multiple Intelligences: Visual/spatial, verbal/linguistic, intrapersonal

Materials: Text, paper, markers or crayons

Procedure:

1. Read a text, and have students create a map of it. Have them start by writing a central word or concept (or drawing a picture) in the center of a sheet of paper. Suggested teacher talk could be, "What words helped to identify the main idea?"

2. Have students draw or write five to seven main ideas that relate to that central word or drawing; these ideas should radiate out from the center. (Students may find it useful to turn their paper on the side in a landscape format for mapping.) By personalizing the map with their own symbols and designs, students will construct visual and meaningful relationships between their ideas and the text.

3. Reread the text, and have students reflect on their maps to better comprehend the text. Suggested teacher talk might be, "How has your thinking changed after drawing the map?"

Note: Adapted from Buzan (1993)

Rewriting a Story

Purpose: To organize and compose thoughts from a specific point of view

Level: Transitional

ELL Technique: No

Multiple Intelligences: Visual/spatial, verbal/linguistic, musical/rhythmic, interpersonal, intrapersonal

Materials: Text

Procedure:

1. After reading a text, have students rewrite a passage from the story in first person from any character's point of view. Suggested teacher talk could be, "What new ideas or information do you have after looking at the text from a different perspective?"

2. Invite students to share with a group any new perspectives they have gained about the character from their rewriting activity. Suggested teacher talk could be, "What made you think that way?"

Motivation/Engagement: Have students use the passage they just edited and revise it into a musical by turning the speaking parts into singing parts. Then, have students perform their musicals.

Say Something

Comprehension: Synthesizing

Purpose: To monitor thinking about text while reading

Level: Transitional

ELL Technique: Yes

Multiple Intelligences: Visual/spatial, verbal/linguistic, interpersonal, intrapersonal

Materials: Text

Procedure:

1. Put students in pairs and assign each pair a text to read (both partners read the same text).

2. Instruct students to determine in advance the intervals at which they will stop in their reading (e.g., after a paragraph, a half page, a whole page) to say something about the text. (The more unfamiliar or complex the text, the smaller the amounts of reading that will need to be done at a time.) Suggested teacher talk could be, "Try to verbalize what is happening in the text."

3. Have the partners read to the designated place in the text and stop to take turns making one statement about what they have just read. Students can state their reflections, a question, a fact, a connection, an inference, and so forth.

4. Have students continue reading the texts, stopping at designated intervals to make statements to each other.

Note: Adapted from Harste, Short, & Burke (1989)

Synthesizing Target

Comprehension: Synthesizing

Purpose: To combine information and form new thoughts

Level: Fluent

ELL Technique: Yes

Multiple Intelligences: Visual/spatial, verbal/linguistic, interpersonal, intrapersonal

Materials: Synthesizing Target reproducible (see CD 💿), texts

Procedure:

1. Copy and distribute target forms. Have students use the form to record their thoughts as they are reading a text. Each ring of the circle represents a new thought, which builds

from their previous ideas. Suggested teacher talk might be, "Try to write down what you are thinking and continue to keep thinking about that thought as you add new thoughts."

2. Students share their forms with a partner to discuss their thought process as they were reading. Suggested teacher talk could be, "What did you think about first? Now what are you thinking?"

3. Reread the text and have students reflect, from the outside in, on their synthesizing targets.

4. Have students share their final thoughts and how the concept on the target supported their understanding of the text.

Comprehension Wrap-Up

Comprehension is a key component of effective reading instruction. Effective comprehension instruction actively engages students in text and motivates them to use strategies and techniques. The NRP report indicates that "a variety of reading comprehension strategies leads to increased learning of strategies to specific transfer of learning, to increased memory and understanding of new passages" (NICHD, 2000, p. 4-52). Such effective comprehension requires explicit and purposeful teaching. "Instruction in comprehension strategies is carried out by a classroom teacher who demonstrates, models, or guides the reader on their acquisition and use. When these procedures have been acquired, the reader becomes independent of the teacher" (NICHD, 2000, p. 4-40).

The strategies, techniques, and teacher talk presented in this chapter and throughout the book support teachers in maximizing their readers' potential of becoming strategic readers.

Assessment Matrix

Assessment	Appropriate Grade Range	Assessment Measures*	Reading Component†	Overview
Assessment Test (Adams et al., 1997, pp. 108–131)	K–2	S, D	PA	Subcomponents include detecting rhymes, counting syllables, matching initial sounds, and counting phonemes.
Broad Assessment System	PreK–12 Online monitoring available Web-based application	S, D, P	PA, P, F, V, C	Features *The Broad Screen* (phonemes, letter-naming sounds, and word reading), *The Broad Diagnostic Inventory* (spelling, vocabulary, and listening and reading comprehension), *The Targeted Diagnostic Inventory (TDI)* (print awareness, blending and deleting phonemes, letter names, letter–sound knowledge and connections, word building, and multisyllable words), and *Progress Monitoring Tasks* (incorporates the TDI tasks).
Developmental Reading Assessment Word Analysis (DRA)	K–5 Online monitoring available Handheld devices available	D, P	PA, P	Includes the following five strands: (1) phonological awareness, (2) metalanguage, (3) letter/high-frequency word recognition, (4) phonics, and (5) structured analysis and syllabication. Helps to determine students' level of control of various word analysis tasks, document students' progress over time, group students according to their instructional needs, and plan effectively for instruction.
Developmental Reading Assessment 2nd Edition (DRA2)	K–3 Online monitoring available	S, D, P	PA, P, F, C	Includes DRA Word Analysis Assessment and has added a WPM fluency rate component. It includes several new and revised Benchmark Books, a simplified *Focus for Instruction,* and *Continuums* to match each assessment text incorporated in the Teacher Observation Guides, which include prediction, retelling and summarizing, interpreting, and reflecting.
Developmental Reading Assessment 2nd Edition (DRA2)	4–8 Online monitoring available and digital pens	S, D, P	F, C	Incorporates the DRA Bridge Pack to seamlessly allow accurate assessment of students reading below fourth-grade level. In addition, the new second edition has added soft covers and more durable binding to the Benchmark Books. Assesses student achievement in engagement, oral reading fluency, and written comprehension.
Diagnostic Assessment of Reading (DAR)	K–adult Online monitoring available	D	PA, P, F, V, C	Assesses print awareness, phonological awareness, letters and sounds, word recognition, word analysis, oral reading accuracy and fluency, silent reading comprehension, spelling, and word meaning.
Dictation Test	1	S, P	PA, P	Assesses sounds represented in print, recognition of sounds within print, and the connection between symbols and clusters of symbols with sounds they represent. The tester reads a sentence, and the student writes down the words in the sentence. The tester writes the words when the student is finished. Scores are given for each phoneme used.
Dynamic Indicators of Basic Early Literacy Skills (DIBELS)	K–6 Online monitoring available	S, P	PA, P, F	Includes identifying letter names, segmenting phonemes, fluency with nonsense words, and fluency with oral reading.
Early Reading Diagnostic Assessment (ERDA)	K–3 Online monitoring available	S, D	PA, P, F, V, C	Assesses letter recognition, pseudoword decoding, rapid automatized naming (RAN), and passage fluency composite, pictorial vocabulary task, oral vocabulary task, and comprehension.
Elementary Spelling Inventory	K–5	S, D	P	Assesses spelling stages of emergent, letter-name, alphabet, within word pattern, syllables and affixes, and derivational relations. The tester says a word, and the student writes down all the sounds he or she hears. The tester scores and analyzes student spelling qualitatively using a feature analysis.

Test	Grade	Type	Components	Description
Fox In A Box	K–2	S, D, P	PA, P, F, V, C	Includes recognizing and generating rhymes, clapping syllables, identifying initial and final consonants, blending and segmenting phonemes, alphabet recognition, alphabet writing, spelling, decoding, reading rate, and oral comprehension. Administered using a hand puppet.
Gray Oral Reading Test–IV (GORT–IV)	1–12	S, D, P	F, C	Subcomponents include accuracy, rate, and responses to questions about content read. The test consists of two parallel forms, each containing 14 developmentally sequenced reading passages with five comprehension questions following each passage.
Iowa Tests of Basic Skills: Vocabulary Subtest (ITBS)	K–8 Online monitoring available	D	PA, P, V, C	Subcomponents include listening (understanding verbal instructions and following directions), word analysis (matching word sounds with pictures), vocabulary (reading and knowing the meaning of words), reading comprehension (understanding what is read in pictures, sentences, and stories), and language (spelling, capitalization, punctuation, usage, and expression).
Lindamood Auditory Conceptualization Test (LAC)	K–12	D, P	PA	Measures an individual's ability to perceive and conceptualize speech sounds using visual medium. Subcomponents are comparing number and order of phonemes, discriminating phonemes, and multisyllabic processing.
NAEP'S Integrated Reading Performance Record: Oral Reading Fluency Scale	1–5	S, D, P	F, C	Assesses phrasing, syntax, expressiveness, accuracy, and rate. Student reads a narrative text silently, answers three comprehension questions orally, then rereads a portion of the text to the tester.
One Minute Reading Fluency Probe (Rasinski, 2003)	K–12+	S	F	Assesses word recognition and accuracy: The student reads aloud for one minute, and the tester records errors and determines accuracy.
Peabody Picture Vocabulary Test–IV (PPVT–IV)	K–12+ Online monitoring available	S, D	V	Measures relational vocabulary (students answer yes or no to questions about words) and picture vocabulary (students indicate which picture best represents a stimulus word).
Texas Primary Reading Inventory (TPRI)	K–2 Online monitoring available	S, D, P	PA, P, F, V, C	Assesses ability to identify and manipulate individual sounds within spoken words. Components of the assessment include graphophonic knowledge (K–1), recognition of letters of the alphabet and the understanding of sound–symbol relationships (2), spelling, word reading (1–2), fluency rate, listening comprehension (K) and reading comprehension (1–2).
Wireless Generation mCLASS: Reading	K–6 Online monitoring available and digital pens	S, P	PA, P, F, V, C	Supports many paper-based assessments, including DIBELS, TPRI, and reading records. mCLASS: DIBELS is a software program for a handheld computer to collect student DIBELS assessment data. The program carefully selects and partners with publishers of proven reading programs to extend the mCLASS:DIBELS solution. Each partner edition directly links mCLASS:DIBELS assessment results to targeted activities and interventions from popular core reading programs.
YOPP Singer Test of Phoneme Segmentation	K–1	S, D	PA	Assesses orally segmenting phonemes: The tester says a word, and the student breaks the word apart and says each sound in the word in order. There are 22 items that are individually administered and require about 5–10 minutes for each student. A correct response is one in which each phoneme in the target word is correctly articulated.

* S = Screening, D = Diagnostic, P = Progress monitoring.
† PA = Phonemic awareness, P = Phonics, F = Fluency, V = Vocabulary, C = Comprehension

References

Adams, M.J. (1990). *Beginning to read: Thinking and learning about print*. Cambridge, MA: MIT Press.

Adams, M.J., Foorman, B.R., Lundberg, I., & Beeler, T. (1997). *Phonemic awareness in young children: A classroom curriculum*. Baltimore, MD: Brookes Publishing.

Afflerbach, P. (2007). *Understanding and using reading assessment, K–12*. Newark, DE: International Reading Association.

Akhavan, N.L. (2007). *Accelerated vocabulary instruction: Strategies for closing the achievement gap for all students*. New York: Scholastic.

Allington, R.L. (2001). *What really matters for struggling readers: Designing research-based programs*. New York: Longman.

Allington, R.L. (2008). *Response to intervention: Research-based designs*. Boston: Allyn & Bacon.

Allington, R.L., & Walmsley, S.A. (2007). *No quick fix, the RTI edition: Rethinking literacy programs in America's elementary schools*. New York: Teachers College Press, Newark, DE: International Reading Association.

Allor, J.H., Gansle, K.A., & Denny, R.K. (2006). The stop and go phonemic awareness game: Providing modeling, practice, and feedback. *Preventing School Failure, 50*(4), 23–30. doi:10.3200/PSFL.50.4.23-30

Amer, A. (2006). Reflections on Bloom's revised taxonomy. *Electronic Journal of Research in Educational Psychology, 4*(1), 213–230.

Amtmann, D., Abbott, R.D., & Berninger, V.W. (2008). Identifying and predicting classes of response to explicit phonological spelling instruction during independent composing. *Journal of Learning Disabilities, 41*(3), 218–234. doi:10.1177/0022219408315639

Anderson, R.C., Hiebert, E.H., Scott, J.A., & Wilkinson, I.A.G. (1985). *Becoming a nation of readers: The report of the Commission on Reading*. Washington, DC: National Institute of Education.

Anderson, L.W., & Krathwohl, D.R. (Eds). (2001). *A taxonomy for learning, teaching and assessing: A revision of Bloom's Taxonomy of educational objectives: Complete edition*. New York: Longman.

Archer, A.L., Gleason, M.M., & Vachon, V. (2000). *Rewards*. Longmont, CO: Sopris West.

Armbruster, B.B., Lehr, F., & Osborn, J. (2001). *Put reading first: The research building blocks for teaching children to read, kindergarten through grade three*. Washington, DC: U.S. Department of Education.

Baldwin, R.S., Ford, J.C., & Readence, J.E. (1981). Teaching word connotations: An alternative strategy. *Reading World, 21*(2), 103–108.

Ball, E.W., & Blachman, B.A. (1991). Does phoneme awareness training in kindergarten make a difference in early word recognition and developmental spelling? *Reading Research Quarterly, 26*(1), 49–66.

Barger, J. (2006). Building word consciousness. *The Reading Teacher, 60*(3), 279–281. doi:10.1598/RT.60.3.8

Baron, F., & Hirst, G. (2004). *Collocations as cues to semantic orientation*. Retrieved July 29, 2009, from ftp.cs.toronto.edu/pub/gh/Baron+Hirst-2003.pdf.

Batsche, G., Elliott, J., Graden, J.L., Grimes, J., Kovaleski, J.F., Prasse, D., et al. (2005). *Response to intervention: Policy considerations and implementation*. Alexandria, VA: National Association of State Directors of Special Education.

Bear, D.R., Invernizzi, M., Templeton, S., & Johnston, F. (2008). *Words their way: Word study for phonics, vocabulary, and spelling instruction* (4th ed.). Upper Saddle River, NJ: Prentice Hall.

Beaver, J.M. (2006). *Teacher guide: Developmental reading assessment, grades K–3* (2nd ed.). Parsippany, NJ: Pearson.

Beck, I.L., McKeown, M.G., & Kucan, L. (2002). *Bringing words to life: Robust vocabulary instruction*. New York: Guilford.

Beck I.L., McKeown, M.G., & Kucan, L. (2008). *Creating robust vocabulary: Frequently asked questions and extended examples*. New York: Guilford.

Behrman, E.H. (2006). Teaching about language, power, and text: A review of classroom practices that support critical literacy. *Journal of Adolescent & Adult Literacy, 49*(6), 490–498. doi:10.1598/JAAL.49.6.4

Ben-Dror, I., Frost, R., & Bentin, S. (1995). Orthographic representation and phonemic segmentation in skilled readers: A Cross-Language Comparison. *Psychological Science, 6*, 176.

Bishop, A., & Bishop, S. (1996). *Teaching phonics, phonemic awareness, and word recognition*. Westminster, CA: Teacher Created Materials.

Blachowicz, C.L.Z. (1986). Making connections: Alternatives to the vocabulary notebook. *Journal of Reading, 29*(7), 643–649.

Blachowicz, C.L.Z., & Fisher, P. (2000). Vocabulary instruction. In M.L. Kamil, P.B. Mosenthal, P.D. Pearson, & R. Barr (Eds.), *Handbook of reading research* (Vol. 3, pp. 503–523). Mahwah, NJ: Erlbaum.

Blachowicz, C.L.Z., & Fisher, P. (2006). *Teaching vocabulary in all classrooms* (3rd ed.). Upper Saddle River, NJ: Merrill/Prentice Hall.

Blevins, W. (1997). *Phonemic awareness activities for early reading success: Easy, playful activities that help prepare children for phonics instruction*. New York: Scholastic.

Blevins, W. (2001). *Building fluency: Lessons and strategies for reading success*. New York: Scholastic.

Block, C.C., Rodgers, L.L., & Johnson, R.B. (2004). *Comprehension process instruction: Creating reading success in grades K–3*. New York: Guilford.

Bloom, B.S., & Krathwohl, D.R. (Eds.). (1956). *Taxonomy of educational objectives: The classification of educational goals, handbook 1: The cognitive domain*. New York: David McKay.

Boulware-Gooden, R., Carreker, S., Thornhill, A., & Joshi, R. (2007). Instruction of metacognitive strategies enhances reading comprehension and vocabulary achievement of third-grade students. *The Reading Teacher, 61*(1), 70–77.

Brassell, D., & Rasinski, T. (2008). *Comprehension that works: Taking students beyond ordinary understanding to deep comprehension*. Huntington Beach, CA: Shell.

Bromley, K. (2007). Nine things every teacher should know about words and vocabulary instruction. *Journal of Adolescent & Adult Literacy, 50*(7), 528–531. doi:10.1598/JAAL.50.7.2

Brophy, J.E. (1983). Conceptualizing student motivation. *Educational Psychologist, 18*, 200–215.

Brown, R. (2008). The road not yet taken: A transactional strategies approach to comprehension instruction. *The Reading Teacher, 61*(7), 538–547. doi:10.1598/RT.61.7.3

Buzan, T. (1993). *The mind map book*. London: BBC.

Caine, G., & Caine, R. (2007). *Natural learning: The basis for raising and sustaining high standards of real world performance: Executive Summary*. Idyllwild, CA: The National Learning Research Institute. Retrieved April 15, 2008, from www.naturallearninginstitute.org/UPDATEDSITE/DOCUMENTS/EXECUTIVE_SUMMARY.pdf

Calkins, L.M. (2001). *The art of teaching reading.* New York: Longman.

Cambourne, B. (1995). Toward an educationally relevant theory of literacy learning: Twenty years of inquiry. *The Reading Teacher, 49*(3), 182–190.

Campbell, K.U. (1995). *Great leaps.* Gainesville, FL: Diarmuid.

Campbell, M.L., Helf, S., & Cooke, N.L. (2008). Effects of adding multisensory components to a supplemental reading program on the decoding skills of treatment resisters. *Education & Treatment of Children, 31*(3), 267–295. doi:10.1353/etc.0.0003

Castiglioni-Spalten, M.L., & Ehri, L.C. (2003). Phonemic awareness instruction: Contribution of articulatory segmentation to novice beginners' reading and spelling. *Scientific Studies of Reading, 7*(1), 25–52. doi:10.1207/S1532799XSSR0701_03

Chard, D.J., & Dickson, S.V. (1999). Phonological awareness: Instructional and assessment guidelines. *Intervention in School and Clinic, 34*(5), 261–270. doi:10.1177/105345129903400502

Cheyney, W.J., & Cohen, E.J. (1998). *Phonics, not if…but how and when: Grades K–2.* Bothell, WA: Wright Group.

Clay, M.M. (2002). *An observational survey of early literacy achievement* (2nd ed.). Portsmouth, NH: Heinemann.

Coffield, F., Moseley, D., Hall, E., & Ecclestone, K. (2004). Learning styles and pedagogy in post-16 learning: A systematic and critical review. *Learning and Skills Research.* Retrieved April 15, 2009, from www.lsda.org.uk/files/PDF/1543.pdf

Collins, A., Brown, J.S., & Newman, S.E. (1989). Cognitive apprenticeship: Teaching the crafts of reading, writing, and mathematics. In L.B. Resnick (Ed.), *Knowing, learning, and instruction: Essays in honor of Robert Glaser* (pp. 453–494). Hillsdale, NJ: Erlbaum.

Collins, N.D. (1993). *Teach critical reading through literature.* Bloomington, IN: Clearinghouse on Reading English and Communication.

Conrad, N.J. (2008). From reading to spelling and spelling to reading: Transfer goes both ways. *Journal of Educational Psychology, 100*(4), 869–878. doi:10.1037/a0012544

Covey, S.R. (1989). *7 habits of highly effective people.* New Work: Free Press.

Covey, S.R. (2006). *Habit 2 begin with the end in mind: The habit of vision* [CD]. New York: Free Press.

Cunningham, A.E., & Stanovich, K.E. (1998). Early reading acquisition and its relation to reading experience and ability 10 years later. *Developmental Psychology, 33*, 934-945.

Cunningham, P.M. (2000). *Phonics they use: Words for reading and writing.* New York: Longman.

Cunningham, P.M., & Allington, R.L. (2007). *Classrooms that work: They can all read and write* (4th ed.). Boston: Allyn & Bacon.

Davis, H.A. (2003). Conceptualizing the role and influence of student-teacher relationships on children's social and cognitive development. *Educational Psychologist, 38*(4), 207–234.

Dewey, J. (1913). *Interest and effort in education.* Boston: Houghton Mifflin.

Dole, J.A., & Smith, E.L. (1987, December). *When prior knowledge is wrong: Reading and learning from science text.* Paper presented at the annual meeting of the National Reading Conference, St. Petersburg, FL.

Dowhower, S. (1994). Repeated reading revisited: Research into practice. *Reading and Writing Quarterly: Overcoming Learning Difficulties, 10*(4), 343–358.

Drieghe, D., Pollatsek, A., Staub, A., & Rayner, K. (2008). The word grouping hypothesis and eye movements during reading. *Journal of Experimental Psychology, 34*(6), 1552–1560.

Duffy, G.G., & Roehler, L.R. (1986). *Improving classroom reading instruction: A decision-making approach.* New York: Random House.

Eber, P. (2007). Assessing student learning: Applying Bloom's taxonomy. *Human Service Education, 27*(1), 45–53.

Edelen-Smith, P.J. (1997). How now brown cow: Phoneme awareness activities for collaborative classrooms. *Intervention in School and Clinic, 33*(2), 103–111. doi:10.1177/105345129703300206

Edwards, P.A., Turner, J.D., & Mokhtari, K. (2008). Balancing the assessment *of* learning and *for* learning in support of student literacy achievement. *The Reading Teacher, 61*(8), 682–684.

Eldredge, J.L., Reutzel, D.R., & Hollingsworth, P.M. (1996). Comparing the effectiveness of two oral reading practices: Round-robin reading and the shared book experience. *Journal of Literacy Research, 28*(2), 201–225.

Farrington, P. (2007). Using context clues: Children as reading detectives. *Literacy Today, 51*, 8–9.

Farstrup, A.E., & Samuels, S.J. (Eds.). (2002). *What research has to say about reading instruction* (3rd ed.). Newark, DE: International Reading Association.

Fink, R., & Samuels, S.J. (Eds.). (2008). *Inspiring reading success: Interest and motivation in an age of high-stakes testing*. Newark, DE: International Reading Association.

Fisher, D., Frey, N., & Lapp, D. (2009). *In a reading state of mind: Brain research, teacher modeling, and comprehension instruction*. Newark, DE: International Reading Association.

Fitzpatrick, J. (1997). *Phonemic awareness: Playing with sounds to strengthen beginning reading skills*. Huntington Beach, CA: Creative Teaching.

Flood, J., Jensen, J.M., Lapp, D., & Squire J.R. (Eds.). (1991). *Handbook of research on teaching the English language arts*. New York: Macmillan.

Fogarty, R. (1997). *Brain-compatible classrooms*. Arlington Heights, IL: Skylight.

Foorman, B.R., & Mehta, P. (2002, November). *Definitions of fluency: Conceptual and methodological challenges*. Paper presented at the Focus on Fluency Forum, San Francisco, CA.

Forbes, S., & Briggs, C. (Eds.). (2003). *Research in reading recovery* (Vol. 2). Portsmouth, NH: Heinemann.

Fountas, I.C., & Pinnell, G.S. (1996). *Guided reading: Good first teaching for all children*. Portsmouth, NH: Heinemann.

Fountas, I.C., & Pinnell, G.S. (1999). *Matching books to readers: Using leveled books in guided reading, K–3*. Portsmouth, NH: Heinemann.

Fredericks, A.D. (2001). *The complete phonemic awareness handbook: More than 300 playful activities for early reading success*. Oxford, UK: Rigby Education.

Freeman, M.S. (1995). *Building a writing community: A practical guide*. Gainesville, FL: Maupin.

Fuchs, L.S., & Fuchs, D. (2008). Best practices in progress monitoring reading and mathematics at the elementary grades. In J. Grimes & A. Thomas (Eds.), *Best practices in school psychology* (Vol. 5, pp. 2147–2164). Bethesda, MD: National Association of School Pyschologists.

Fuchs, L.S., Fuchs, D., Hosp, M.K., & Jenkins, J.R. (2001). Oral reading fluency as an indicator of reading competence: A theoretical, empirical, and historical analysis. *Scientific Studies of Reading, 5*(3), 239–256. doi:10.1207/S1532799XSSR0503_3

Gardner, H. (1983). *Frames of mind: The theory of multiple intelligences*. New York: Basic.

Gardner, H. (1993). *Multiple Intelligences: The theory in practice*. New York: Basic.

Gaskins, I.W. (2005). *Success with struggling readers: The benchmark school approach*. New York: Guilford.

Gaskins, I.W., Ehri, L.C., Cress, C., O'Hara, C., & Donnelly, K. (1996/1997). Procedures for word learning: Making discoveries about words. *The Reading Teacher, 50*(4), 312–327.

Gentry, J.R. (1989). *Spel is a four-letter word*. Portsmouth, NH: Heinemann.

Gentry, J.R. (2006). *Breaking the code: The new science of beginning reading and writing*. Portsmouth, NH: Heinemann.

Gentry, J.R., & Gillet, J.W. (1992). *Teaching kids to spell*. Portsmouth, NH: Heinemann.

Gillet, J.W., & Kita, M.J. (1979). Words, kids, and categories. *The Reading Teacher, 32*(5), 538–546.

Goals 2000: Educate America Act of 1994, Pub. L. 103–277, 108 Stat.125.

Graves, D.H. (1982). *Writing: Teachers and children at work*. Portsmouth, NH: Heinemann.

Graves, M.F. (2000). A vocabulary program to complement and bolster a middle-grade comprehension program. In B.M. Taylor, M.F. Graves, & P.W. van den Broek (Eds.), *Reading for meaning: Fostering comprehension in the middle grades* (pp. 116–135). Newark, DE: International Reading Association.

Graves, M.F., Juel, C., & Graves, B.B. (1998). *Teaching reading in the twenty-first century*. Englewood Cliffs, NJ: Prentice Hall.

Graves, M.F., & Watts-Taffe, S. (2008). For the love of words: Fostering word consciousness in young readers. *The Reading Teacher, 62*(3), 185–193. doi:10.1598/RT.62.3.1

Greenwood, S.C., & Flanigan, K. (2007). Overlapping vocabulary and comprehension: Context clues complement semantic gradients. *The Reading Teacher, 61*(3), 249–254. doi:10.1598/RT.61.3.5

Hall, L., & Piazza, S. (2008). Critically reading texts: What students do and how teachers can help. *The Reading Teacher, 62*(1), 32–41. doi:10.1598/RT.62.1.4

Hamner, D. (n.d.). Writing poetry with rebus and rhyme [Lesson plan]. ReadWriteThink.org. www.readwritethink.org/lessons/lesson_view.asp?id=273

Harackiewicz, J.M., Durik, A.M., Barron, K.E., Linnenbrink-Garcia, L., & Tauer, J.M. (2008). The role of achievement goals in the development of interest: Reciprocal relations between achievement goals, interests, and performance. *Journal of Educational Psychology, 100*(1), 105–122. doi:10.1037/0022-0663.100.1.105

Harste, J.C., Short, K.G., & Burke, C.L. (1989). *Creating classrooms for authors: The reading-writing connection*. Portsmouth, NH: Heinemann.

Harvey, S., & Goudvis, A. (2000). *Strategies that work: Teaching comprehension to enhance understanding* (2nd ed.). York, ME: Stenhouse.

Heckelman, R.G. (1969). A neurological-impress method of remedial-reading instruction. *Academic Therapy Quarterly, 4*(4), 277–282.

Henderson, E.H. (1990). *Teaching spelling* (2nd ed.). Boston: Houghton Mifflin.

Henderson, E.H., Bear, D.R., & Templeton S. (Eds.). (1992). *Development of orthographic knowledge and the foundations of literacy: A memorial Festschrift for Edmund H. Henderson*. Hillsdale, NJ: Erlbaum.

Herber, H.L. (1984). *Teaching reading in content areas* (2nd ed.). Englewood Cliffs, NJ: Prentice Hall.

Herron, J. (2008). Why phonics teaching must change: Of course, we must teach decoding, but we must teach it meaningfully. *Educational Leadership, 66*(1), 77–81.

Hiebert, E.H. (2005). *Quickreads: A research-based fluency program*. Upper Saddle River, NJ: Pearson Education.

Hiebert, E.H., Pearson, P.D., Taylor, B.M., Richardson, V., & Paris, S.G. (1998). *Every child a reader: Applying reading research to the classroom*. Ann Arbor: Center for the Improvement of Early Reading Achievement, University of Michigan School of Education.

Hilden, K., & Pressley, M. (2007). Self-regulation through transactional strategies instruction. *Reading and Writing Quarterly, 23*(1), 51–75.

Hill, M. (1998). Reaching struggling readers. In G.K. Beers & B.G. Samuels (Eds.), *Into focus: Understanding and creating middle school readers* (pp. 81–104). Norwood, MA: Christopher-Gordon.

Hodgkinson, H. (2006). *The whole child in a fractured word*. Retrieved March, 15, 2009, from www.ascd.org/ASCD/pdf/fracturedworld.pdf

Holdaway, D. (1979). *The foundations of literacy*. Sydney, Australia: Ashton Scholastic.

Horner, S.L, & O'Connor, E.A. (2007). Helping beginning and struggling readers to develop self-regulated strategies: A reading recovery example. *Reading & Writing Quarterly, 23*(1), 97–109.

Hoyt, L. (1992). Many ways of knowing: Using drama, oral interactions, and visual arts to enhance reading comprehension. *The Reading Teacher, 45*(8), 580–584.

Hoyt, L. (2008). *Revisit, reflect, retell: Time-tested strategies for teaching reading comprehension* (Updated ed.). Portsmouth, NH: Heinemann.

Hoyt, L., & Therriault, T. (2008). *Mastering the mechanics: Ready-to-use lessons for modeled, guided, and independent editing, grades 4–5.* New York: Scholastic.

International Reading Association. (1998). *Phonemic awareness and the teaching of reading* (Position statement). Newark, DE: Author.

Irwin, J.W. (1991). *Teaching reading comprehension processes* (2nd ed.). Boston: Pearson.

Irwin, J.W., & Baker, I. (1989). *Promoting active reading comprehension strategies: A resource book for teachers.* Englewood Cliffs, NJ: Prentice Hall.

Israel, S.E., & Duffy, G.G. (Eds.). (2009). *Handbook of research on reading comprehension.* New York: Routledge.

Jang, H. (2008). Supporting students' motivation, engagement, and learning during an uninteresting activity. *Journal of Educational Psychology, 100*(4), 798–811. doi:10.1037/a0012841

Jensen, E. (2000). *Different brains, different learners: How to reach the hard to reach.* San Diego, CA: The Brain Store.

Jensen, E. (2005). *Teaching with the brain in mind* (2nd ed.). Alexandria, VA: Association for Supervision and Curriculum Development.

Jensen, E., & Nickelsen, L. (2008). *Deeper learning: 7 powerful strategies for in-depth and longer-lasting learning.* Thousand Oaks, CA: Corwin.

Jewitt, C., & Kress, G.R. (Eds.). (2003). *Multimodal literacy.* New York: Peter Lang.

Johnson, D.D., & Pearson, P.D. (1984). *Teaching reading vocabulary* (2nd ed.). New York: Holt, Rinehart and Winston.

Johnston, A.M., Barnes, M.A., & Desrochers, A. (2008). Reading comprehension: Developmental processes, individual differences, and interventions. *Canadian Psychology, 49*(2), 125–132. doi:10.1037/0708 -5591.49.2.125

Juel, C. (1988). Learning to read and write: A longitudinal study of fifty-four children from first through fourth grades. *Journal of Educational Psychology, 80*(4), 437–447.

Keene, E.O., & Zimmermann, S. (1997). *Mosaic of thought: Teaching comprehension in a reader's workshop.* Portsmouth, NH: Heinemann.

Keene, E.O., & Zimmermann, S. (2007). *Mosaic of thought: The power of comprehension strategy instruction* (2nd ed.). Portsmouth, NH: Heinemann.

Kendrick, M., & McKay, R. (2004). Drawings as an alternative way of understanding young children's construction of literacy. *Journal of Early Childhood Literacy, 4*(1), 109–128. doi:10.1177/1468798404041458

Kinniburgh, L., & Shaw, E.L., Jr. (2007). Building reading fluency in elementary science through readers' theatre. *Science Activities, 44*(1), 16–20. doi:10.3200/SATS.44.1.16-22

Kinniburgh, L.H., & Shaw, E.L., Jr. (2009). Using question–answer relationships to build. Reading comprehension in science. *Science Activities, 45*(4), 19–28.

Klauda, S.L., & Guthrie, J.T. (2008). Relationships of three components of reading fluency to reading comprehension. *Journal of Educational Psychology, 100*(2), 310–321. doi:10.1037/0022-0663.100.2.310

Knapp, M.S. (1995). *Teaching for meaning in high-poverty classrooms.* New York: Teachers College Press.

Kohn, A. (1993). *Published by rewards: The trouble with gold stars, incentive plans, A's, praise, and other bribes*. Boston: Houghton Mifflin.

Kohn, A. (2005). Unconditional Teaching. *Educational Leadership, 63*(1), 20–24.

Kuhn, M.R., & Stahl, S.A. (2003). Fluency: A review of developmental and remedial practices. *Journal of Educational Psychology, 95*(1), 3–21.

Kunen, S., Cohen, R., & Solman, R. (1981). A levels-of-processing analysis of Bloom's taxonomy. *Journal of Educational Psychology, 73*(2), 202–211. doi:10.1037/0022-0663.73.2.202

Kuo, L., & Anderson, R.C. (2006). Morphological awareness and learning to read: A cross-language perspective. *Educational Psychologist, 41*(3), 161–180. doi:10.1207/s15326985ep4103_3

LaBerge, D., & Samuels, S.J. (1974). Toward a theory of automatic information processing in reading. *Cognitive Psychology, 6*, 293–323.

Langer, J.A. (1981). From theory to practice: A prereading plan. *Journal of Reading, 25*(2), 152–156.

Lavoie, R.D. (2007). *The motivation breakthrough: 6 steps to turning on the tuned-out child*. New York: Touchstone.

Lenz, B.K. (2006). Creating school-wide conditions for high-quality learning strategy classroom instruction. *Intervention in School and Clinic, 41*(5), 261–266. doi:10.1177/10534512060410050201

Lenz, B.K., & Hughes, C.A. (1990). A word identification strategy for adolescents with learning disabilities. *Journal of Learning Disabilities, 23*(3), 149–158. doi:10.1177/002221949002300304

LeVasseur, V.M., Macaruso, P., & Shankweiler, D. (2008). Promoting gains in reading fluency: A comparison of three approaches. *Reading and Writing, 21*(3), 205–230. doi:10.1007/s11145-007-9070-1

Levine, M.D. (2002). *A mind at a time*. New York: Simon & Schuster.

Liow, S.J.R., & Lau, L.H.-S. (2006). The development of bilingual children's early spelling in English. *Journal of Educational Psychology, 98*(4), 868–878. doi:10.1037/0022-0663.98.4.868

Love, E., & Reilly, S. (1996). *A sound way: Phonics activities for early literacy*. York, ME: Stenhouse.

Lundberg, I., Frost, J., & Petersen, O.P. (1988). Effects of an extensive program for stimulating phonological awareness in preschool children. *Reading Research Quarterly, 23*(3), 263–284.

Lyons, C.A. (2003). *Teaching struggling readers: How to use brain-based research to maximize learning*. Portsmouth, NH: Heinemann.

Many, J.E., Taylor, D.L, Wang, Y., Sachs, G.T., & Schreiber, H. (2007). An examination of preservice literacy teachers' initial attempts to provide instructional scaffolding. *Reading Horizons, 48*(1), 19–40.

Manyak, P.C. (2008). Phonemes in use: Multiple activities for a critical process. *The Reading Teacher, 61*(8), 659–662. doi:10.1598/RT.61.8.8

Martin, M.A. (1985). Students' application of self-questioning study techniques: An investigation of their efficiency. *Reading Psychology, 6*(1), 69–83.

Marzano, R.J. (2007). *The art and science of teaching: A comprehensive framework for effective instruction*. Alexandria, VA: Association for Supervision and Curriculum Development.

Marzano, R.J., & Haystead, M.W. (2008). *Making standards useful in the classroom*. Alexandria, VA: Association for Supervision and Curriculum Development.

Marzano, R.J., Pickering, D., & Pollock, J.E. (2001). *Classroom instruction that works: Research-based strategies for increasing achievement*. Alexandria, VA: Association for Supervision and Curriculum Development.

Maslow, A. (1943). A theory of human motivation. *Psychological Review, 50*(4), 370–396.

McEwan, E.K. (2002). *Teach them all to read: Catching the kids who fall through the cracks*. Thousand Oaks, CA: Corwin.

McGinley, W.J., & Denner, P.R. (1987). Story impressions: A prereading/writing activity. *Journal of Reading, 31*(3), 248–253.

McKeown, M.G. (1993). Creating effective definitions for young word learners. *Reading Research Quarterly, 28*(1), 16–33.

McMaster, J.C. (1998). "Doing" literature: Using drama to build literacy classrooms: The segue for a few struggling readers. *The Reading Teacher, 51*(7), 574–584.

Menzies, H.M., Mahdavi, J.N., & Lewis, J.L. (2008). Early intervention in reading: From research to practice. *Remedial and Special Education, 29*(2), 67–77. doi:10.1177/0741932508315844

Miller, D. (2002). *Reading with meaning: Teaching comprehension in the primary grades.* York, ME: Stenhouse.

Miller, J., & Schwanenflugel, P.J. (2006). Prosody of syntactically complex sentences in the oral reading of young children. *Journal of Educational Psychology, 98*(4), 839–853. doi:10.1037/0022-0663.98.4.839

Miller, P., & Eilam, B. (2008). Development in the thematic and containment-relation-oriented organization of word concepts. *The Journal of Educational Research, 101*(6), 350–362. doi:10.3200/JOER.101.6.350 -362

Misulis, K. (1999). Making vocabulary development manageable in content instruction. *Contemporary Education, 70*(2), 25–29.

Montelongo, J. (2008). Text guides: Scaffolding summarization and fortifying reading skills. *The International Journal of Learning, 15*(7), 289–296.

Morris, D. (1992). *Case studies in teaching beginning readers: The Howard Street tutoring manual.* Boone, NC: Fieldstream.

Morrow, L.M., & Tracey, D.H. (1997). Strategies used for phonics instruction in early childhood classrooms. *The Reading Teacher, 50*(8), 644–651.

Mountain, L. (2002). Flip-a-chip to build vocabulary. *Journal of Adolescent & Adult Literacy, 46*(1), 62–68.

Moustafa, M. (1997). *Beyond traditional phonics: Research discoveries and reading instruction.* Portsmouth, NH: Heinemann.

Murray, B.A., & Lesniak, T. (1999). The letterbox lesson: A hands-on approach for teaching decoding. *The Reading Teacher, 52*(6), 644–650.

Nagy, W.E. (2003). *Teaching vocabulary to improve reading comprehension.* Newark, DE: International Reading Association.

Nagy, W.E., Anderson, R.C., & Herman, P.A. (1987). Learning word meanings from context during normal reading. *American Educational Research Journal, 24*(2), 237–270.

Nagy, W.E., Diakidoy, I.N., & Anderson, R.C. (1991). *The development of knowledge of derivational suffixes* (Tech. Rep. No. 536). Champaign, IL: Center for the Study of Reading.

Nathan, R.G., & Stanovich, K.E. (1991). The causes and consequences of differences in reading fluency. *Theory Into Practice, 30*(3), 176–184.

National Institute of Child Health and Human Development. (2000). *Report of the National Reading Panel. Teaching children to read: An evidence-based assessment of the scientific research literature on reading and its implications for reading instruction* (NIH Publication No. 00-4769). Washington, DC: U.S. Government Printing Office.

Nations, S., & Alonso, M. (2001). *Primary literacy centers: Making reading and writing stick.* Gainesville, FL: Maupin House.

Nelson, D.L. (2008). A context-based strategy for teaching vocabulary. *English Journal, 97*(4), 33–37.

Newbury, M. (2007). Sounds system. *Times Educational Supplement,* Great Britain Issue 4753, 40–41.

Nilsen, A.P., & Nilsen, D.L.F. (2003). Vocabulary development: Teaching vs. testing. *English Journal, 92*(3), 31–37. doi:10.2307/822257

Nist, S.L., & Olejnik, S. (1995). The role of context and dictionary definitions on varying levels of word knowledge. *Reading Research Quarterly, 30*(2), 172–193.

O'Connor, P., & Jackson, C. (2008). The factor structure and validity of the learning styles profiler. *European Journal of Psychological Assessment, 24*(2), 117–123. doi:10.1027/1015-5759.24.2.117

O'Connor, R.E., White, A., & Swanson, H.L. (2007). Repeated reading versus continuous reading: Influences on reading fluency and comprehension. *Council for Exceptional Children, 74*(1), 31–46.

Ogle, D. (1986). K-W-L group instructional strategy. In A.S. Palincsar, D. Ogle, B.F. Jones, & E.G. Carr (Eds.), *Teaching reading as thinking* (Teleconference Resource Guide, pp. 11-17). Alexandria, VA: Association for Supervision and Curriculum Development.

Ogle, D. (2000). Make it visual: A picture is worth a thousand words. In M. McLaughlin & M. Vogt (Eds.), *Creativity and innovation in content area teaching* (pp. 55–71). Norwood, MA: Christopher Gordon.

Olson, M.W., & Gee, T.C. (1991). Content reading instruction in the primary grades: Perceptions and strategies. *The Reading Teacher, 45*(4), 298–307.

Opitz, M., & Rasinski, T.V. (1998). *Good bye round robin: 25 effective oral reading strategies.* Portsmouth, NH: Heinemann.

Paris, S.G., Wasik, B.A., & Turner, J.C. (1991). The development of strategic readers. In R. Barr, M.L. Kamil, P.B. Mosenthal, & P.D. Pearson (Eds.), *Handbook of reading research* (Vol. 2, pp. 609–640). White Plains, NY: Longman.

Parsons, S.A. (2008). Providing all students ACCESS to self-regulated literacy learning. *The Reading Teacher, 61*(8), 628–635. doi:10.1598/RT.61.8.4

Paulson, E.J. (2005). Viewing eye movements during reading through the lens of chaos theory: How reading is like the weather. *Reading Research Quarterly, 40*(3), 338–358. doi:10.1598/RRQ.40.3.3

Pearson, P.D., & Duke, N.K. (2002). Comprehension instruction in the primary grades. In C.C. Block & M. Pressley (Eds.), *Comprehension instruction: Research-based best practices* (pp. 247–258). New York: Guilford.

Pearson, P.D., & Gallagher, M. (1983). The instruction of reading comprehension. *Contemporary Educational Psychology, 8*(3), 317–344.

Perfetti, C.A., Beck, I.L., Bell, L., & Hughes, C. (1987). Phonemic knowledge and learning to read are reciprocal: A longitudinal study of first grade. *Merrill-Palmer Quarterly, 33*(3), 283–319.

Perry, N.E., Hutchinson, L., & Thauberger, C. (2007). Mentoring student teachers to design and implement literacy tasks that support self-regulated reading and writing. *Reading & Writing Quarterly, 23*(1), 27–50. doi:10.1080/10573560600837636

Pinnell, G.S., & Fountas, I.C. (1998). *Word matters: Teaching phonics and spelling in the reading/writing classroom.* Portsmouth, NH: Heinemann.

Pinnell, G.S., Pikulski, J.J., Wixon, K.K., Campbell, J.R., Gough, P.P., & Beatty, A.S. (1995). *Listening to children read aloud data from NAEP's integral reading performance record CIRPR at grade 4* (Report No. 23-FR-04 prepared by the Educational Testing Service). Washington DC: Office of Educational Research and Improvement, U.S. Department of Education.

Pittelmann, S.D., Heimlich, J.E., Berglund, R.L., & French, M.P. (1991). *Semantic feature analysis: Classroom applications.* Newark, DE: International Reading Association.

Pressley, M. (2002). Metacognition and self-regulated comprehension. In A.E. Farstrup & S.J. Samuels (Eds.), *What research has to say about reading instruction* (3rd ed., pp. 291–309). Newark, DE: International Reading Association.

Pressley, M., El-Dinary, P.B., Gaskins, T., Schuder, T., Bergman, J.L., Almasi, J.F., et al. (1992). Beyond direct explanation: Transactional instruction of reading comprehension strategies. *The Elementary School Journal, 92*(5), 513–555. doi:10.1086/461705

Pressley, M., Goodchild, F., Fleet, J., Zajchowski, E., & Evan, E. (1989). The challenges of classroom strategy instruction. *The Elementary School Journal, 89*(3), 301–342.

Raphael, T.E. (1986). Teaching question-answer relationships, revisited. *The Reading Teacher, 39*(6), 516–522.

Raphael, T.E., Highfield, K., & Au, K.H. (2006). *QAR now: Question answer relationships*. New York: Scholastic.

Rashotte, C.A., & Torgesen, J.K. (1985). Repeated reading and reading fluency in learning disabled children. *Reading Research Quarterly, 20*(2), 180–188.

Rasinski, T.V. (2000). Speed does matter in reading. *The Reading Teacher, 54*(2), 146–150.

Rasinski, T.V. (2003). *The fluent reader: Oral reading strategies for building word recognition, fluency, and comprehension*. New York: Scholastic.

Rasinski, T.V. (2006). Reading fluency instruction: Moving beyond accuracy, automaticity, and prosody. *The Reading Teacher, 59*(7), 704–706. doi:10.1598/RT.59.7.10

Rasinski, T.V., & Lenhart, L.A. (2007/2008). Explorations of fluent readers. *Reading Today, 25*(3), 18.

Rasinski, T.V. (1989). Fluency for everyone: Incorporating fluency instruction in the classroom. *The Reading Teacher, 42*(9), 690–693.

Rayner, K. (1998). Eye movement in reading and informational processing: Twenty years of research. *Psychological Bulletin, 124*(3), 372–422.

Readence, J.E., Bean, T.W., & Baldwin, R.S. (2007). *Content area literacy: An integrated approach* (9th ed.). Dubuque, IA: Kendall/Hunt.

Redfield, D.L., & Rousseau, E.W. (1981). Meta-analysis of experimental research on teacher questioning behavior. *Review of Educational Research, 51*(2), 237–245.

Reutebuch, C. (2008). Succeed with a response-to-intervention model. *Intervention in School and Clinic, 44*(2), 126–128. doi:10.1177/1053451208321598

Robb, L. (1997). Stretch your students' reading vocabulary. *Instructor, 106*(8), 34–36.

Robbie, S., Ruggierello, T., & Warren, B. (2001). *Using drama to bring language to life: Ideas, games, and activities for teachers of languages and language arts*. Concord, ON: Captus Press.

Robinson, E., & Robinson, S. (2003). *What does it mean? Discourse, text, culture: An introduction*. Sydney, Australia: McGraw-Hill.

Robinson, F. (1961). Study skills for superior students in secondary schools. *The Reading Teacher, 25*(1), 29–33.

Routman, R. (2000). *Conversations: Strategies for teaching, learning, and evaluating*. Portsmouth, NH: Heinemann.

Routman, R. (2003). *Reading essentials: The specifics you need to teach reading well*. Portsmouth, NH: Heinemann.

Runge, T.J., & Watkins, M.W. (2006). The structure of phonological awareness among kindergarten students. *School Psychology Review, 35*(3), 370–386.

Rupley, W.H., Logan, J.W., & Nichols, W.D. (1999). Vocabulary instruction in a balanced reading program. *The Reading Teacher, 52*(4), 336–346.

Samuels, S.J. (1979). The method of repeated readings. *The Reading Teacher, 32*(4), 403–408.

Samuels, S.J. (2002). Reading fluency: Its development and assessment. In A.E. Farstrup & S.J. Samuels (Eds.), *What research has to say about reading instruction* (3rd ed., pp. 166–183). Newark, DE: International Reading Association.

Samuels, S.J., & Farstrup, A.E. (Eds.). (2006). *What research has to say about fluency instruction*. Newark, DE: International Reading Association.

Santa, C.M., Havens, L.T., & Maycumber, E. (1996). *Project CRISS: Creating independence through student-owned strategies*. Dubuque, IA: Kendall/Hunt.

Schmidt, B., & Buckley, M. (1990). Plot relationships chart. In J.M. Bacon, D. Bewell, & M. Vogt (Eds.), *Responses to literature: Grades K–8* (p. 7). Newark, DE: International Reading Association.

Schulman, M.B., & Payne, C.D. (2000). *Guided reading: Making it work*. New York: Scholastic.

Schwartz, R.M. (1988). Learning to learn vocabulary in content area textbooks. *Journal of Reading, 32*(2), 108–118.

Schwartz, R.M., & Raphael, T.E. (1985). Concept of definition: A key to improving students' vocabulary. *The Reading Teacher, 39*(2), 198–205.

Shanahan, T. (2002, November). *A sin of the second kind: The status of reading fluency in America*. Paper presented at the Focus on Fluency Forum, San Francisco, CA.

Shanahan, T., & Shanahan, C. (2008). Teaching disciplinary literacy to adolescents: Rethinking content-area literacy. *Harvard Educational Review, 78*(1), 40–59.

Sharp, A.C., Sinatra, G.M., & Reynolds, R.E. (2008). The development of children's orthographic knowledge: A microgenetic perspective. *Reading Research Quarterly, 43*(3), 206–226. doi:10.1598/RRQ.43.3.1

Shaywitz, S.E., & Shaywitz, B.A. (2007). What neuroscience really tells us about reading instruction. *Educational Leadership, 64*(5), 74–76.

Shepard, A. (1994). From script to stage: Tips for Readers' Theatre. *The Reading Teacher, 48*(2), 184–185.

Short, K.G., Harste, J.C., & Burke, C.L. (1996). *Creating classrooms for authors and inquirers*. Portsmouth, NH: Heinemann.

Short, R.J., & Talley, R.C. (1997). Rethinking psychology and the schools: Implications of recent national policy. *American Psychologist, 52*(3), 234–240. doi:10.1037/0003-066X.52.3.234

Silver, H.F., Strong, R.W., & Perini, M.J. (2001). *Tools for promoting active, in-depth learning* (2nd ed.). Woodbridge, NJ: Thoughtful Education.

Sippola, A.E. (1995). K-W-L-S. *The Reading Teacher, 48*(6), 542–543.

Skinner, E.A., & Belmont, M.J. (1993). Motivation in the classroom: Reciprocal effects of teacher behavior and student engagement across the school year. *Journal of Educational Psychology, 85*(4), 571–581. doi:10.1037/0022-0663.85.4.571

Sloyer, S. (1982). *Readers Theatre: Story dramatization in the classroom*. Urbana, IL: National Council of Teachers of English.

Snow, C.E., Burns, M.S., & Griffin P. (Eds.). (1998). *Preventing reading difficulties in young children*. Washington, DC: National Academy Press.

Sprenger, M. (2005). How to teach so students remember. Alexandria, VA: Association for Supervision and Curriculum Development.

Stahl, S.A., Duffy-Hester, A.M., & Stahl, K.A. (1998). Everything you wanted to know about phonics (but were afraid to ask). *Reading Research Quarterly, 33*(3), 338–355.

Stahl, S.A., & Nagy, W.E. (2006). *Teaching word meanings*. Mahwah, NJ: Erlbaum.

Stayter, F.Z., & Allington, R.L. (1991). Fluency and comprehension. *Theory Into Practice, 30*(3), 143–148.

Stiggins, R., & Chappuis, J. (2008). Enhancing student learning. *January District Administrator, 44*(1), 42–44.

Strickland, D.S. (1998). *Teaching phonics today: A primer for educators*. Newark, DE: International Reading Association.

Strickland, D.S., Ganske, K., & Monroe, J.K. (2002). *Supporting struggling readers and writers: Strategies for classroom intervention, 3–6.* Newark, DE: International Reading Association.

Stull, A.T., & Mayer, R.E. (2007). Learning by doing verses learning by viewing: Three experimental comparisons of learner-generated verses author-provided graphic organizers. *Journal of Educational Psychology, 99*(4), 808–820. doi:10.1037/0022-0663.99.4.808

Taberski, S. (2000). *On solid ground: Strategies for teaching reading K–3.* Portsmouth, NH: Heinemann.

Tate, M.L. (2003). *Worksheets don't grow dendrites: Twenty instructional strategies that engage the brain.* Thousand Oaks, CA: Corwin.

Taylor, B. (2008). Tier I: Effective classroom reading instruction in the elementary grades. In D. Fuchs, L. Fuchs, & S. Vaughn (Eds.), *Response to Intervention: A framework for reading educators* (pp. 5–26). Newark, DE: International Reading Association.

Thompson, M. (2008) Multimodal teaching and learning: Creating spaces for content teachers. *Journal of Adolescent & Adult Literacy 52*(2), 144–153.

Tierney, R.J., & Readence, J.E. (2005). *Reading strategies and practices: A compendium* (6th ed.). Boston: Allyn & Bacon.

Tomlinson, C.A., & McTighe, J. (2006). *Integrating differentiated instruction & understanding by design: Connecting content and kids.* Alexandria, VA: Association for Supervision and Curriculum Development.

Tompkins, G.E. (2000). *Teaching writing: Balancing process and product.* Upper Saddle River, NJ: Prentice Hall.

Tompkins, G.E. (2001). *Literacy for the twenty-first century: A balanced approach* (2nd ed.). Englewood Cliffs, NJ: Prentice Hall.

Torgesen, J.K., Rashotte, C.A., & Alexander, A.W. (2001). Principles of fluency instruction in reading: Relationships with established empirical outcomes. In M. Wolf (Ed.), *Dyslexia, fluency, and the brain* (pp. 333–355). Timonium, MD: York.

Traill, L. (1995). *Highlight my strengths: Assessment and evaluation of literacy learning.* Crystal Lake, IL: Rigby.

Trelease, J. (2001). *The read-aloud handbook* (5th ed.). New York: Penguin.

Tyner, B. (2004). *Small-group reading instruction: A differentiated teaching model for beginning and struggling readers.* Newark, DE: International Reading Association.

Unsworth, L., & Heberle, V. (2009). *Teaching multimodal literacy in English as a foreign language.* Oakville, CT: Brown Publishing.

Vacca, J.L., Vacca, R.T., & Gove, M.K. (1995). *Reading and learning to read* (3rd ed.). Reading, MA: Addison-Wesley.

Vacca, R.T., & Vacca, J.L. (1996). *Content area reading* (5th ed.). Glenview, IL: Scott Foresman.

Vadasy, P.F., & Sanders, E.A. (2008). Repeated reading intervention: Outcomes and interactions with readers' skills and classroom instruction. *Journal of Educational Psychology, 100*(2), 272–290. doi:10.1037/0022-0663.100.2.272

Vaughn, S., Linan-Thompson, S., & Hickman, P. (2003). Response to instruction as a means of identifying students with reading/learning disabilities. *Exceptional Children, 69*(4), 391–409.

Vygotsky, L.S. (1978). *Mind in society: The development of higher psychological processes* (M. Cole, V. John-Steiner, S. Scribner, & E. Souberman, Eds & Trans.). Cambridge, MA: Harvard University Press.

Wagner, R.K., Torgesen, J.K., & Rashotte, C.A. (1994). Development of reading-related phonological processing abilities: New evidence of bidirectional causality from a latent variable longitudinal study. *Developmental Psychology, 30*(1), 78–87.

Waldo, B. (1991). Story pyramid. In J.M. Macon, D. Bewell, & M.E. Vogt (Eds.), *Responses to literature: Grades K–8* (pp. 23–24). Newark, DE: International Reading Association.

White, T.G. (2005). Effects of systematic and strategic analogy-based phonics on grade 2 students' word reading and reading comprehension. *Reading Research Quarterly, 40*(2), 234–255. doi:10.1598/RRQ.40.2.5

Whitin, P. (2009). Tech-to-stretch: Expanding possibilities for literature response. *The Reading Teacher, 62*(5), 408-418.

Wiggins, G.P., & McTighe, J. (2005). *Understanding by design* (2nd ed.). Upper Saddle River, NJ: Prentice Hall.

Williams, R.M.-C. (2008). Image, text, and story: Comics and graphic novels in the classroom. *Art Education, 61*(6), 13–19.

Wood, K.D., Lapp, D., & Flood, J. (1992). *Guiding readers through text: A review of study guides*. Newark, DE: International Reading Association.

Wylie, R.E., & Durell, D.D. (1970). Teaching vowels through phonograms. *Elementary English, 47*(6), 787–790.

Yopp, H.K. (1992). Developing phonemic awareness in young children. *The Reading Teacher, 45*(9), 696–700.

Young, T.A., & Vardell, S. (1993). Weaving Readers Theatre and nonfiction into the curriculum. *The Reading Teacher, 46*(5), 396–406.

Zgonc, Y. (1999). *Phonological awareness: The missing piece to help crack the reading code*. Eau Claire, WI: Otter Creek Institute.

Zigler, E., & Finn-Stevenson, M. (2007). From research to policy and practice: The school of the 21st century. *Americal Journal of Orthopsychiatry, 77*(2), 175–181. doi:10.1037/0002-9432.77.2.175

Zinger, E., Singer, D.G., & Bishop-Josef, S.J. (Eds.). (2004). *Children's play: The roots of reading*. Washington, DC: Zero to Three Press.

Zutell, J. (1998). Word sorting: A developmental spelling approach to word study for delayed readers. *Reading & Writing Quarterly, 14*(2), 219–238.

RECOMMENDED RESOURCES

Abercrombie, B. (1990). *Charlie Anderson*. New York: M.K. McElderry.

Adams, P. (1990). *This is the house that Jack built*. New York: Child's Play.

Arnold, T. (1997). *Parts*. New York: Penguin Books.

Banks, K. (2006). *Max's words*. New York: Farrar, Straus & Giroux.

Benjamin, A. (1987). *Rat-a-tat, pitter pat*. New York: HarperCollins.

Bennett, R. (1988). The gingerbread man. In B. Schenk de Regniers, E. Moore, M. White, & J. Carr (Eds.), *Sing a song of popcorn: Every child's book of poems* (p. 50). New York: Scholastic.

Biel, T. (2003). *Zoobooks: Tigers*. Poway, CA: Wildlife Education.

Braun, W., & Braun, C. (2000). *A Readers Theatre treasury of stories*. Winnipeg, Canada: Portage and Main.

Brinckloe, J. (1986). *Fireflies*. New York: Aladdin.

Brooke, L. (2000–2008). Heartland series. New York: Scholastic

Brown, M. (1998). *Buster's dino dilemma (Arthur Chapter Book #7)*. New York: Little, Brown.

Bunting, E. (1988). *How many days to America? A Thanksgiving story*. New York: Clarion.

Bunting, E. (1991). *Fly away home*. New York: Clarion.

Burns, M. (2008). *The greedy triangle*. New York: Scholastic.

Burt, A., & Vandyck, W. (2005). *Spelling repair kit: Improve your spelling skills*. London: Hodder & Stoughton.

Cannon, J. (1993). *Stellaluna*. New York: Scholastic.

Carle, E. (1983). *The very hungry caterpillar*. New York: Philomel.

Carle, E. (2002). *"Slowly, slowly, slowly," said the sloth*. New York: Penguin Putnam.

Cherry, L. (1990). *The great kapot tree: A tale of the Amazon rain forest*. San Diego, CA: Gulliver Green/
Harcourt.

Cleary, B. (1981). *Ramona Quimby, age 8*. New York: Morrow.

Clinton, C., & Quails, S. (2008). *Phillis's big test*. New York: Houghton Mifflin.

Cosgrove, B. (2007). *Weather*. New York: DK Children.

Cowley, J. (1996). *Annabel*. Bothell, WA: Wright Group.

Dealey, E. (2002). *Goldie Locks has Chicken Pox*. New York: Aladdin Paperbacks.

Degross, M. (1994). *Donavan's word jar*. New York: HarperCollins.

dePaola, T. (1973). *Andy: That's my name*. New York: Prentice Hall.

DiCamillo, K. (2000). *Because of Winn-Dixie*. Cambridge, MA: Candlewick.

Donnelly, J. (1988). *The Titantic: Lost—and found*. New York: Random House.

Eaton, D., & Lee, J. (1996). The three silly cowboys. Parsippany, NJ: Pearson.

Flocabulary: www.Flocabualry.com

Freeman, M. (2002). *Go facts: Insects*. Littleton, MA: Newbridge/Sundance.

Harrison, B., & Rappaport, A. (2006). *Flocabulary: The Hip-Hop Approach to SAT-Level Vocabulary
Building*. City: Kennebunkport, ME: Cider Mill Press.

Hartmann, J. (2001). Rockin' rhymin' teddy bear 1 and 2. On *Language play & listening fun for everyone*
[CD]. St. Petersburg, FL: Planet Visions. Available: www.jackhartman.com

Hartmann, J. (2002a). Do the word stretch. On *Shake, rattle 'n read* [CD]. St. Petersburg, FL: Planet Visions.
Available: www.jackhartmann.com

Hartmann, J. (2002b). Special soup. On *Shake, rattle 'n read* [CD]. St. Petersburg, FL: Planet Visions.
Available: www.jackhartmann.com

Henkes, K. (1988). *Chester's way*. New York: Greenwillow.

Henkes, K. (1991). *Chrysanthemum*. New York: Greenwillow.

Henkes, K. (1993). *Owen*. New York: Greenwillow.

Hoose, P., & Hoose, A. (1998). *Hey little ant*. Berkley, CA: Tricycle.

Hutchins, P. (1986). *The doorbell rang*. New York: Greenwillow.

Keats, E.J. (1992). *Over in the meadow*. New York: Scholastic.

Kesselman, W. (1993). *Emma*. New York: Bantam Doubleday Dell.

KIDiddles: www.kididdles.com/lyrics

Konigsburg, E.L. (1997). *The view from Saturday*. New York: Scholastic.

Kramer, S.H. (2008). *Adaptive dance and rhythms for all ages with basic lesson plans*. Netherlands:
SusanKramer.

Langstaff, J. (1989). *Oh, a-hunting we will go*. Lexington, MA: Heath.

Lasky, K. (1994). *The librarian who measured the Earth*. New York: Little, Brown.

Layne, S. (2006). *Mergers*. Gretna, LA: Pelican

Layne, S., & Hoyt, A. (2007). *Love the baby*. Gretna, LA: Pelican.

Lionni, L. (1970). *Fish is fish*. New York: Knopf.

Lionni, L. (1976). *A color of his own*. New York: Knopf.

Martin, A. (2005). *A dog's life: The autobiography of a stray*. New York: Scholastic.

Martin, B., Jr (1974). *Sounds of a powwow*. New York: Holt, Rinehart and Winston.

Martin, B., Jr, & Archambault, J. (1987). *Knots on a counting rope*. New York: Henry Holt.

Martin, B., Jr, & Archambault, J. (1988). *Barn dance*. New York: Holt.

Martin, B., Jr, & Archambault, J. (1989). *Chicka chicka boom boom*. New York: Scholastic.

Marzollo, J. (2000). *I love you: A rebus poem*. New York: Scholastic.

Mazzoni, D., & Dannenberg, R. (1999). *Audacity* [Computer software]. Available: audacity.sourceforge.net

Miranda, A. (1997). *To market, to market*. Orlando, FL: Harcourt.

Most, B. (1996). *Cock-a-doodle-moo*. San Diego, CA: Harcourt Brace.

Naylor, P.R. (1992). *Shiloh*. New York: Bantam Doubleday Dell.

Noble, T. (1980). *The day Jimmy's boa ate the wash*. New York: Dial.

Numeroff, L. (2002). *If you take a mouse to school*. New York: Laura Geringer.

Obligato, L. (1986). *Faint frogs feeling feverish and other terrifically tantalizing tongue twisters*. New York: Vikings Children's Books.

O'Conner, J. (2009). *Fancy Nancy: The dazzling book report*. New York: HarperCollins.

Pallotta, J. (1990). *The frog alphabet book*. Watertown, MA: Charlesbridge.

Parish, H. (1995). *Good driving, Amelia Bedelia*. New York: Greenwillow.

Penn, A. (1993). *The kissing hand*. Washington, DC: Child Welfare League of America.

Plater, I. (1998). *Jolly Olly*. Crystal Lakes, IL: Rigby.

Polacco, P. (1988). *The keeping quilt*. New York: Simon & Schuster.

Prelutsky, J. (1982). *The baby uggs are hatching*. New York: Greenwillow.

Prelutsky, J. (1983). *The Random House book of poetry for children*. New York: Random House.

Priddy, R. (2001). *My big book of everything*. New York: Dorling Kindersley.

Raffi. (1990). *Down by the bay*. New York: Crown.

Rayevsky, K., & Rayevsky, R. (2006). *Antonyms, synonyms, and homonyms*. New York: Holiday House.

Readers-theatre.com: www.readers-theatre.com

Rovetch, L. (2001). *Ook the book*. San Francisco: Chronicle.

Rylant, C. (1985). *The relatives came*. New York: Atheneum.

Rylant, C. (1996). *Henry and Mudge*. New York: Simon & Schuster.

Sava, S.C. (2006). *Dreamland chronicles: Book one*. Blue Dream Studios. Available: www.thedreamland-chronicles.com

Schlein, M. (1990). *The year of the panda*. New York: Crowell.

Seuss, D. (1963). *Hop on pop*. Boston: Houghton Mifflin.

Seuss, D. (1974). *There's a wocket in my pocket*. Boston: Houghton Mifflin.

Shihab Nye, N. (2008). *Honeybee: Poems and prose*. New York: HarperCollins.

Showers, P. (1991). *The listening walk*. New York: HarperCollins.

Silverstein, S. (1996). Furniture bash. In *Falling up* (p. 32). New York: HarperCollins.

Silverstein, S. (1974). *Where the sidewalk ends*. New York: HarperCollins.

Spier, P. (1992). *The star spangled banner*. New York: Dell Publishing.

Stevenson, J. (1998). *Popcorn: Poems*. New York: Greenwillow.

Suen, A. (2005). *Finding a way: Six historic U.S. routes*. Parsippany, NJ: Celebration Press, Pearson Learning Group.

Taback, S. (1997). *There was an old lady who swallowed a fly*. New York: Viking.

Tocci, S. (2006). *Mercury*. New York: Scholastic.

Tokuda, W., Hall, R., & Wakiyama, H. (1992). *Humphrey the lost whale: A true story*. Torrance, CA: Heian.

Vaughan, M. (1995). *Tingo tango mango tree*. Morristown, NJ: Silver Burdett.

Westerskov, K. (2004). *Penguins*. Carlsbad, CA: Dominie Press.

White, E.B. (1974). *Charlotte's web*. New York: HarperTrophy.

Whyte, D., & Record, S. (2008). *Hop, skip, and jump to learn* [CD]. Peterborough, NH: Crystal Springs Books.

Wikipedia: www.wikipedia.com

Winstead, A., Dacey, B., & Banelin, D. (2003). *The star-spangled banner*. Nashville, TN: Ideals.

Wood, A. (1984). *The napping house*. New York: Harcourt Brace.

Wordsmith.org: www.wordsmith.org

Yolen, J. (1991). *Greyling*. New York: Philomel.

Young, E. (1992). *Seven blind mice*. New York: Philomel.

Zolotow, C. (1994). *The seashore book*. New York: HarperTrophy.

Index

Note: Page numbers followed by *f* and *t* indicate figures and tables, respectively.